Understanding
Research Methods

An Overview of the Essentials

Sixth Edition

Mildred L. Patten

P y r c z a k   Publishing
P.O. Box 250430 • Glendale, CA 91225

"Pyrczak Publishing" is an imprint of Fred Pyrczak, Publisher, A California Corporation.

This edition was written in collaboration with Randall R. Bruce.

Project director: Monica Lopez.

Editorial assistance provided by Cheryl Alcorn, Brenda Koplin, Jack Petit, Erica Simmons, and Sharon Young.

Cover design by Robert Kibler and Larry Nichols.

Printed in the United States of America by Malloy, Inc.

ISBN 1-884585-73-6

CONTENTS

Continued →

iv

NOTES

INTRODUCTION TO THE SIXTH EDITION

This book provides an overview of basic research methods.

The distinctive features of this book are:

- The division of the material into short sections instead of long chapters, which will help students take small steps through this exciting—but highly technical—field of study. The long chapters in other research methods books prompt students to take big gulps, which often are not easily digested.

- When one topic builds directly on the previous one, the second one begins with a reminder of what students should have mastered in the previous topic. This helps students keep their eyes on the big picture and make a smooth transition from one topic to the next.

- Technical jargon is defined in plain English to the extent possible, and numerous examples make abstract research concepts concrete. Students' reactions in field tests attest to success in the effort to make this book comprehensible.

- The material on statistics is presented at the conceptual level. It shows how to interpret statistical reports but does not include computational details.

- The exercises at the end of the topics encourage students to pause to make sure they have mastered one topic before moving on to another. This is important because much of the material in this book is cumulative. Thorough mastery of an earlier topic is frequently a prerequisite for ease in mastering a later topic. The first part of each exercise tests comprehension of factual material. The second part asks students to interpret and apply the material they have mastered. This will help students internalize the concepts as well as stimulate classroom discussions. Finally, the third part provides questions that help students consider major issues in planning a research project.

Why should students have an overview of research methods? Because...

- Leaders in all fields are increasingly relying on the results of research to make important decisions, such as how to help those who are dependent on welfare, which types of educational programs to fund, and how to adjust work environments to improve employees' output and satisfaction. If students hope to become decision-makers in their field, they must master research methods in order to be effective in sorting through the conflicting claims often found in the research literature on a topic.

- Many students will be expected to do simple but important research on the job. For instance, clinical psychologists are expected to track improvements made by their clients, teachers are expected to experiment with new methods in the classroom, and social workers are expected to collect data on their clients.

- All students will be making lifestyle decisions based on research reported in the media. Should an individual take vitamin supplements? How should individuals dress for success on the job? Which make of automobile is superior if the buyer's primary concern is safety? Answers based on research are often offered in newspapers, magazines, and television newscasts. As a result of studying research methods, students will become knowledgeable, critical consumers of research.

- Finally, students may need to read and report on published research in other classes. Such students will be more skilled at doing this if they have a solid understanding of basic methods of research.

New to the Sixth Edition

In this edition, the following topics have been added: Topic 18 (Creating a Synthesis [when writing a literature review]), Topic 24 (Sampling and Demographics), Topic 33 (Internal Consistency and Reliability), Topic 42 (Confounding in Experiments), Topic 71 (The Structure of a Research Report), and Topic 72 (Reporting Research Results). Also, throughout the book, updated examples from published research literature have been incorporated.

Acknowledgments

Dr. Anne Hafner and Dr. Robert Morman, both of California State University, Los Angeles, provided many helpful comments on the first draft of this book. New material for subsequent editions was reviewed by Dr. Robert Rosenthal of Harvard University and the University of California, Riverside; Dr. Deborah M. Oh of California State University, Los Angeles; and Dr. Richard Rasor of American River College. All these individuals made important contributions to the development of this book.

Mildred L. Patten

PART A

INTRODUCTION TO RESEARCH METHODS

This part of the book defines what is meant by the term *empirical research* and provides an overview of the characteristics of the major approaches to this type of research. Broad issues that underlie all types of research—such as the nature of research hypotheses, how researchers define the variables they plan to study, ethical considerations in research, and the relationship between theory and research—are also covered in this part.

NOTES

The **empirical approach** to knowledge is based on observations.[1] Everyone uses the empirical approach in everyday living. For instance, if a teacher observes students becoming restless during a certain lesson, he or she might say they "know" the lesson is boring. As useful as everyday observations often are, they can be misleading and are often misinterpreted. For instance, the teacher may have misinterpreted the reasons for the students' restlessness. The time and day, such as a warm Friday afternoon, might be the source of the students' restlessness and *not* the "boringness" of the lesson. Even if the lesson is indeed boring to this teacher's students, the teacher might conclude that the lesson is boring to students *in general*, when it might, in fact, be interesting to other students at other ability levels, with different backgrounds, and so on.

When researchers use the empirical approach, they strive to avoid misleading results and poor interpretations. The key to doing so is careful planning of **why** they want to make observations, **whom** they want to observe, as well as **how** and **when** to observe.

The question of *why to observe* establishes the need for the study. Perhaps a better method for helping students acquire a certain mathematics skill is needed. After considering their own experiences and reviewing related literature on the topic, researchers prepare a formal statement of their research purpose, such as "whether the use of hands-on manipulatives to teach Topic X will result in greater student achievement than a workbook approach." A researcher might also have a **hypothesis**, which is a statement indicating what results are expected. For instance, a researcher might hypothesize that students who use manipulatives will have higher scores than those who are exposed to a workbook approach. The question of *why* is explored throughout Parts A and B of this book.

When researchers plan *whom to observe*, they first decide whether to observe an entire population (such as all fifth-grade students in a school district) or just a sample of the population. If a sample is to be observed, which is often done, researchers consider how to obtain a sample that is not biased against any types of individuals or subgroups. For instance, asking students to volunteer to take a mathematics lesson might result in a sample of students who are more interested in mathematics than the students in the population as a whole. Such a sample would be biased against those who are less interested. Methods of drawing unbiased samples are discussed in Part C of this book.

When researchers plan *how to observe*, they select among available instruments such as objective tests, interviews, and direct observation of behavior, with an eye to selecting the most valid instrument(s). If none is judged to be reasonably valid for their purposes, they develop new instruments. In addition, researchers need to decide *when* they will use the instruments to obtain the most valid results. These issues are explored in detail in Part D of this book.

The observations researchers make may result in **data** in the form of numbers, which are analyzed statistically. Widely used statistical techniques are described in Part F of this book. Note that some scientific observations are *not* reduced to numbers but are expressed in words. For instance, interview data may be described in a narrative that points out themes and trends. Such research is referred to as *qualitative research*. The differences between qualitative and quantitative research are described in Topics 9 and 10. In addition, qualitative research methods are discussed in some detail in Part H of this book.

One of the most fundamental distinctions in scientific research is whether research is **experimental** or **nonexperimental**. In *experimental* research, treatments are given for the research purpose, such as treating some students with hands-on manipulatives and others with a workbook approach in order to determine which treatment *causes* greater math achievement.[2] Of course, researchers are not always interested in cause-and-effect questions. For instance, they might want to know whether teachers believe they need more training in the use of manipulatives for teaching mathematics. For this particular research purpose, a researcher should ask teachers about their needs without giving treatments, such as training them how to use manipula-

---

[1] Examples of other approaches are (1) *deduction*, such as when one deduces a proof in mathematics based on certain assumptions and definitions, and (2) *reliance on authority*, such as relying on a dictator's pronouncements as a source of knowledge.

[2] The design of experiments is discussed in Part E of this book.

tives. Thus, *nonexperimental* research is needed for this research purpose. The distinction between experimental and nonexperimental research is explored in the next two topics of this book.

EXERCISE ON TOPIC 1

1. The empirical approach to knowledge is based on what?

2. Is the empirical approach used in everyday living?

3. What does the question of *why* establish?

4. How is the term *hypothesis* defined in this topic?

5. According to the topic, are samples often observed?

6. What do researchers do when they plan *how* to observe?

7. The results from which type of research ("quantitative" *or* "qualitative") are *not* reduced to numbers?

8. Are treatments given for the research purpose in "experimental research" *or* in "nonexperimental research"?

9. If a researcher asked students for their opinions on switching from the semester system to the quarter system, would the researcher be conducting "experimental research" *or* "nonexperimental research"?

Questions for Discussion

10. Briefly describe a time when you were misled by everyday observation (i.e., when you reached a conclusion based on an everyday observation that you later decided was an incorrect conclusion).

11. You have probably encountered conflicting research reported in the mass media. For example, one study might indicate that X increases blood pressure while another study indicates that X does not. Speculate on the reasons why various researchers might obtain different results when studying the same problem.

For Students Who Are Planning Research

12. Name a general problem area in which you might conduct research. At this point, your problem area may still be broad, such as "social phobia," *or* it may be narrow, such as "effectiveness of behavior modification in the treatment of social phobia among children." Note that you may want to name several problem areas for research and make a final selection at a later time.

13. Have you already made observations in your problem area(s)? If so, briefly describe them. (Keep in mind that observations may be direct, such as observing aggressive behavior on a playground, *or* indirect, such as asking adolescents for self-reports on their alcohol consumption.)

In **experiments**, researchers give treatments and observe to see if they cause changes in behavior. A classic simple experiment is one in which a researcher forms two groups at random and gives each group a different treatment. To form two groups at random, a researcher can put the names of the available participants on slips of paper, mix them thoroughly, and pull some names for each group.[1] Notice that random assignment gives each participant an equal chance of being in either group.

Below are three examples of experiments.

EXAMPLE 1
Fifty students were divided into two groups at random. One group received math instruction via a correspondence course on the Internet. The other group was given instruction on the same math skills using a traditional textbook. The purpose was to see if instruction via the Internet was more effective than traditional textbook instruction.

In Example 1, the group receiving the new type of instruction via the Internet is referred to as the **experimental group** while the group receiving the instruction with a textbook is called the **control group**.

When the participants are divided at random (such as drawing names out of a hat to determine who will be in the experimental group and who will be in the control group), the experiment is called a **true experiment**. Not all experiments are true experiments,[2] as illustrated by Example 2.

EXAMPLE 2
A psychiatrist identified 100 clinically depressed clients who volunteered to take a new drug under her direction. She also identified 100 nonvolunteers with the same diagnosis and similar demographics (i.e., background characteristics such as age and gender) to serve as controls. The study was conducted to investigate the effectiveness of the new drug in treating depression.

In Example 2, the experiment was conducted by comparing the volunteers who were given the new drug with a group of nonvolunteers who were *not* given the new drug. This study is an experiment even though random assignment was not used. Note that if a researcher administers treatments or ar-

ranges for their administration, the study is called an experiment regardless of whether the groups of participants are formed at random.

Some experiments are conducted with only one group of participants, as illustrated in Example 3, in which the extra verbal praise is the treatment.

EXAMPLE 3
The students in one classroom were observed for an hour each day for a week in order to count the number of inappropriate out-of-seat behaviors. During the next week, the teacher provided extra verbal praise when students were in their seats at appropriate times. During the third week, the teacher stopped providing the extra verbal praise. The results showed less inappropriate out-of-seat behavior during the second week of the experiment than in the other two weeks.

In **nonexperimental studies**, researchers do not give treatments. Rather, they observe participants in order to describe them as they naturally exist without experimental treatments. One of the most common types of nonexperimental studies is a survey or poll in which participants are interviewed, questioned, or otherwise observed in order to determine their attitudes, beliefs, and behaviors as they exist without experimental intervention.

Nonexperimental studies come in many forms, which are explored in more detail in Topic 4. At this point, however, readers should be able to distinguish between nonexperimental studies and experiments by determining whether treatments were administered for experimental purposes.

Note that consumers of research cannot distinguish between nonexperimental and experimental studies on the basis of the type of instrument (i.e., measuring tool) used. Instruments such as paper-and-pencil tests, interview schedules, and personality scales are used in both types of studies. The act of measurement is usually not considered to be a treatment. In fact, researchers try to measure in such a way that the act of measuring does not affect or change the participants. This is true in both experimental and nonexperimental studies.

By now, it should be clear that the purpose of an experiment is to explore cause-and-effect relationships (i.e., treatments are given to see how they affect the participants). The next topic describes how nonexperimental studies are also sometimes used for this purpose.

---

[1] Other methods for drawing random samples are discussed in Part C of this book.
[2] Types of experiments are explored more fully in Part E, where the advantages of true experiments are discussed.

Exercise on Topic 2

1. Are treatments given in nonexperimental studies?

2. In an experiment, Group A was given verbal praise for being on time for appointments while Group B was given no special treatment. Which group is the control group?

3. Is it necessary to have at least two groups of participants in order to conduct an experiment?

4. What is the purpose of a nonexperimental study?

5. Is a survey an experiment?

6. Does knowing that a multiple-choice test was used in a study help a consumer of research determine whether the study was experimental *or* nonexperimental?

7. What is the purpose of an experiment?

8. A political scientist polled voters to determine their opinions on a decision by the Supreme Court. Is this an "experimental study" *or* "nonexperimental study"?

9. A teacher compared the effectiveness of three methods of teaching handwriting by using different methods with different students. Did the teacher conduct an "experimental study" *or* "nonexperimental study"?

Questions for Discussion

10. Suppose you read that an outbreak of intestinal disorders occurred in a town and the source was traced to contaminated chicken served in a popular restaurant. Is it likely the study that identified the source was "experimental" *or* "nonexperimental"? Why?

11. Have you ever conducted an informal experiment by giving a treatment to a person or a group and then observing the effects? If so, briefly describe it. Would you have obtained better information by including a control group? Explain.

12. Suppose you wanted to know whether having parents read to preschool children has a positive effect on the children's subsequent reading achievement. Do you think it would be better to conduct an "experimental study" *or* "nonexperimental study"? Why?

For Students Who Are Planning Research

13. At this point, do you anticipate using an "experimental" *or* "nonexperimental" approach in your research? If it will be experimental, what treatments do you plan to administer?

14. If you plan to conduct experimental research, have you already conducted an informal experiment on your topic? If so, did you use a control group? Was it a true experiment? How will the experiment you are planning differ from the informal experiment you already conducted?

As indicated in Topic 2, an **experiment** is a study in which treatments are given in order to observe their effects. When researchers conduct experiments, they ask, "Does the treatment (i.e., the input or stimulus) given by the researcher *cause* changes in participants' behavior (i.e., changes in the output or response)?"

When researchers want to investigate cause-and-effect relationships, they usually prefer experimental over nonexperimental studies. However, sometimes it is not possible to conduct an experiment for physical, ethical, legal, or financial reasons. An example is the effects of smoking on health. It would be unethical (because of potential harm to the participants) to treat some participants with smoke (such as requiring them to smoke a pack of cigarettes a day for 15 years) in order to observe the effects in comparison with a nonsmoking control group (which is forbidden to smoke for 15 years). Clearly, for this research problem, researchers cannot conduct an experiment. Notice that even if it were ethical to conduct such an experiment, it might not be practical because researchers probably would not want to wait 15 years to determine the answer to such an important question.

When it is impossible or impractical to conduct an experiment to answer a causal question, a researcher must settle for information derived from nonexperimental studies. For instance, a researcher could identify individuals who currently have lung cancer as well as a control group without lung cancer but with similar **demographics** (i.e., background characteristics such as socioeconomic status). Then, the researcher could examine differences between the two groups in terms of previous lifestyle characteristics that might affect health such as diet, exercise, smoking, prescription drug use, illicit substance abuse, and so on.

A finding that smoking differentiates between the two groups that have similar demographics suggests that smoking is a possible cause of lung cancer. However, there are several dangers in this interpretation. First, smoking and cancer might have a common cause. For example, perhaps stress causes cancer and also causes individuals to smoke excessively. If this is the case, banning smoking will not prevent cancer, only reducing stress will. Another danger is that the researcher may have failed to identify control participants who were properly matched with those who have lung cancer. For in-stance, perhaps most of those with lung cancer reside in urban areas while most of those in the control group reside in rural areas. Because urban areas tend to have more smog than rural areas, smog might be the cause, and smoking might be coincidental. These types of problems would not arise in an experiment in which participants are divided at random to form two groups: one of which is made to smoke and the other forbidden to smoke. They would *not* exist because the random assignment would produce two groups that are equally likely to experience stress and equally likely to live in either rural or urban areas and, in fact, be about equal[1] in terms of all other potential causes of cancer.[2]

The example of smoking and lung cancer illustrates a specific type of nonexperimental study known as a **causal–comparative study** (sometimes called an **ex post facto study**).[3] The essential characteristics of this type of nonexperimental study are (1) researchers observe and describe some current condition (such as lung cancer) and (2) researchers look to the past to try to identify the possible cause(s) of the condition. Notice that researchers do *not* give treatments in causal–comparative studies. Instead, they only describe observations. Hence, they are conducting nonexperimental studies.

Although the causal–comparative method has more potential pitfalls than the experimental method, it is often the best researchers can do when attempting to explore causality. Note that when it is used properly, and the comparison groups are selected carefully, the causal–comparative method is a powerful scientific tool that provides data on many important issues in all the sciences.

---

[1] Because of the laws of probability, the larger the sample, the more likely that two groups formed at random will be equal in terms of their characteristics. Sample size is covered in Topics 25 and 26.

[2] The relationship between smoking and health has been examined in many hundreds of causal–comparative studies. On this basis, almost all experts agree that alternative interpretations are without merit. However, the results of some of the early studies on the effects of smoking on health were disputed because the studies were not true experiments (i.e., did not have random assignment to groups).

[3] Other types of nonexperimental studies are covered in the next topic.

EXERCISE ON TOPIC 3

1. According to the topic, do "experimental" *or* "causal–comparative" studies have more potential pitfalls when trying to identify cause-and-effect relationships?

2. Researchers look to the past for a cause in which type of study?

3. Is causal–comparative research a type of experiment?

4. Are treatments given by researchers in causal–comparative studies?

5. Random assignment to treatments is used in which type of study?

6. How is the term *demographics* defined in this topic?

7. A researcher compared the health of low-income adolescents who had received free lunches during their elementary school years with the health of a comparable group of low-income adolescents who had not received free lunches. The purpose was to determine the effects of free lunches on health. Did the researcher conduct an "experimental" *or* a "causal–comparative" study?

8. A researcher divided patients with diabetes who were being released from the hospital into two groups. Upon their release, the researcher provided brief counseling for individuals with diabetes to one group while providing the other group with extended counseling. The purpose was to determine the effects of the two types of counseling on patients' compliance with physicians' directions during the first month after hospitalization. Did the researcher conduct an "experimental" *or* a "causal–comparative" study?

9. What is another name for the term *causal–comparative study*?

Questions for Discussion

10. If you wanted to investigate the causes of child abuse, would you use the "experimental" *or* the "causal–comparative" method? Explain.

11. Suppose you read that a causal–comparative study indicates that those who take vitamins A and E tend to be less overweight than the general population. Are there any possible dangers in the interpretation that the vitamins *cause* people to maintain a healthy weight?

For Students Who Are Planning Research

12. If you will be conducting a nonexperimental study, will it be causal–comparative (i.e., looking to the past for the causes of some current condition)? If yes, briefly explain why you chose this method of research instead of the experimental method.

TOPIC 4 TYPES OF NONEXPERIMENTAL RESEARCH

As indicated in Topics 2 and 3, researchers do not give treatments to participants in nonexperimental studies. Rather, they observe (i.e., measure) in order to describe the participants without trying to change them.

Nonexperimental studies take many forms because they serve many purposes. The most common types of nonexperimental studies are briefly described here.

As indicated in the previous topic, **causal–comparative research** is research in which researchers look to the past for the cause(s) of a current condition. It is used primarily when researchers are interested in causality, but it is *not* possible to conduct an **experiment**.

Another type of nonexperimental research is the **survey** or *poll*. The purpose of surveys is to describe the attitudes, beliefs, and behaviors of a population. Researchers draw a sample of a population, study the sample, and then make inferences to the population from the sample data. For instance, a researcher could survey a sample of individuals receiving food stamps to determine what types of food they purchase with the stamps. The results obtained from studying the sample can be generalized to the population (assuming that a good sample has been drawn).[1] Note that if a researcher decides not to sample but, instead, interviews everyone in the population (i.e., all individuals receiving food stamps), the study would be called a **census**. A census is a count (or study) of all members of a population.

While surveys usually include hundreds or even thousands of participants, a **case study** usually involves only one. For instance, some important theories in clinical psychology were developed based on intensive one-on-one case studies of individuals. In a case study, the emphasis is on obtaining thorough knowledge of an individual, sometimes obtained over a long period of time. Researchers do not confine themselves to asking a limited number of questions on a one-shot basis as they would do in a survey.

When researchers repeatedly measure traits of the participants over a period of time in order to trace developmental trends, they are conducting **longitudinal research**. For instance, a researcher could measure the visual acuity of a sample of infants each week for a year to trace their development.

In **correlational research**, researchers are interested in the degree of relationship among two or more *quantitative variables*. For instance, scores on a college admissions test and GPAs are quantitative, and because individuals *vary* or differ on both of them, they are variables.[2] If a researcher conducts a study in which he or she is asking, "Did those with high admissions scores tend to earn high GPAs?" the researcher is asking a correlational question. To the extent that the answer to the question is true, the researcher can assert that the test works (i.e., has validity for predicting GPAs).[3]

Experiments and all the types of research mentioned so far in this topic belong to the class of research called **quantitative research**. A distinctive feature of quantitative research is that researchers gather data in such a way that the data are easy to quantify, allowing for statistical analysis of the data. For instance, to measure attitudes toward Asian American immigrants, a quantitative researcher might use a questionnaire and count how many times respondents answer "yes" to statements about Asian Americans and then calculate the percentage who answered "yes" to each statement.

In contrast, in **qualitative research**, researchers gather data (such as responses to open-ended interview questions on attitudes toward Asian Americans) that must be analyzed using informed judgment to identify major and minor themes expressed by participants. Most published qualitative research is collected using semi-structured interviews in which there is a core list of questions from which the interviewers may deviate as needed to obtain in-depth information.

Other differences between qualitative and quantitative research are explored in Topics 9 and 10. In addition, Part H of this book describes qualitative research methods in detail.

In **historical research**, information is examined in order to understand the past. Note that good his-

---

[1] Characteristics of good samples for quantitative research are explored in detail in Part C of this book. Considerations in sampling for qualitative research are described in Topics 64 and 65 in Part H of this book.

[2] Types of variables are described in Topics 5 and 6.

[3] Validity is explored in Part D of this book. Correlational studies employ a statistic called a *correlation coefficient*, which is described in Topic 53.

torical research is not just a matter of developing a chronological list of so-called facts and dates. Rather, it is an attempt to understand the dynamics of human history. As such, it is driven by theories and hypotheses. In other words, by reviewing historical evidence, researchers are able to develop theories that may explain historical events and patterns. These theories lead to hypotheses, which are evaluated in terms of additional historical data that are collected. Historical researchers may use qualitative methods (e.g., examining historical documents using insight and judgment to identify themes) or qualitative methods (e.g., counting certain types of statements made in historical documents). Historical research is typically taught in history departments and is not considered further in this book.

EXERCISE ON TOPIC 4

1. Suppose a researcher administered an intelligence test to young children each year for five years in order to study changes in intelligence over time. The researcher was conducting what type of study?

2. Is the study in Question 1 experimental?

3. If a researcher conducts a poll to estimate public support for free child care for mothers on welfare, the researcher is conducting what type of nonexperimental study?

4. An investigator determined the degree of relationship between vocabulary scores and reading comprehension scores. The researcher was conducting what type of nonexperimental study?

5. According to this topic, what is a distinctive feature of quantitative research?

6. Most published qualitative research is collected using what?

Questions for Discussion

7. Name a topic in your field of study that you might explore with a nonexperimental study. Which type of nonexperimental study would be most appropriate for your topic?

8. Think of a survey in which you were asked to serve as a participant. (You may have been sent a questionnaire in the mail, such as a consumer satisfaction survey, or you may have been contacted in person or by phone.) Did you cooperate and respond? Why? Why not?

9. Name two quantitative variables that might be studied using correlational research.

10. Suppose someone prepared a list of educational events and their dates of occurrence in the last 100 years. Would the list be an example of "good" historical research? Explain.

For Students Who Are Planning Research

11. If you will be conducting a nonexperimental study, which type will it be? Explain the basis for your choice.

A **variable** is a trait or characteristic with two or more categories. Participants *vary* in terms of the categories to which they belong. Example 1 has two variables.

EXAMPLE 1
A sample of registered voters was surveyed. Each voter was asked first to name his or her gender (male or female) and then to name the candidate for whom he or she planned to vote (Doe, Jones, or Smith). The purpose was to explore gender differences in voting preferences.

The two variables in Example 1 are (1) gender, with two categories and (2) the preferred candidate, with three categories (i.e., three possible candidates).

Be careful not to confuse a variable with its categories. For instance, "male" is one of the two categories of the variable called "gender." "Male" is not a variable. Here is how to visualize it:

One Variable ⇨   *GENDER*
Two Categories ⇨ | Male | Female |

All variables have **mutually exclusive categories**. That is, each respondent to the survey in Example 1 will belong to one—and *only one*—category. For instance, the categories for "preferred candidate" are mutually exclusive because a researcher would ask, "For which *one* candidate do you plan to vote?" When conducting such a survey, a researcher would not allow a participant to name two candidates (i.e., two categories) for the same political office.

Researchers define variables in such a way that the categories are **exhaustive**. To be exhaustive, a variable must have a category for each respondent's opinion. For instance, a researcher would want to add a fourth choice of "undecided" for respondents who have not yet chosen among the three candidates in Example 1.

Notice that both variables in Example 1 are "naming" variables (more properly called "categorical" variables).[1] Each participant "names" his or her gender and "names" the preferred candidate. Other variables have quantitative categories that describe the amount of a characteristic. Consider Example 2.

EXAMPLE 2
The college admissions scores on the *Scholastic Aptitude Test* (*SAT*) were compared with students' freshman GPAs to determine how valid the *SAT* is for predicting GPAs.

Both the College Board's *SAT* scores (ranging from 200 to 800 per subtest) and GPAs (usually ranging from 0.00 to 4.00) are quantitative. In other words, each possible score is a category. A student who earns a *SAT* score of 550 belongs to the category called "550." Likewise, a student who has a GPA of 2.9 belongs to the category called "2.9."

Variables in nonexperimental studies are sometimes classified as being either **independent** or **dependent**. For instance, when researchers conduct a causal–comparative study (see Topic 3 to review), the presumed cause (such as smoking) is called the *independent* variable, and the response or outcome (such as lung cancer) is called the *dependent* variable. Remember:

> The *independent variable* (stimulus or input)
> causes changes in the
> *dependent variable* (response or output).

Some researchers refer to any variable that comes first (whether or not it is presumed to be a cause) as "independent" and to the one that comes later as "dependent." For instance, *SAT* scores (the predictor variable) are usually determined before students earn their college GPAs. Thus, some researchers would call the *SAT* the independent variable and the GPA the dependent variable. It is also common to call the independent variable the **predictor** and the outcome variable (such as GPA) the **criterion**. The term "criterion" means "standard." Hence, GPA is the standard by which the *SAT* is often judged. Ideally, high scores on the *SAT* should be associated with high GPAs, while low *SAT* scores should be associated with low GPAs. To the extent that this is true, the *SAT* is judged to be valid. To the extent that it is not true, the *SAT* is judged to be invalid. Procedures for determining the validity of a test are described in Part D of this book.

---

[1] *Naming data* are obtained from the *nominal scale of measurement*. Scales of measurement are discussed in Topic 45.

EXERCISE ON TOPIC 5

1. Adults who were taking a course to learn English as a second language were asked to name their country of birth and their number of years of formal education. In this example, how many variables were being studied?

2. In Question 1, which variable is a categorical variable?

3. In Question 1, which variable is quantitative?

4. A sample of adults was asked their level of agreement with the statement, "The President of the United States is doing a good job in handling foreign relations." They were permitted to respond either "strongly agree," "agree," "disagree," or "strongly disagree." How many variables were being studied?

5. What is meant by *mutually exclusive categories*?

6. A researcher looked for the causes of social unrest by examining economic variables such as poverty, income, and so on. Is social unrest an "independent" *or* "dependent" variable?

7. If a researcher administers a basic math test to middle school children to see if the basic math test scores predict grades in high school algebra, what is the criterion variable?

8. Suppose a researcher asks participants to identify their age group using these categories: "under 21," "21–39," "40–55," and "56+." Are these exhaustive categories?

9. In Question 8, how many variables are being studied?

10. What is the minimum number of categories that each variable must have?

Questions for Discussion

11. Suppose you want to measure income on a self-report questionnaire on which each participant will check off his or her income category. Name the categories you would use. Are they exhaustive and mutually exclusive? Explain.

12. Name a quantitative variable of interest to you and name its categories. Are the categories mutually exclusive and exhaustive? Explain.

For Students Who Are Planning Research

13. If you will be conducting a nonexperimental study, name the major variables you will be studying. For each, indicate whether the categories will be quantitative.

All experiments have at least one **independent variable** and one **dependent variable**. The purpose of experiments is to estimate the extent to which independent variables cause changes in dependent variables.

As indicated in the previous section, an independent variable is a stimulus or input variable. Note that in experiments, researchers *physically manipulate* independent variables. Examples of physical manipulation are (1) giving a new drug to some participants while giving a placebo to others, (2) providing some students with computers while denying computers to others, and (3) using group counseling with some clients while using individual counseling with others. Thus, to *physically manipulate* means to physically administer treatments.

Note that in *nonexperimental* studies, researchers do *not* physically manipulate independent variables. Instead, they observe independent variables as they occur (or have occurred) naturally. For instance, researchers observe the health of individuals who have smoked cigarettes in nonexperimental studies—researchers do not provide participants with cigarettes, nor do they expose participants to smoke. (See Topic 3 to review other differences between experimental and nonexperimental studies of causation.)

In a simple experiment, there is only one independent variable and only one dependent variable, as in Example 1.

EXAMPLE 1
On alternative weeks, a disruptive first-grade student is given extra praise for being in her seat when appropriate. The purpose of the study is to see if the extra praise will increase the amount of appropriate in-seat behavior.

In Example 1, the physical manipulation is giving or not giving extra praise, which is the independent variable (i.e., the stimulus or input variable). The dependent variable (i.e., response or outcome variable) is the change in the student's in-seat behavior.

Often, experiments have more than one dependent variable. For instance, in Example 1, a researcher could observe to see not only if the treatment causes (1) more in-seat behavior, but also (2) improvement in the student's achievement and (3) improvement in the student's attitude toward school during the weeks the extra praise is given. If a researcher did this, the researcher would have three dependent variables.

Many experiments also have more than one independent variable. Often, these experiments are more interesting than those with only one independent variable because they provide insights into the causal effects of combinations of variables. Consider Example 2, which has two independent variables (i.e., child care and transportation money).

EXAMPLE 2
Voluntary, free job training was offered to all mothers on welfare in a small city. Four groups of the mothers were formed at random to explore the effects of these two independent variables: (1) providing or not providing free child care while in training and (2) providing or not providing transportation money to get to the job-training site. Each group was assigned at random to one of the four treatment conditions shown here:

GROUP 1 child care *and* transportation money	GROUP 3 *no* child care *and* transportation money
GROUP 2 child care *and* *no* transportation money	GROUP 4 *no* child care *and* *no* transportation money

It was predicted that those in Group 1 (the group that was given *both* child care and transportation money) would have the highest attendance rates, those in Group 2 would have the next highest, those in Group 3 would have the next highest, and those in Group 4 would have the lowest rates of attendance in the job-training program.

Notice that in Example 2, a researcher can determine (1) how effective child care is, (2) how effective transportation money is, and (3) the effectiveness of both child care *and* transportation money *in combination*. Thus, a researcher would get more information by looking at two independent variables in one study than by looking at each independent variable in a separate experiment (in which case, a researcher could determine only points 1 and 2).

EXERCISE ON TOPIC 6

1. All experiments have at least how many dependent variables?

2. In an experiment, what is the name of a stimulus or input variable?

3. What does *physically manipulate* mean in an experimental context?

4. Are dependent variables physically manipulated?

5. Can an experiment have more than one independent variable?

6. Every other customer entering a shoe store was given a different coupon. One coupon offered a second pair of shoes for 50% off. The other coupon offered to reduce the total price by 25% if two pairs of shoes were purchased. The purpose was to determine which coupon was more effective in getting individuals to buy two pairs of shoes. In this experiment, what is the independent variable?

7. In Question 6, what is the dependent variable?

8. A teacher showed an educational film on daily nutritional needs to one group of students and gave a handout on the same material to another group. The purpose was to determine which method of instruction was more effective in increasing students' knowledge of daily nutritional needs. In this experiment, what is the dependent variable?

9. In Question 8, what is the independent variable?

Questions for Discussion

10. Name a variable that would be easy for a researcher to physically manipulate in an experiment. Then, name a variable that might be affected by the manipulation.

11. Name a variable that you would be unwilling to physically manipulate due to ethical or legal concerns.

For Students Who Are Planning Research

12. If you will be conducting an experiment, name the independent and dependent variables you will be studying.

TOPIC 7 RESEARCH HYPOTHESES, PURPOSES, AND QUESTIONS

A **research hypothesis** is a prediction of the outcome of a study. The prediction may be based on an educated guess or a formal theory. Example 1 is a hypothesis for a nonexperimental study.

EXAMPLE 1
It is hypothesized that first-grade girls have better reading comprehension than first-grade boys.

In Example 1, the researcher is predicting that he or she will find higher reading comprehension among girls than boys. To test the prediction, a nonexperimental study would be appropriate because nothing in the hypothesis suggests that treatments will be given.

A simple research hypothesis predicts a relationship between two variables. The two variables in Example 1 are (1) gender and (2) reading comprehension. The hypothesis states that reading comprehension is related to gender.

Example 2 is a hypothesis for an experimental study.

EXAMPLE 2
It is hypothesized that children who are shown a video with mild violence will be more aggressive on the playground than those who are shown a similar video without violence.

In Example 2, the *independent variable* is violence (mild vs. no violence), and the *dependent variable* is aggressiveness on the playground.

The hypotheses in Examples 1 and 2 are examples of **directional hypotheses**. In a directional hypothesis, researchers predict which group will be higher or have more of some attribute.

Sometimes researchers have a **nondirectional hypothesis**. Consider Example 3.

EXAMPLE 3
It is hypothesized that the child-rearing practices of Tribe A are different from those of Tribe B.

The author of Example 3 is saying that there will be a difference but does not predict the direction of the difference. This is perfectly acceptable when there is no basis for making an educated guess as to the outcome of a study.

Instead of a nondirectional hypothesis, a researcher might state a **research purpose**. Example 4 shows a research purpose that corresponds to the nondirectional hypothesis in Example 3.

EXAMPLE 4
The research purpose is to explore the differences in child-rearing practices between Tribe A and Tribe B.

A **research question** may also be substituted for a nondirectional hypothesis. Example 5 shows a research question that corresponds to the nondirectional hypothesis in Example 3 and the research purpose in Example 4.

EXAMPLE 5
The research question is, "How do the child-rearing practices in Tribe A and Tribe B differ?"

When using a research question as the basis for research, researchers usually do *not* state it as a question that can be answered with a simple "yes" or "no," as is done in Example 6.

EXAMPLE 6
The research question is, "Do the child-rearing practices in Tribe A and Tribe B differ?"

Example 6 merely asks, "Do they differ?" This is not a very interesting research question because it implies that the results of the research will be only a simple "yes" or "no." Example 5 is superior because it asks, "*How* do they differ?"—a question that implies that the results will be complex and, thus, more interesting and informative.

The choice between a nondirectional hypothesis, a research purpose, and a research question is purely a matter of personal taste—all are acceptable in the scientific community. Of course, when researchers are willing and able to predict the outcome of a study, they state a directional hypothesis—not a research purpose or question. In other words, a research purpose or a research question are suitable substitutes for a nondirectional hypothesis. It is inappropriate to use these as substitutes for a directional hypothesis.

Those who have read research reports in journals may have encountered references to another type of hypothesis: the **null hypothesis**. This is a *statistical hypothesis*, which needs to be considered when analyzing results obtained from samples in quantitative research studies. The null hypothesis need not be considered at this point. However, it will be explored in detail in Part F of this book.

EXERCISE ON TOPIC 7

1. Which type of statement (hypothesis, purpose, or question) predicts the outcome of a study?

2. "It is hypothesized that college students who have firm career goals achieve higher GPAs than those who do not have firm career goals." Is this a "directional" *or* "nondirectional" hypothesis?

3. "It is hypothesized that children of immigrants and children of native-born citizens differ in their attitudes toward school." Is this a "directional" *or* "nondirectional" hypothesis?

4. "The goal of this study is to examine college students' attitudes toward religion." Is this statement a "hypothesis" *or* "purpose"?

5. "Are children of alcoholics different from children of nonalcoholics in their social adjustment?" Is this research question stated appropriately? Why? Why not?

6. When researchers are willing to predict the outcome of a study, should they state a "directional" *or* "nondirectional" hypothesis?

7. What are the two alternatives to stating a nondirectional hypothesis?

8. Consider nondirectional hypotheses, research purposes, and research questions. Are "all three acceptable in the scientific community" *or* is "one type preferred over the others"?

Questions for Discussion

9. Restate this hypothesis as a research purpose: "It is hypothesized that there is a difference in job satisfaction between those who receive regular feedback on their job performance and those who receive irregular feedback."

10. Is the hypothesis in Question 9 "directional" *or* "nondirectional"? Explain.

11. Could an experiment be conducted to test the hypothesis in Question 9? Explain.

12. Restate the following hypothesis as a research question: "It is hypothesized that those who exercise regularly and those who do not exercise regularly differ in other behaviors that affect health."

For Students Who Are Planning Research

13. State a research hypothesis, purpose, or question for the research you are planning. (Note: You may have more than one of each.)

14. If you stated a hypothesis in response to Question 13, is it "directional" *or* "nondirectional"?

TOPIC 8   OPERATIONAL DEFINITIONS OF VARIABLES

Dictionaries provide **conceptual definitions** of variables. For instance, a researcher in speech communication might be interested in students' ability to *recite*, which has a dictionary definition along these lines: "to repeat or speak aloud from or as from memory, especially in a formal way." This definition is perfectly adequate if a researcher merely wants to communicate the general topic of his or her research to other individuals.

Suppose, however, that the researcher wants to conduct an experiment on the effectiveness of two memory aids on the ability to recite. As the researcher plans the research, it will become clear that a conceptual definition is not adequate because it does not indicate the precise concrete or physical steps the researcher will take in order to identify the variable. Redefining a variable in terms of physical steps is called *operationalizing* a variable. When a researcher operationalizes a variable, he or she is creating an **operational definition**. Example 1 shows the first attempt at creating an operational definition of students' ability to recite.

EXAMPLE 1
For the research project, the ability to recite is defined as the number of words mispronounced, missing, or misplaced when students repeat aloud from memory Christian Abzab's poem *The Road Taken* in front of a panel of three teachers.

Notice that the definition in Example 1 is not fully operational because there might still be questions about the *physical arrangements* such as, "Will the students stand while reciting?" "In what type of room will the recitation take place (a classroom or auditorium)?" "Will the teachers be male or female?" and "Will the teachers already know the students?"

It is important to note that no attempt at operationalizing a variable will result in a completely operational definition because there are an infinite number of physical characteristics that might be addressed in any definition (e.g., the humidity in the room, the level of lighting, the type of flooring, the color of the walls). Thus, instead of striving for completely operational definitions, researchers try to produce definitions that are adequate to permit a **replication** in all important respects by another researcher. A replication is an attempt to confirm the results of a study by conducting it again in the same way. Of course, there is much subjectivity in applying this criterion of adequacy (i.e., sufficiently operational to permit replication), and researchers may not all agree on when it has been met.[1]

Notice that a highly operational definition is not necessarily meaningful or relevant. For example, clients' self-esteem could be operationalized with the definition in Example 2.

EXAMPLE 2
Positive self-esteem is defined as answering "yes" to the written question, "Do you feel good about yourself?"

The definition in Example 2 is reasonably operational because it indicates what specific question to ask in writing and what response to look for. However, the definition is quite narrow. For instance, it does not tap self-esteem in the various dimensions of clients' lives, such as self-esteem in the workplace, in social settings, and so on. Thus, Example 2 illustrates that a definition can be operational without being adequate in other respects, such as being fully multidimensional.

Treatments given in experiments also should be operationalized. For instance, "verbal praise" given in an experiment could be operationalized in terms of the types of words used when giving praise, the frequency of the praise, the conditions under which the praise will be given, and so on.

Notice that if a researcher fails to provide operational definitions of all key variables in a research report, the report is vague at best, and the results are often of limited usefulness. For instance, if research shows that a certain program is helpful in reducing spousal abuse, but the researcher fails to provide a highly operational definition, consumers of research will not know how to conduct the program in applied settings.

---

[1] Confidence in results of a study is increased when the results have been independently replicated by other researchers. This is the case because a given researcher may have blind spots, unconscious biases, etc. Also, a given researcher may have been unlucky and have results that were influenced by large random errors. Independent replications by others reduce the odds that these factors are the cause of a particular finding.

EXERCISE ON TOPIC 8

1. Which type of definition indicates physical steps?

2. In practice, are operational definitions ever fully operationalized?

3. Which of the following definitions of *gregarious* is more operational?
   A. Talking on the phone with friends for at least two hours each week.
   B. Being open and friendly when in social gatherings with others.

4. Which of the following definitions of being *computer literate* is more operational?
   A. Having taken at least two formal courses of instruction on the use of computers in an accredited school.
   B. Having knowledge of the origins and uses of computers in modern society and their implications.

5. Which of the following definitions of administering *nonverbal praise* (in an experiment) is more operational?
   A. Using various positive gestures involving various body parts without speaking.
   B. Nodding the head slightly in an up-down direction while smiling lightly with the lips closed.

6. To replicate the research of others, do researchers need "operational" *or* "conceptual" definitions?

7. Is it possible for a definition to be highly operational, yet be inadequate in other respects?

Questions for Discussion

8. Suppose you read a research report claiming that low socioeconomic status (SES) children have lower self-concepts than high SES children. In the report, the only definition of self-concept is "feeling good about oneself." How much credence would you give the results in light of the definition? What additional information, if any, would you want about the definition if you were planning to replicate the study?

9. In a research report, job satisfaction is defined as "the number of times each participant said 'yes' to a set of questions such as 'Do you look forward to going to work most mornings?'" Is this definition completely operational? If not, what is missing from the definition?

10. Is the definition in Question 9 too narrow in terms of how you normally think about job satisfaction? Why? Why not?

11. Write a highly operational definition of "success in college."

12. Write a highly operational definition of "motivation to succeed on the job."

For Students Who Are Planning Research

13. Name the major variables you will be studying. Define each, trying to be as operational as possible. (Note: After you have read published research on your topic, you may want to come back here and redefine some of your definitions in light of how other researchers have defined them.)

The results of **quantitative research** are presented as quantities or numbers (i.e., statistics). In **qualitative research**, the results are presented as discussions of trends and/or themes based on words, not statistics. In addition to the difference in how results are presented, there are a number of characteristics that distinguish the two types of research. To understand some of the major ones, consider this research problem: A metropolitan police force is demoralized, with signs such as high rates of absenteeism, failure to follow procedures, and so on. Furthermore, the press has raised questions about the effectiveness of the force and its leadership. In response, the police commission is planning to employ a researcher to identify possible causes and solutions.

If a researcher with a quantitative orientation is retained, he or she would probably begin with a review of the research literature on demoralized police departments. From the review, the researcher would attempt to develop hypotheses to be tested by research. This is a *deductive approach* to planning the research. That is, the researcher is deducing from the literature possible explanations (i.e., hypotheses) to be tested. In contrast, a qualitative researcher would tend to use an *inductive approach* to planning the research. He or she might, for example, begin to gather data on the specific police force in question by making preliminary observations and conducting informal interviews. The resulting preliminary findings might be used as a basis for planning what additional types of information to collect and how to collect them. Thus, rather than approaching the research task with preconceived notions based on published theory and research, a qualitative researcher would emphasize induction from the preliminary data that he or she collected.

Note that qualitative researchers (like quantitative researchers) typically examine previously published literature and include reviews of it in their research reports. However, quantitative researchers use literature as the basis for planning research while qualitative researchers tend to deemphasize it.

When deciding what types of instruments (i.e., measuring tools) to use, quantitative researchers prefer those that produce data that can be easily reduced to numbers, such as structured questionnaires, or interview schedules with objective formats, such as multiple-choice questions. In contrast, qualitative researchers prefer instruments that yield words that are not easily reduced to numbers. These can be obtained using instruments such as unstructured interviews or direct, unstructured observations of police officers and their administrators.

When deciding how many members of the police force to use as participants, [1] quantitative researchers tend to select large samples. Quantitative researchers are able to work with large samples because objective instruments such as an anonymous, objective questionnaire usually are easy to administer to large numbers of participants in a short amount of time. In contrast, qualitative researchers tend to use smaller samples because of the amount of time required to use their instruments, such as extended, in-depth, one-on-one unstructured interviews and extensive observations over time.

When deciding which individuals to use as research participants, quantitative researchers prefer to select a *random sample* in which all participants have an equal chance of being selected. This can be done, for instance, by drawing names out of a hat. (The uses of random samples and their relationship to statistics are discussed in later topics.) Qualitative researchers, on the other hand, are more likely to select a *purposive sample* of individuals that the researcher believes are key informants in terms of social dynamics, leadership positions, job responsibilities, and so on. In other words, qualitative researchers prefer to use informed judgment in selecting participants, while quantitative researchers prefer to leave the selection of participants to chance (i.e., random selection).

While working with the participants, qualitative researchers would be open to the possibility of making adjustments in the instrumentation, such as rewording questions or adding questions based on earlier responses by participants. On the other hand, quantitative researchers seldom make such adjustments during the course of a research project. Instead, quantitative researchers plan their research in detail in advance and follow the plan closely throughout the study because mid-stream deviations might be viewed as introducing subjectivity into the study. It is important to note that while quantitative

---

[1] Note that the term "participants" implies that the individuals being studied have voluntarily agreed to participate in a given research project. When individuals are being observed without their consent, they are more likely to be called "subjects."

researchers emphasize "objectivity," qualitative researchers believe all observational processes are inherently subjective and open to interpretation. Because of this, qualitative researchers sometimes mention relevant details of their personal backgrounds (such as having a mother who was a police officer) in order to inform readers of their research of possible sources of bias in collecting and interpreting the data.

For data analysis, quantitative researchers tend to summarize all responses with statistics and seldom report on the responses of individual participants. Qualitative researchers, on the other hand, tend to cite individuals' responses (such as quoting individual participants) in the Results section of a research report.

Finally, quantitative researchers tend to generalize the results to one or more populations, while qualitative researchers tend to limit their conclusions to only the individuals who were directly studied.

Should the police commission select a researcher with a "quantitative" or "qualitative" orientation? Criteria for making such a decision are described in the next topic.

EXERCISE ON TOPIC 9

1. Do "qualitative" or "quantitative" researchers tend to rely more on published research literature in planning research?

2. Which method of research relies on the inductive approach?

3. Which method of research is more likely to lead to a statistical report of results?

4. In which method of research would a researcher be more likely to make adjustments to the interview questions during the course of a research project?

5. Which method of research tends to have smaller samples?

6. Do "qualitative" or "quantitative" researchers prefer random sampling?

7. There are more likely to be quotations from participants in the Results sections of reports on which type of research?

8. In which type of research do researchers have more interest in generalizing the results to populations?

Questions for Discussion

9. In general, are you more likely to believe research results that are presented as themes and trends expressed in words or results described with statistics? Explain. (If you have not read academic research extensively, consider secondary reports of research such as those found in newspapers, magazines, and textbooks.)

10. Do you believe both qualitative and quantitative research have valuable roles in advancing knowledge in your field of study? Why? Why not?

For Students Who Are Planning Research

11. At this point, are you leaning toward conducting "qualitative" or "quantitative" research? Explain the basis for your choice. (Note that you will be learning more about qualitative research in the next topic.)

TOPIC 10 QUANTITATIVE VS. QUALITATIVE RESEARCH: II

The last topic finished with the question, "Should the police commission select a researcher with a 'quantitative' or 'qualitative' orientation?" Some of the criteria that should be considered when making such a decision are:

A. Some research questions inherently lend themselves more to the quantitative than the qualitative approach. For instance, "What is the impact of terrorism on the U.S. economy?" is a question that lends itself to quantitative research because economic variables readily lend themselves to quantitative analysis. On the other hand, "What is the emotional impact of terrorism on at-risk health care workers?" is a question that lends itself more to the qualitative approach because this question focuses on emotional impact, which is more difficult to quantify. Note, however, that the second question could be examined with either qualitative or quantitative research.

B. When little is known about a topic, qualitative research should usually be initially favored. New topics are constantly emerging in all fields, such as new diseases like SARS, new criminal concerns such as domestic terrorism, and new educational techniques such as using the Internet for instructional purposes in classrooms. On new topics, there often is little, if any, previously published research. In its absence, quantitative researchers may find it difficult to employ the deductive approach (i.e., deduct hypotheses from previously published research). Also, quantitative researchers might find it difficult to write structured questions about a little-known topic. (How can a researcher know exactly what to ask when he or she knows little about a topic?) In contrast, qualitative researchers could start with broad questions and refine them during the course of the interviews as various themes and issues start to emerge. Based on the qualitative results, theories might be developed from which hypotheses could be deduced and subsequently tested by using quantitative research.

C. When the participants belong to a culture that is closed or secretive, qualitative research should usually be favored. A skilled qualitative researcher who is willing to spend considerable time breaking through the barriers that keep researchers out is more likely to be successful than a quantitative researcher who tends to spend much less time interacting with participants.

D. When potential participants are not available for extensive interactions or observation, the quantitative approach should be considered. For instance, it might be difficult to schedule extensive interviews with chief executives of major corporations. However, the chief executives might be willing to respond to a brief objective-type questionnaire, which would provide data that can be analyzed with statistics.

E. When time and funds are very limited, quantitative research might be favored. Although this is an arguable criterion for selecting between the two types of research, it is suggested because quantitative research can be used to provide quick, inexpensive snapshots of narrow aspects of research problems. Qualitative methods do not lend themselves to the more economical snapshot approach.

F. When audiences require "hard numbers" (such as legislators or funding agencies sometimes do), quantitative research should be favored or, at least, incorporated into a qualitative research project. When someone says, "Just the numbers, please," themes and trends illustrated with quotations are unlikely to impress them. For such an audience, one should start by presenting statistics when possible. This might open the door to consideration of more qualitative aspects of the findings. Notice that implicit in this criterion is the notion that both qualitative and quantitative approaches might be used in a given research project, with each approach contributing a different type of information.

Up to this point, quantitative and qualitative research have been presented as though they are opposites. However, some researchers conduct research that is a blend of the two approaches. For instance, a quantitative researcher who uses semistructured interviews to collect data, reduces the data to statistics, but also reports quotations from participants to support the statistics, is conducting research that has some of the characteristics of both approaches.

Clearly, the hypothetical police commission needs to make a complex decision. How would you answer the question in the first paragraph of this topic? What is the basis for your answer? For more information on the characteristics of qualitative research, consult Part H of this book.

EXERCISE ON TOPIC 10

1. Which of the following lends itself more to quantitative research?
    A. How do the social relations of adolescents who use illicit drugs differ from those who do not use them?
    B. How do school attendance and grades earned in school differ between adolescents who use illicit drugs and those who do not use them?

2. Which of the following lends itself more to qualitative research?
    A. What are the differences between the social interactions of college students on commuter campuses and students on campuses where most students live on campus?
    B. To what extent does family income predict whether a student will choose to attend a commuter college or a college where most students live on campus?

3. Suppose a researcher wants to do research on members of a secretive fraternity. According to the information in this topic, which type of researcher is more likely to be successful in conducting the research?

4. If little is known about a new topic, which type of research is recommended for initial use?

5. For which type of research must participants usually be available for extensive interactions with researchers?

6. Which type of research is more suitable for getting a quick snapshot of a problem?

Questions for Discussion

7. How would you answer the two questions in the last paragraph of this topic?

8. Suppose a team of researchers wants to conduct research to identify the characteristics of professors whom students perceive as being excellent. Would you advise them to do "qualitative" *or* "quantitative" research? Why?

9. Name a problem in your field of study that would probably lend itself more to the quantitative than the qualitative approach.

For Students Who Are Planning Research

10. In light of the information in this topic, have you changed your mind about your answer to Question 10 in the Exercise on Topic 9? Explain.

TOPIC 11 PROGRAM EVALUATION

Consider a school that receives a foundation grant for a new program that emphasizes parental involvement and shared decision-making. In this program, decisions are made by an administrator with the advice and consent of both teachers and parents. The ultimate purpose is to help students improve in a variety of academic and social skills. In this case, as in most others, granting agencies require a report on the implementation and effectiveness of the programs for which they provide funding. To prepare such a report, researchers conduct a **program evaluation** by engaging in *evaluation research*.

At first glance, it might appear that a researcher should conduct *experimental research*. As indicated in Topic 2, experimental research is research in which researchers give treatment(s) (in this case, a program) in order to observe their effects. Indeed, while elements of evaluation research resemble experimental work, there are some major differences.

First, program evaluation is almost always *applied research* (i.e., research in which researchers wish to apply the findings directly to such practical decisions as whether to continue funding the program and whether to modify it). Experimental research, on the other hand, is often *basic research* in which researchers are attempting to understand underlying theories that explain behavior without necessarily looking for direct, immediate applications.

Second, new programs are, or should be, based on a *needs assessment*. A needs assessment is nonexperimental research in which researchers attempt to determine the practical needs of those who will be served by the program. For a school-based program, a researcher might ask questions such as, "What types of skills do the students need to acquire?" and "What types of program interventions to promote these skills will be most readily accepted by students, parents, and teachers?" Pure experimental research is seldom preceded by a formal needs assessment, which is associated with program evaluation because a major focus of evaluation is to estimate the extent to which a program has met the needs revealed in an earlier needs assessment.

Third, the programs, which are analogous to treatments in an experiment, are usually subject to change during the course of the evaluation. For instance, perhaps a program is designed to give teachers a major role in decision-making, with only a minor role for parents. If, in midstream, it is found that the parents are seeking more involvement, adjustments may be made in the program procedures to give parents a greater voice in decision-making. Although it is almost unheard of for an experimental researcher to make changes in the nature of a treatment during the course of an experiment, skilled program evaluators are open to such modifications. In fact, program evaluators collect information during the course of a program that assists in the process of modifying the program while it is being implemented. Collecting this information is called **formative evaluation**.

Formative evaluation has two prongs. First, information is collected on the *process* of implementing a program. For instance, when looking at the process, a researcher might ask, "Were the parents notified of the program in a timely manner?" and "Were the proposed meetings of parents and teachers conducted?" These questions clearly ask about the process, not the ultimate goals of student improvement. The second prong of formative evaluation involves collecting information on the *progress toward the ultimate goals*. For example, periodic achievement tests might be administered to see if students are showing signs of improvement. If not, evaluators and program administrators might rethink the program they are implementing and make appropriate changes. By looking at *progress*, those responsible for the program can often prevent disappointment in the final results of a program evaluation.

When evaluators collect information about participants' attainment of the ultimate goals at the end of the program (such as at the end of a school year), the activity is called **summative evaluation**. A summative evaluation report contains information about the final or long-term benefits of the program for its ultimate clients (such as students). Summative evaluation often involves a comparison with a control group. For instance, students in a program might be compared with similar students in other schools who are not in the program. Note that while experimental researchers typically strive to use random assignment (like pulling names out of a hat) to form experimental and control groups, program evaluators usually have to find an external group (such as students at another school) to serve as the control group.

The final program evaluation research report should provide an overview of the needs assessment that led to the development of the program, the results of the formative evaluation (i.e., data on program implementation and client progress), as well as data on the summative evaluation (i.e., the extent to which clients reached the ultimate program goals). It should also contain recommendations regarding extending the program in the future, including recommendations for improving the program's implementation.

EXERCISE ON TOPIC 11

1. Is "program evaluation" *or* "experimental research" almost always *applied research*?

2. Is a needs assessment associated with "experimental research" *or* "program evaluation"?

3. Is it acceptable to modify the treatments (programs) during the course of a program evaluation?

4. Suppose, as part of a program evaluation, an evaluator asks, "How many children were reading at grade level by the end of the program?" Is this question relevant to "formative" *or* to "summative" evaluation?

5. Suppose that as part of a program evaluation, an evaluator asks, "Are the clients in the job-placement program writing better résumés?" Is this question relevant to "formative" *or* "summative" evaluation?

6. Suppose, as part of a program evaluation, an evaluator asks, "Were key program personnel hired on time?" Is this question relevant to "formative" *or* "summative" evaluation?

7. When a researcher looks at the process of implementing a program, is the researcher conducting "formative" *or* "summative" evaluation?

8. Is examining program participants' *progress* toward attaining the ultimate goals of the program part of "formative" *or* "summative" evaluation?

9. Is the attainment of the final goals of a program by participants a topic for "formative" *or* "summative" evaluation?

Questions for Discussion

10. Suppose you were on the board of a foundation that was giving a grant for a program to a social welfare agency. Would you prefer to have the program evaluated by an employee of the program (such as the program director) *or* by an external, independent evaluator? Why?

11. Government agencies and organizations sometimes fund certain programs despite prior negative summative evaluations. Speculate on some of the reasons for this. Are any of the reasons justifiable?

For Students Who Are Planning Research

12. Will you be evaluating a program in your research? If yes, name the program and indicate whether you will be conducting both "formative" *and* "summative" research.

When planning research, it is imperative to consider potential harm to participants that might result from their participation. Often, certain treatments that researchers might want to administer in experimental studies present hazards. For instance, a research psychologist might expose an experimental group to an anxiety-provoking stimulus in a study designed to advance a theory on the sources and effects of anxiety. Clearly, some participants might suffer mental anguish as a result of being exposed to the treatment.

Participants also might be harmed in nonexperimental studies. For instance, the process of exploring sensitive traits (e.g., relationships with abusive parents) might cause participants to focus on them again, leading to renewed anxiety, sleeplessness, and so on.

Because of such potential problems, the research community has developed a body of ethical values regarding the use of humans as participants. The primary value is that participants must be *protected from both physical and psychological harm.* Unfortunately, it is not always possible to anticipate all the potential for harm, especially when using new treatments or measuring tools. Because of this, most universities and large school districts have research committees that review research plans for potential harm to participants.

Another important value is that participants *have a right to privacy.* For instance, most individuals would probably agree that it would be a violation of parents' rights to privacy for researchers to question children about discord between their parents without parental consent, even if the results might be very useful to educators, sociologists, psychologists, and other professionals.

A related value is that participants have a right to have the data collected about them as individuals kept *confidential.* Even if participants freely and knowingly provide information to researchers, the researchers have an obligation not to disclose the information to others *unless* the identities of the participants are disguised or hidden, which is often accomplished by using statistics such as group averages.

Also, almost all researchers agree that participants have a right to *knowledge of the purpose* of the research before they participate. Having this knowledge, they are in a better position to determine whether they want to participate. Unfortunately, complete honesty with participants about the purpose of a study sometimes makes it difficult or impossible to conduct research on important topics. For instance, suppose researchers want to study the influence of lobbyists on a group of state legislators. The researchers might get some legislators to allow the researchers to "shadow" them (i.e., follow them around unobtrusively) if the purpose is only vaguely described as "to understand the state's political process." However, how many legislators (especially those who allow themselves to be unduly influenced by lobbyists) would agree to being shadowed if researchers reveal the true purpose? Is it ethical to present only a vague general purpose that does not reveal specific goals? Do government employees have a right to privacy on the job? These types of questions illustrate the difficulties in balancing the need to protect participants with the need to collect information of benefit to society.[1]

A key to promoting ethical values is *informed consent.* To use informed consent, researchers inform the participants of (1) the general purpose of the research, (2) what will be done to them during the research, (3) what the potential benefit(s) to them and others might be, (4) what the potential for harm to them might be, and (5) the fact that they may withdraw at any time without penalty, even at midstream during the research. This information should be provided in writing, and the participants (or their guardians) should sign an informed consent form to indicate that they understand it and freely agree to participate.

Another key to promoting ethical values is to *debrief* participants after their participation in a study. Debriefing consists of reviewing the purpose(s) of the study and the procedure(s) used as well as offering to share the results with the participants when the results become available. The process of debriefing should also include reassurances that the data will remain confidential. In addition, participants should be allowed to ask for information about any aspect of the study in which they participated. During debriefing, researchers should try to identify participants who may need more help in overcoming unanticipated harm to them than a

---

[1] For more information on this topic, refer to *Ethical Principles in the Conduct of Research with Human Subjects*, published by the American Psychological Association. Visit www.apa.org for more information.

standard debriefing session provides. At the debriefing session, information should be provided on how to contact the researchers after the debriefing session so that participants can contact the researchers for more information in the future or to request assistance with any harmful effects that might reveal themselves at a later date.

EXERCISE ON TOPIC 12

1. Should researchers take steps to prevent psychological harm as well as physical harm to participants?

2. Should participants be told that they are free to withdraw from a study at any time without penalty?

3. Under the principle of informed consent, is it acceptable to hide the general purpose of a study from the participants?

4. Should informed consent be in writing?

5. Is debriefing done "before" or "after" a study is conducted?

6. What does debriefing cover?

7. Should information about participants be kept confidential even if the participants freely provided it to researchers?

Questions for Discussion

8. How would you answer these two rhetorical questions that are posed in the topic?
   - Is it ethical to present only a vague general purpose that does not reveal specific goals?
   - Do government employees have a right to privacy on the job?

9. Suppose a researcher wants to keep a class of third-grade students in from recess to administer an attitude-toward-school scale. The purpose is to help teachers understand their students' attitudes and how they might affect students' achievement in school. Is there potential for harm in this case? Would it be wise to seek informed consent from the parents? Why? Why not?

10. A researcher interviewed adolescents on their possible use of marijuana (with their informed consent). During the course of the interviews, some participants named other individuals who use marijuana but who have not provided informed consent to the researcher. Does this raise ethical concerns? What, if anything, can the researcher do to protect the other individuals?

11. Suppose one of your instructors asks you to be a participant in a research project but does not tell you the purpose of the research. Would you ask for information on the purpose before deciding whether to participate? Would you feel pressured to participate because the researcher is your instructor?

For Students Who Are Planning Research

12. Do you anticipate that the study you are planning has the potential to harm the participants? Will you be obtaining informed consent? Will you have your consent form reviewed by your professor? By a university committee? By others? Explain.

TOPIC 13   THE ROLE OF THEORY IN RESEARCH

A **theory** is a unified explanation for discrete observations that might otherwise be viewed as un-related or contradictory. One of the most widely studied theories in learning is reinforcement theory. It defines positive reinforcement as anything that increases the frequency of a response from an animal or individual. For instance, it is common to give praise as a reward to a dog for sitting. To the extent that the praise increases the sitting behavior, it constitutes positive reinforcement.

At first, reinforcement theory sounds obvious, and in a way, it is self-defining. So why has it been so carefully studied? Because it explains many apparently contradictory observations. For instance, suppose at first an individual praises a dog regularly for sitting and after a while becomes lax and offers praise intermittently. Common sense might suggest that the sitting behavior will decrease with the decrease in praise. However, the individual might actually observe an increase in sitting because reinforcement theory indicates that intermittent reinforcement[1] is, under many circumstances, more effective than consistent reinforcement. Thus, reinforcement theory is a unified set of principles that helps explain why certain behaviors increase in their frequency. Without it, behaviors that do not seem to be consistent or related to each other would be observed.

One of the major functions of research is to test hypotheses derived from an existing theory. To do this, a researcher *deduces* hypotheses that are consistent with the theory. For instance, an axiom of self-regulated learning theory states that the goals students adopt determine their level of cognitive engagement. From this, a researcher might deduce that when students know they will be tested again on the same material, those who have lower goals (e.g., a goal of getting 70% right) should ask for less feedback about wrongly answered test items than those who have higher goals.[2] A study that confirms this hypothesis lends support to the underlying theory. Assuming the study is methodologically strong, failure to confirm a hypothesis calls the theory (or parts of it) into question, causing theorists to consider reformulating it to account for the discrepancy.

Another major function of research is to provide the observations and conclusions on which researchers can *induce* theory. That is, researchers try to develop theories that explain events they have observed. Researchers who practice *qualitative research* often refer to this as **grounded theory** (i.e., theory that is grounded on observations).[3] Grounded theory is often thought of as evolutionary. That is, it usually is developed during the process of making observations, and it is regularly revised (i.e., evolves) as new observations warrant.

The desire by scientists to develop theories on all major aspects of human experience should not be surprising. Unified explanations of phenomena are clearly more useful than a collection of unrelated "facts" collected via nontheoretical research.

Students who are looking for a research topic for a thesis or term project would be well advised to consider a theory of interest. Testing some aspect of the theory makes a potential contribution to the understanding of all aspects of behavior related to the theory. In addition, students will find it easier to defend their selection of a research topic and write the introduction to the research report if it can be shown that the study has implications for validating and refining an important theory.

When thinking about theory as a basis for research, keep in mind that no theory of human behavior is universal (i.e., there almost always are exceptions to the rule). This is why researchers usually examine *trends across groups* in order to test or develop theories. However, do not overlook the possibility of designing a study specifically to examine those individuals who do not perform as predicted by a theory. Understanding how the dynamics of their behavior differ from those who act in the way predicted by theory may help in refining a theory to take account of exceptions.

---

[1] Technical terms for various schedules of reinforcement are not discussed here.

[2] For more information on this theory and to see an example of research based on the theory, see Azevedo, R., & Cromley, J. G. (2004). Does training on self-regulated learning facilitate students' learning with hypermedia? *Journal of Educational Psychology, 96,* 523–535.

[3] For more information on the use of the grounded theory approach to research, see Part H of this book. For an example of a study that employs grounded theory, see Pressley, M., Gaskins, I. W., Solic, K., & Collins, S. (2006). A portrait of Benchmark School: How a school produces high achievement in students who previously failed. *Journal of Educational Psychology, 98,* 282–306.

EXERCISE ON TOPIC 13

1. How is a *theory* defined in this topic?

2. Do researchers use "induction" *or* "deduction" to derive a hypothesis from a theory?

3. What are the two major functions of research mentioned in this topic?

4. If a hypothesis derived from a theory is not confirmed, what implications does this have for the theory?

5. Is grounded theory based on "induction" *or* "deduction"?

6. Is the use of grounded theory more likely to be associated with "qualitative" *or* "quantitative" research?

Question for Discussion

7. Examine the discussion of a theory in a textbook in your field. Does the author of the textbook cite research that supports it? Does he or she suggest unresolved issues relating to the theory that might be explored in future research? Explain.

For Students Who Are Planning Research

8. Is the purpose of your research to test a hypothesis deduced from a theory? (This is typically done by quantitative researchers. See Topics 9 and 10 for a brief explanation of the differences between qualitative and quantitative research.) Explain.

9. Is the purpose of your research to make observations on which a theory may be built? (This is typically done by qualitative researchers. See Topics 9 and 10 for a brief explanation of the differences between qualitative and quantitative research.) Explain.

10. Will you be conducting research without reference to theory? (Note that it is possible to plan and conduct research on practical matters without explicit reference to theory. For instance, suppose your local schools went on double shifts because of overcrowding, and you want to investigate the effects of the double shifts on students' attitudes and achievements. While there may be several theories that relate to this situation, you might conduct your research *as a practical, nontheoretical matter* in order to better inform decision-makers and taxpayers on this matter.) If you will not be referencing theory, will the results of your research still have important practical implications? Explain.

PART B

REVIEWING LITERATURE

Reviewing the research conducted by others is often the first step in planning a new research project. In this part, the reasons for reviewing literature and how it helps researchers identify a suitable idea for additional research are discussed. Because it is assumed that you already know how to locate books and articles in mass-circulation periodicals and newspapers, the emphasis here is on how computerized databases can make a search of academic journals more efficient and precise. Finally, some basic principles for writing literature reviews, including how to cite references, are described.

NOTES

TOPIC 14 REASONS FOR REVIEWING LITERATURE

A researcher begins by identifying a broad problem area. This could be a practical problem such as "the education of bilingual children" or it could be a more theoretical one such as "How valid is attribution theory in informal learning situations?"

Next, a researcher examines the literature about the problem area. Examining both the theoretical and research literature may help in identifying a testable hypothesis or a specific research purpose or research question.[1] In fact, authors of published research often make specific suggestions for future research in the last section of their research reports.[2]

After examining the literature, a researcher may decide to *replicate* a study that has already been published.[3] In a *strict replication*, researchers try to mimic the original study in all important respects because the purpose of a strict replication is to see if the same types of results as in the original study will be obtained. Of course, a strict replication should be undertaken only for studies with potentially important implications. Note that if the results of a study cannot be replicated by other researchers, the results of the original study may be viewed as invalid.

Another possibility is to locate an important study and conduct a *modified replication* (i.e., a replication with some major modification(s) such as examining a new population or using an improved measurement technique.

Because there are many topics on which the results of published research are conflicting, a third possibility is to plan a study designed to resolve a conflict. Published reviews of research often point out such conflicts and offer possible explanations of them.

After examining the existing research in a problem area, a researcher may arrive at a creative idea that is *not* a direct extension of existing research. While there are important cases of this in the history of science, they are rare. Thus, it is extremely unlikely that a novice researcher will have such an insight at the beginning of his or her professional career. Put another way, new research almost always has its origins in existing research.

In addition to helping to identify purposes for future research, reviewing published research provides three additional benefits. First, researchers may identify measuring tools (called *instruments*) that were used successfully by other researchers. He or she may also identify instruments found to be seriously flawed, which can be avoided in future research.

Second, a researcher may be able to identify and avoid dead ends (i.e., ideas for research may have already been thoroughly investigated and shown to be not fruitful, such as treatments that failed in experiments to produce the desired effects).

Third, researchers can get ideas on how to organize and write research reports by paying careful attention to the style and organization used by previous researchers.

When writing research reports, researchers are expected to cite relevant research. When writing a research report for publication in a journal, it is typical to integrate the literature into the introduction. (In theses and dissertations, the **literature review** is often presented in a separate chapter immediately following the chapter that contains the introduction.) Note that a well-crafted review of research shows readers the context within which the researcher was working. It can also help to justify a study if the literature is used to establish the importance of a research topic and to show how the research being reported on flows from previously published research.

For students who are conducting research, writing reviews of research allows the students to demonstrate to instructors, thesis committee members, and others that they were able to locate research relevant to their research purposes and write critical reviews that synthesize what is known about a topic.

In the next topic, methods for searching for literature electronically are explored. Then, specific techniques for writing literature reviews are explored in the remaining topics in this part of this book.

---

[1] See Topic 7 to review hypotheses as well as purposes and questions, which are alternatives to hypotheses, as the heart of research. A testable hypothesis is one that can be tested through direct observation.

[2] The last section is usually labeled "Discussion." See Part I of this book for more information on the typical structure of research reports.

[3] Check with your professor to see if this is acceptable in light of the objectives for the course.

EXERCISE ON TOPIC 14

1. When planning research, which should come first?
   A. Identify a broad problem area.
   B. Develop a testable hypothesis or research problem.

2. Suppose a researcher conducted a replication of a study but used a sample from a population different from the one used in the first study. What type of replication did the researcher conduct?

3. Should a researcher be surprised to find conflicting results in the research literature on a given topic?

4. "According to this topic, students would be wise to try to find a creative, new research idea (not derived from the literature) to explore in their first research project." Is this statement "true" or "false"?

5. In journal articles, the literature review is usually integrated into which part of the article?

6. How can a researcher use a review of literature to help justify a study the researcher has undertaken?

Question for Discussion

7. Has the information in this topic convinced you that reviewing published literature is an important part of the research planning process? Explain.

For Students Who Are Planning Research

8. Have you begun reading the literature on your problem area? If yes, are you planning a strict replication of a previous study? A modified replication? A study that might resolve a conflict in the literature? Explain.

9. Was your research purpose or hypothesis explicitly suggested in the literature you have read? Explain.

TOPIC 15 LOCATING LITERATURE ELECTRONICALLY

The use of electronic databases (i.e., databases accessible via computers) to locate articles in academic journals is explored. Note that journal articles are the major source of original reports of empirical research as well as the primary source of information on established and emerging theories.

Three of the major databases in the social and behavioral sciences are (1) *Sociological Abstracts*, which contains *Sociological Abstracts* and *Social Planning/Policy & Development Abstracts*, covering journal articles published in more than 1,800 journals; (2) *PsycINFO*, which contains *Psychological Abstracts*, with abstracts of journal articles worldwide since 1974; and (3) *ERIC*, which contains abstracts of articles in education found in more than 600 journals dating from 1966 to the present.[1] While the following examples illustrate the use of the *ERIC* database, the principles for searching all three databases are quite similar.

The best access point for the *ERIC* database is at www.eric.ed.gov. Unlike most other databases, access is free of charge to any user, and it can be accessed from any computer connected to the Internet without restrictions such as passwords. (Other electronic databases are usually free of charge to students through their college libraries, which pay license fees that permit students and professors to use them without additional charge.)

The first step in searching a database is to examine its thesaurus. At www.eric.ed.gov, click on the "Thesaurus" tab near the top of the screen. At this point, a researcher can browse the terms used by *ERIC* (either alphabetically or within broad categories). Also, any term can be entered to find out if the term is used by *ERIC* in classifying journal articles in the database.

A thesaurus can help in refining a research topic. For instance, if "Drinking" is entered as a search term (to the right of "Search For:") in the *ERIC* Thesaurus, five terms (called "descriptors") related to drinking appear, including "drinking," "drinking drivers" and "drinking water." By clicking on the word "drinking," the user finds a brief definition called a "Scope Note," which indicates that the term

"drinking" is defined as "consumption of alcoholic beverages." It also indicates that "alcohol abuse" is a narrower term. By clicking on "alcohol abuse," the user finds that the Scope Note defines this term as "excessive or otherwise inappropriate ingestion of alcoholic beverages, often causing risk or injury to health and impaired social functioning." In addition, the Thesaurus indicates that "alcoholism" is a "narrower term" than "alcohol abuse," while a "broader term" is "substance abuse." Related terms such as "alcohol education," "antisocial behavior," and "fetal alcohol syndrome" are also given. With this information from the Thesaurus, a researcher can determine which of the *ERIC* terms will be most appropriate for a literature search.

Suppose a user decided that the term "alcohol abuse" was the most appropriate for his or her purposes. By clicking on the "*ERIC* Search" tab near the top of the screen, then clicking on the "Advanced Search" tab and typing in "alcohol abuse" (with the box to limit the results to "journal articles" checked under "Publication Type(s):"), the user finds references for 1,870 articles (as of the time of this writing).[2]

Frequently, researchers want to narrow their database searches in order to make them more precise. An important instruction for doing this is *AND*. For instance, if a researcher uses the instruction to locate articles with "*alcohol abuse AND treatment*," *ERIC* will identify only 258 journal articles that deal with *both* alcohol abuse *and* its treatment.

A search can be made more precise by using *NOT*. Using the instruction "*alcohol abuse NOT college*" will identify all articles relating to alcohol abuse but exclude those that relate to alcohol abuse at the college level.

A researcher can conduct a search for all articles containing either (or both) of two keywords by using *OR*. For instance, the instruction to find "*dyslexia OR learning disabilities*" will locate all articles with either one of these descriptors. Thus, using *OR* broadens a search.[3]

In the Advanced Search mode, it is sometimes useful to search for authors by selecting the "Au-

[1] The emphasis in this topic is on journal articles. Note that *PsycINFO* also abstracts books, *Sociological Abstracts* also abstracts dissertations, and *ERIC* also abstracts unpublished documents, such as convention papers, which are available on microfiche.

[2] Before beginning the search, click on the "Advanced Search" link and change the check mark from "Any Publication Type" to "Journal Articles."
[3] The terms *AND*, *NOT*, and *OR* are known as "Boolean operators" or as "logical operators."

thor" box in the "Keywords (all fields)" pull-down menu. This is especially useful if the name of an important researcher (or theorist) in the research area is known and the researcher wants to identify additional publications by him or her.

While in the Advanced Search mode, it is possible to search for articles that have the keywords in their titles. For instance, as noted above, a search for "alcohol abuse" in any field in journal articles yields an unmanageable 1,870 publications. Restricting the search to articles containing the term *alcohol abuse* in their titles yields only 161 articles. These are the 161 of the 1,870 that are most likely to deal directly with alcohol abuse (as opposed to publications in which it is dealt with as a side issue) because the authors mentioned alcohol abuse in the titles of their articles.

Other important electronic databases for locating journal articles and other types of literature are described in Appendix A. Whichever database is used, it is important to first read carefully the instructions for using the particular database being accessed. (Instructions can usually be accessed from the home page of a database.) While all databases permit searches for publications that deal with particular keywords, many have special features to assist users.

For more information on accessing electronic databases, consult a college reference librarian.

EXERCISE ON TOPIC 15

1. Which database is free of charge to any user?

2. What is the first step in searching a database?

3. In *ERIC*, what is a "scope note"?

4. The terms found in the *ERIC* Thesaurus are known as what?

5. Which of the following will yield a larger number of references?
   A. A search using "alcohol abuse *AND* treatment."
   B. A search using "alcohol abuse *OR* treatment."

6. If a researcher wanted to search for journal articles on Term A but wanted to exclude articles that also include Term B, which logical operator should the researcher use?

7. Which of the following will yield a smaller number of references?
   A. A search for the keyword "discipline" as well as a separate search for the keyword "rewards."
   B. A search for "discipline *AND* rewards."

Question for Discussion

8. If you have searched for journal articles electronically in the past, briefly describe your experience(s). Was it easy to do? What suggestions do you have for others who will be doing it for the first time?

For Students Who Are Planning Research

9. Name some keywords you might use in an electronic search of the literature. Have you checked in a thesaurus to see if they are valid for use in the database you plan to access?

10. Have you (or will you) use the logical operators described in this topic? Explain.

A straightforward approach for beginning a literature review is to identify the broad problem area and indicate why it is important. Example 1 shows the first two sentences of a literature review. The first sentence clearly identifies the topic (substance abuse among Latino youth) and the second sentence asserts that it is an important problem.

EXAMPLE 1
Substance use and abuse are among the most well-documented behavioral risks for Latino youth. There is evidence that lifetime drug-use rates for Latinos are increasing, and that use and related outcomes pose a significant public health problem for Latino communities (Martinez, Eddy, & DeGarmo, 2003; Vega & Gil, 1999).[1]

The importance of a topic may also be established by citing statistics that indicate how many individuals are affected by a particular problem (e.g., how many individuals were victims of armed assault last year) or how many individuals are in the population of interest (e.g., how many children are enrolled in special classes for the gifted). Some major sources for statistics are described in Appendix B.

Another straightforward way to begin a literature review is to start with a conceptual definition[2] of a key variable. Example 2 illustrates the beginning of a review that starts with a definition.

EXAMPLE 2
Narcissism is defined as a pervasive pattern of grandiosity and self-importance (American Psychiatric Association, 2000). Narcissistic individuals are preoccupied with dreams of success, power, beauty, brilliance, or ideal love. Such individuals appear as though they are on an interpersonal stage....[3]

Note that it is acceptable to cite a published conceptual definition, as was done in Example 2 above.

If a literature review starts with definitions, the definitions should be followed by statements (and statistics, if any) indicating the importance of the problem area. See Appendix C for examples of how various researchers started their reviews.

After establishing the importance of the research topic and providing definitions of key terms, the next step is to write a *topic-by-topic* description of relevant research. Provide major and minor subheadings to guide readers through a long literature review. For instance, some of the **major headings** and *minor subheadings* used by Vaitl et al. (2006) in their review of research on altered states of consciousness are shown in Example 3.

EXAMPLE 3
Spontaneously Occurring Altered States of Consciousness (ACS)
States of Drowsiness
Daydreaming
Sleep and Dreaming
Near-Death Experiences
Physically and Physiologically Induced ASC
Extreme Environmental Conditions
Starvation and Diet
Respiratory Maneuvers[4]

Avoid writing a series of abstracts (i.e., writing a summary of one article, then a summary of another article, and so on). Instead, group references together when they have something in common. For instance, in Example 4, the authors make two points and cite two references to substantiate each one.

EXAMPLE 4
In addition to economic disadvantage and poor working conditions, research has noted that Latino migrant farm workers experience racial and ethnic discrimination (Dalla & Christensen, 2005; With & Dollar, 2004). The effects of racial and ethnic stereotypes depicting Latinos as "defective" are particularly deleterious at the level of service delivery (Dalla et al., 2004; Jackson, 1995).[5]

---

[1] Martinez, C. R. Jr. (2006). Effects of differential family acculturation on Latino adolescent substance use. *Family Relations*, *55*, 306–317.

[2] See Topic 8 for a discussion of the differences between conceptual and operational definitions. Conceptual definitions may also be integrated throughout a literature review as new terms are introduced. Operational definitions are usually provided in the Methods section of research reports.

[3] Otway, L. J., & Vignoles, V. L. (2006). Narcissism and childhood recollections: A quantitative test of psychoanalytic predictions. *Personality and Social Psychology Bulletin*, *32*, 104–116.

---

[4] Vaitl, D. et al. (2006). Psychobiology of altered states of consciousness. *Psychological Bulletin*, *131*, 98–127.

[5] Parra-Cardona, J. R., Bulok, L. A., Imig, D. R., Villarruel, F. A., & Gold, S. J. (2006). "Trabajando duro todos los días": Learning from the life experiences of Mexican-origin migrant families. *Family Relations*, *55*, 361–375.

At the end of a long literature review, it is appropriate to present a brief summary.

EXERCISE ON TOPIC 16

1. This topic suggests two ways that a writer might begin a literature review. What is the first way that is mentioned?

2. This topic suggests two ways that a writer might begin a literature review. What is the second way that is mentioned?

3. This topic suggests that statistics can be cited to establish what?

4. What should be provided in order to guide readers through a long literature review?

5. Instead of writing a series of abstracts, what should the writer do?

6. Examine the last sentence in Example 1 in this topic. Note that two references are given for the sentence. Is this appropriate?

Question for Discussion

7. Consider the six literature review excerpts in Appendix C. Each excerpt shows the beginning paragraph(s) of a literature review in a research article. In your opinion, do they all convince you of the importance of the respective problem areas? Explain.

For Students Who Are Planning Research

8. Name some of the headings and subheadings you anticipate you might use to organize your literature review. (Note that these may change after you have carefully examined all the literature on your topic.)

A literature review should be a *critical* assessment of the literature on a topic. Novice writers often make two common mistakes that lead to *noncritical* reviews. First, they often take the results of each study to be "facts" that have been proven. As indicated below, all studies should be presumed to be flawed and, therefore, offer only degrees of evidence, not "truths" to be accepted noncritically. Second, novice writers often discuss all studies as though they were equal in quality, when, in fact, some studies are methodologically superior to others.

To prepare to write a critical review, the writer should assess the quality of each research article that will be cited. The first important area that requires critical assessment is sampling. More often than not, researchers work with samples that are less than ideal (such as volunteers instead of random samples of the populations of interest). Weaknesses in sampling limit the generalizability of the results. For instance, the results of a study on learning theory using a sample of psychology students who volunteered to serve as participants in a study would have limited generalizability to nonvolunteers.

The second important area that requires critical assessment is instrumentation (i.e., measurement instruments). It is safe to presume that all instruments are flawed to some extent. Furthermore, it is safe to presume that various methods of measuring a given variable might lead to somewhat different results. For instance, one researcher on nutrition might measure by asking overweight adolescents to keep diaries of what they eat throughout a day. Fearing that participants might not be completely truthful in diaries, another researcher on nutrition might observe the food choices of overweight adolescents in the school cafeteria. The second method has the limitation of being conducted in a highly structured environment, where the food choices might be limited. Neither method is either "right" or "wrong." Instead, they are two methods that have limitations, which should be considered when critically assessing the results of the studies.

The third important area to consider when critically assessing studies that will be cited in a literature review applies only to experiments (i.e., studies in which treatments are administered to participants in order to estimate the effects of the treatments on the participants' subsequent behaviors). Experiments are often flawed by having inappropriate control conditions (such as comparing a treatment group consisting of volunteers with a control group from the general population). Also, laboratory experiments (e.g., receiving rewards for making appropriate food choices in a laboratory setting) may have limited generalizability to receiving rewards in a natural environment (i.e., the rewards may have different effects in the natural environment than in the laboratory setting).

Issues in sampling are discussed in detail in Part C of this book, while issues in instrumentation are covered in Part D, and considerations in the evaluation of experiments are covered in Part E. Careful attention to these parts of the book will help in making informed assessments of the results of published studies.

Fortunately, researchers often discuss the limitations of their studies, usually in the last section of their research reports. Examining researchers' self-assessments of the limitations of their research can help writers of literature reviews in which the studies will be cited. Example 1 shows a portion of such a discussion of limitations.

EXAMPLE 1
One limitation of this study is that the sample was composed entirely of college students. It is possible that this group is more acculturated than the general Hispanic population. A second limitation has to do with the fact that our sample is predominantly female…. In addition, these students volunteered to come in for counseling, thus suggesting a possible volunteer bias.[1]

Because flaws are widespread in research, it is important to assess the seriousness of the flaws and use appropriate terms when describing the results. For instance, Example 2 shows some terms that might be used to describe the results of research with serious weaknesses.

EXAMPLE 2
Doe's (2006) study provides some evidence that….

Recent research by Doe (2006) raises the possibility that….

Preliminary evidence suggest that…(Doe, 2006)….

---

[1] Martinez, S., Stillerman, L., & Waldo, M. (2005). Reliability and validity of the SCL-90-R with Hispanic college students. *Hispanic Journal of Behavior Sciences, 27*, 254–264.

Of course, some studies provide strong evidence such as a national survey using a large, representative sample. Also, sometimes there is a series of studies on the same topic, all of which have similar results, making the overall findings of the series highly reliable. Terms that might be used to refer to strong evidence are shown in Example 3.

EXAMPLE 3

Overall, this set of studies clearly indicates that....

In summary, the five studies described above provide nearly conclusive evidence that....

Doe's (2006) national survey demonstrates that....

It is not necessary to use terms such as those in Examples 2 and 3 to qualify every comment about each study cited in a literature review However, keep in mind that when a writer presents a finding or statement from the literature without qualification, readers are likely to assume that the writer believes the underlying methodology and logic are reasonably sound.

EXERCISE ON TOPIC 17

1. According to the topic, novice writers often make two common mistakes. What is the first one that is mentioned in this topic?

2. According to the topic, novice writers often make two common mistakes. What is the second one that is mentioned in this topic?

3. "More often than not, researchers work with samples that are less than ideal." According to this topic, is this statement "true" *or* "false"?

4. "It is safe to assume that flawed instruments are rare in research." According to this topic, is this statement "true" *or* "false"?

5. Do researchers often discuss the limitations of their own studies?

6. When a writer presents a finding or statement from the literature without qualification, readers are likely to assume what?

Question for Discussion

7. Suppose this statement appeared in a literature review: "The results of Doe's (2006) study clearly prove that A is higher than B." In light of the information in this topic, is such a statement justified? Explain.

For Students Who Are Planning Research

8. In the past, have you ever written an *uncritical* literature review for a term project? Has this topic convinced you that such reviews can be misleading? Explain.

TOPIC 18   CREATING A SYNTHESIS

As indicated in the previous topic, a literature review should be based on a critical assessment of the literature on a topic. However, it should consist of more than just critical summaries of individual studies. Instead, a literature review should be a **synthesis**—providing a "whole" picture of what is known and what is not known as well as an attempt to show how diverse pieces of information fit together and make sense.

A key to creating a synthesis is to write a review that moves from subtopic to subtopic (not from one study to another), while citing whatever studies are relevant for each topic. See Example 3 in Topic 16 for an example of a topic outline for writing a literature review.

To further the creation of a synthesis, the writer of a review should explicitly point out major trends and commonalities in the results of previous research. Example 1 illustrates how this might be done.

EXAMPLE 1
People tend to become entrapped in previously chosen situations and throw away good money after bad decisions. As a result, ultimate losses are heavily increased. This has been demonstrated as a reliable and robust phenomenon (Bazerman, Giuliano, & Appelman, 1984; Brockner, 1992; Brockner & Rubin, 1985; Garland, 1990; Staw, 1976, 1997; Teger, 1980). Laboratory findings and field studies simply confirm what has been noted as a recurrent tragedy in everyday life....[1]

In addition, when there are major discrepancies in results, they should be pointed out, and possible explanations for the discrepancies should be noted. This is done in Example 2 by pointing out an important difference in the samples used in the studies.

EXAMPLE 2
While the studies described above support the prediction that X is greater than Y in samples of college students, a recent study of young adolescents found no difference in X and Y. It may be that X and Y operate differently within different age groups.

A "whole" picture of the literature on a research topic should also explicitly point out gaps in the literature, which is illustrated in Example 3. Note that the purpose of research is often to fill in a gap found in the literature.

EXAMPLE 3
Research on the affective consequences of being a target of social discrimination has mainly focused on depressed emotions (for an overview, see Major, Quinton, & McCoy, 2002). So far, anger—and especially self-directed anger—has not been taken into account.[2]

To facilitate providing readers with an overview, writers of reviews should avoid providing extensive, detailed descriptions of the research methodology used in each study. In other words, it is usually not necessary to provide details on how studies were conducted. The main exceptions are when the writer of the review wants to document a particular weakness in a study being cited (e.g., use of a small, unrepresentative sample) or when the details of the methodology might help explain why two studies on the same topic arrived at substantially different results.

In addition, one or more paragraphs (or even whole sections) might be devoted to describing a particular author's written work when the work is central to one or more points being made in the literature review.

Because direct quotations break the flow of a presentation, they should be used very sparingly. Quotations normally should be used only for (1) presenting especially well-crafted definitions of key terms, (2) presenting concepts that are explained especially well with a particular set of words, and (3) clarifying differences of opinion in the literature when seeing that the differences in wording (such as the wording of theories) might help readers understand the issues involved.

The flow of presentation can be facilitated through the use of appropriate transitional terms and phrases (e.g., "however," "as a consequence," and "indeed") both within and between paragraphs.

Finally, a brief summary of the literature review placed at the end of a review can help readers grasp the "whole" of the literature review.

---

[1] Zhang, L., & Baumeister, R. F. (2006). Your money or your self-esteem: Threatened egotism promotes costly entrapment in losing endeavors. *Personality and Social Psychology Bulletin, 32*, 881–893.

[2] Hansen, N., & Sassenberg, K. (2006). Does social identification harm or serve as a buffer? The impact of social identification on anger after experiencing social discrimination. *Personality and Social Psychology Bulletin, 32*, 983–996.

Exercise on Topic 18

1. "An effective literature review should consist solely of a set of critical summaries of individual studies." Is this statement "true" or "false"?

2. "A key to creating a synthesis is to write a review that moves from subtopic to subtopic." Is this statement "true" or "false"?

3. Is it desirable to point out major trends and commonalities in the results of previous research?

4. Is it desirable to point out gaps in the literature?

5. Should the methodology employed in each of the studies cited in a review be described in detail?

6. When would it be appropriate to devote one or more paragraphs to describing a particular author's written work?

7. Why should direct quotations be used sparingly?

8. What can be placed at the end of a review to help readers grasp the "whole" of the literature review?

Questions for Discussion

9. When you wrote term papers in the past, did you include many direct quotations from the authors you cited? Are you surprised by the suggestion made in this topic regarding quotations? Explain.

10. Before you read this topic, would you have been likely to write a series of summaries of previous research in the belief that the series would produce an effective literature review? Explain.

For Students Who Are Planning Research

11. Have you started writing a literature review on your topic? If yes, what types of changes will you make in it based on what you learned in this topic?

TOPIC 19 CITING REFERENCES

While there are a number of methods (called *styles*) for citing references, the Harvard method is the one most widely used in the social and behavioral sciences. This method is also known as the author-date referencing system.

The American Psychological Association (APA) has adopted and modified the Harvard method, and the *Publication Manual of the American Psychological Association* describes in detail how to use this method.[1] In this topic, some of the basics for citing sources and preparing a reference list using this method are described.

In the text of a literature review, the last name(s) of the author(s) of a reference can be made the subject of the sentence, as in Example 1, or referred to parenthetically, as in Example 2. The form shown in Example 1 obviously emphasizes the authorship, while the form shown in Example 2 emphasizes the content of the statement (in this case, by making "managerial sociology" the subject of the sentence).

EXAMPLE 1
Doe and Smith (2006) point out that despite being a relatively new field of inquiry, managerial sociology has made important contributions to our understanding of this issue. Specifically....

EXAMPLE 2
Despite being a relatively new field of inquiry, managerial sociology has made important contributions to our understanding of this issue (Doe & Smith, 2006). Specifically....

Making the authors' last names the subjects of sentences is helpful when a reviewer wants to compare and contrast the findings (or thoughts) of two or more authors, as shown in Example 3.

EXAMPLE 3
While Lopez (2005) reported that X increased as a function of Y, Jones (2006) reported no increase. The reason for this discrepancy is difficult to determine. However, Jones used a larger sample and better....

As indicated in previous topics, it is often a good idea to group authors together when they make a common point. However, except for school assignments where a student might be required to show all references, long strings of references for a single point should usually be avoided. To do this, use the abbreviation "e.g.," meaning "for example," which is done in Example 4. Note that by using "e.g." the author is pointing out that there are more studies with the same type of result but only some of the most important ones are being cited.

EXAMPLE 4
The superiority of X over Y in the treatment of Z has been widely reported in the literature. The strongest evidence to date has been obtained by numerous researchers who have used large, national samples (e.g., Solis, 2003; Wong, 2004; Smith & West, 2005; Brett, 2006). These studies tend to confirm the principle that....

The reference list at the end of a research report should include references for only those citations that were cited in the body of the report. Do not include all relevant references, as might be done in a bibliography or suggested reading list.

The items in a reference list should be listed alphabetically by authors' last names, as shown in Example 5. Note that the first two references in Example 5 are for journal articles, the third one is for a book, and the last one is for material found on a Web site.

EXAMPLE 5
Adams, J. G. (2006). The effects of anything on everything. *Journal of Behavior Therapy and Analysis*, *23*, 55–72.

Brennan, K. P., & Strang, T. S. (2005). The reliability of popular measures of depression. *Personality and Social Disorders in Education*, *44*, 145–157.

Chin, W. D. (2005). *The art of being kind*. New York: Brooks Publishing.

Lopez, F. L. (2005). "Cognitive structure of intelligence." Retrieved February 23, 2006 from www.apa.org/info/st1445

When using APA style in preparing a reference list, it is important to note details of the style such as the following:

For a journal article: The title of the article is in lowercase except for the first word (or first word following a colon), and the title of the journal is in upper- and lowercase and is italicized. It is followed by the volume number, which is also italicized.

For a book: The title of the book is in lowercase except for the first word (or first word following a colon) and is italicized.

---

[1] Copies of the manual can be found in psychology departments' required textbook sections of most college and university bookstores. Copies can also be purchased at www.apa.org.

For material found on the Web: Provide the date on which the material was accessed because the content of a Web site might vary from day to day.

For all sources: Follow the punctuation used in the examples carefully. For instance, when writing in English, a comma is not necessary between two elements in a list. However, in APA style, a comma is used between the names of two authors (e.g., Brennan, K. P., & Strang, T. S.).

Regardless of the particular style being followed, apply it accurately and consistently. Failure to do so will raise questions about the care taken with other aspects of the research project.

Exercise on Topic 19

1. The American Psychological Association (APA) adopted and modified which method for citing references?

2. When citing a reference in the text by putting authors' surnames in parentheses, what is the writer emphasizing?

3. In addition to emphasizing authorship, what is the other reason why a writer might want to make the authors' surnames the subjects of sentences in a literature review?

4. Instead of citing all references relevant to a particular topic, a writer can use what abbreviation to begin the list of some sample references?

5. In APA style, should the reference list include references for additional readings not cited in the literature review *or* should the reference list contain only references for citations made in the body of the literature review?

6. In the citation for a journal article, should the title of the article be put in italics?

7. In the reference for a book, should the title of the book be put in italics?

8. When there are two authors for a reference, should a comma be placed between their names (in APA style)?

Question for Discussion

9. Is the APA style widely used in your area of study? If no, what is the name of the most dominant style? (Examining journal articles in your field will help you determine the answer to this question. Also, some journals include instructions to authors near the beginning or end of each issue of the journal.)

For Students Who Are Planning Research

10. Have you used APA style in the past? Will you be using it when you write the report of your research? Explain.

PART C

SAMPLING

When it is impractical to study an entire population, researchers draw a sample, study it, and infer that what is true of the sample is probably also true of the population. Because an inference to a population is only as good as the method used to draw the sample, the advantages and disadvantages of various methods of sampling are explored in detail in this part of the book. The issue of sample size is also considered.

NOTES

Topic 20 Biased and Unbiased Sampling

Researchers frequently draw a **sample** from a **population**, which is the group in which researchers are ultimately interested. A population may be large, such as all social workers in the United States, or small, such as all social workers employed by a specific hospital. If a researcher studies every member of a population, the researcher is conducting a **census**. For large populations, however, it is more efficient to study a sample instead of conducting a census. After drawing a sample, researchers study it and then make inferences to the population. That is, researchers infer that the characteristics of the sample probably are the characteristics of the population.[1]

Obviously, the quality of a sample affects the quality of the inferences made from a sample to the population. Thus, a poor sample is likely to lead to incorrect inferences. The two questions researchers ask when evaluating a sample are: "Is the size adequate?" (a question that is discussed in Topics 25 and 26) and "Is the sample biased?"

A researcher can select an **unbiased** sample by giving every member of a population an equal chance of being included in the sample. One way to do this is to put the names of all individuals in the population on slips of paper, mix them up, and draw as many as needed for the sample. The result is called a **simple random sample**.[2]

Note that researchers cannot give every member of a population an equal chance of being included unless the researchers are able to identify all members of the population of interest. Failure to identify all members of a population is a major source of bias in sampling. For instance, if the population of interest consists of all homeless individuals in a city, but researchers can identify only those who seek public assistance, researchers can sample only from these members of the population. This creates a bias against the less-visible homeless who may be less resourceful, more destitute (or less destitute), and so on. To the extent that a sample is biased against less-visible homeless individuals, the inferences about all homeless individuals will be incorrect to an unknown extent (i.e., it is not possible to estimate how much error a bias of this type has caused because researchers do not have information on less-visible homeless individuals).

Researchers also obtain biased samples when they use **samples of convenience** (also known as *accidental samples*). For instance, if a psychology professor wants to study a principle of learning theory as it applies to all college sophomores but only uses those students who happen to be enrolled in his or her introductory psychology class, the sample is biased against all other college sophomores. This introduces many possibilities for error. For instance, the professor may have a reputation for giving high grades and thus may attract students with learning styles that are different from those of the general population of college sophomores. Also, of course, different colleges attract different types of students, and this professor has sampled only from students enrolled at the college where the professor teaches.

A third major source of bias is **volunteerism**. Volunteerism takes two forms. First, sometimes researchers simply issue a call for volunteers. This is often done in medical research in which researchers advertise for potential participants, such as those with chronic heart conditions, in order to test new methods of treatment. What is wrong with this? The possibilities are almost endless. For instance, some individuals may volunteer because they are becoming desperate as their condition worsens, whereas those who are doing better may be less inclined to expose themselves to experimental treatment, *or* those who volunteer may be more persistent and resourceful (and thus in better health) than the general population of those with heart conditions. These two opposing possibilities illustrate why researchers strive to eliminate bias—because they often cannot even speculate accurately on the direction in which a given bias might affect the results of a study.

Second, volunteerism might bias a sample even if a researcher begins by identifying a random sample from an entire population. For instance, a researcher might draw a random sample of all freshmen at a college and contact them to take part in a study of attitudes toward the use of instructional technology in higher education. For a variety of reasons, many of those in the random sample the researcher has selected may refuse to participate. Those who do participate, in effect, are volunteers

---

[1] The process of *inferring* from a sample to a population is also called *generalizing*. Inferential statistics, which are described in Part F of this book, assist in determining the reliability of inferences made from samples to populations.

[2] Another method for drawing a simple random sample is described in the next topic.

and may be fundamentally different from nonvolunteers—such as by being more interested in technology and more concerned about being successful in their educational pursuits.

Exercise on Topic 20

1. In this topic, how is *population* defined?

2. If a researcher studies every member of a population, what type of study is the researcher conducting?

3. How can a researcher draw an unbiased sample?

4. Suppose a researcher drew a random sample from a population of college students but some of those selected refuse to take part in the study. Are the students who participated in the study a "biased" *or* an "unbiased" sample of the population?

5. If a researcher mails questionnaires to all clients of a social worker, and 50% of them are completed and returned, is the sample "biased" *or* "unbiased"?

6. Suppose a psychologist has his or her clients participate in an experiment simply because they are readily accessible (not drawn at random from the population of interest). What type of sample is being used?

7. Briefly describe one way a researcher can draw a simple random sample.

Questions for Discussion

8. Individuals who receive questionnaires in the mail often fail to return them, creating a bias because those who do return them are volunteers. Speculate on some things a researcher can do to get more individuals to respond. (Consider mailed questionnaires you have received in the past and your reasons for responding or not responding.)

9. Are you convinced by the text that researchers should go to great lengths to avoid bias in their samples? Why? Why not?

10. Suppose you drew a random sample of all licensed clinical psychologists in your community to interview by phone. On the days you made the phone calls, some of them were not available to be interviewed, so you drew replacements for them at random from the population of licensed clinical psychologists. Speculate on whether the sample is biased *or* unbiased in light of the fact that replacements were drawn at random.

For Students Who Are Planning Research

11. Do you anticipate you will be drawing a sample for your study *or* will you be conducting a census?

12. If you will be sampling, do you anticipate that you will be using a biased sample? If yes, what do you anticipate will be the source of the bias? Is there anything you can do to reduce the bias? Explain.

As indicated in the previous section, **a simple random sample** is one in which every member of a population is given an equal chance of being included in a sample.

Putting names on slips of paper and drawing them from a hat is one way to obtain a random sample. Another way is to use a table of random numbers, a portion of which is reproduced in Table 1 near the end of this book. It consists of numbers that are unrelated to each other or to anything else. To use such a table, a researcher must give each member of a population a *number name*, and each name must contain the same number of digits. For instance, if there are 70 members of a population, the researcher should name one of the individuals 00 (it does not matter who the first individual is because the researcher is only renaming individuals with "number names" at this point—not selecting individuals). The researcher should name a second individual 01, name a third individual 02, and so on.[1]

After giving each individual a unique number name, the researcher can flip to any page in a book of random numbers (there is only one page of such a book in Table 1) and, without looking, point to a number—this is the number of the first individual selected. Assume that the first number pointed to is the first digit in the first row (Row #1) in Table 1, which is the number 2. The digit to the right of it is 1; together, they constitute the number 21. Thus, individual number 21 has been selected. Now, move two digits to the right. The next two digits (ignoring the space between them, which is there only to help guide your eye) are 0 and 4. Thus, individual number 04 has been selected. The next two digits are 9 and 8. Because there are only 70 individuals in the population, no one is named 98. Thus, this number does not select anyone, so the researcher should continue to the right in the first row in the table. The next two digits are 0 and 8, which selects individual number 08. The researcher should continue in this manner until he or she has the number of participants needed for the sample.[2]

It is important to note that random samples are subject to error. For instance, quite by chance a random sample might contain a disproportionately large number of males, high achievers, and so on. Error created by random sampling is simply called **sampling error** by statisticians. Fortunately, if researchers use samples of adequate size (a topic discussed in Topics 25 and 26), sampling errors are minimized. In addition, researchers can evaluate the effects of sampling errors by using inferential statistics, which are discussed in detail in Part F of this book.

Notice that bias also creates errors when sampling (see Topic 20). However, errors due to bias are nonchance errors, which are not reduced by increasing sample size. For instance, if a researcher samples for a political survey and the researcher's method is biased against Republicans (for example, by including too many urban voters, who tend to be Democrats), increasing the sample size using the same biased sampling method yields a larger sample of voters who tend not to be Republicans. The larger sample is no less biased than the smaller one (it is just as biased as the smaller one). Thus, increasing sample size does not necessarily decrease bias.

Another method of sampling that many researchers regard as being essentially equivalent to simple random sampling is **systematic sampling**. In this type of sampling, every *n*th individual is selected. The number "*n*" can be any number such as two, in which case a researcher would select every second individual.[3] However, there is a potential problem with this method. Suppose someone has arranged the population in such a way that every second individual is somehow different from the others. Perhaps the population has been arranged in this order: man next to woman, next to man, next to woman, and so on. If a researcher draws every other individual, the researcher will obtain a sample of all males or all females. Because a researcher cannot be sure that no one has ordered a list of the population in a way that might affect the sample, an alphabetical list (as opposed to any other kind, such as a classroom seating chart) is preferred when using systematic sampling. Note that a researcher should go completely through the alphabetical list

---

[1] Notice that because the population size (70) contains two digits, every member of the population is being given a two-digit number name.
[2] Computer programs may also be used to select random samples. For instance, consult: www.random.org and/or www.randomizer.org/form.htm.

---

[3] Divide the population size by the desired sample size to determine the value of *n*.

(through the letter *z*) because different national origin groups tend to concentrate at different points in the alphabet. Following this procedure yields a good sample, but note that it is a *systematic sample*, and it should *not* be referred to as a random sample.

EXERCISE ON TOPIC 21

1. Is there a sequence or pattern to the numbers in a table of random numbers?

2. This topic covers how to use a table of random numbers to draw what type of sample?

3. What is the name for errors created by random sampling?

4. How can researchers minimize sampling errors?

5. Can researchers minimize the effects of a bias in sampling by increasing the sample size?

6. Suppose a researcher wants to sample from a population of 99 clients and the random starting point in Table 1 is the first digit in the last row (Row #26). What are the numbers of the first two clients selected?

7. Suppose a researcher wants to sample from a population of 500 clients and the random starting point in Table 1 is the first digit in the fifth row (Row #5). What are the numbers of the first two clients selected?

8. If a researcher draws every other individual from a list of the population, the researcher is using what type of sampling?

9. What is the potential problem with systematic sampling?

10. How can a researcher get around the problem you named in the answer to Question 9?

Questions for Discussion

11. Suppose a friend was planning to use simple random sampling in a research project from which he or she wants to generalize to all students on a campus. Would you recommend drawing names from a hat *or* using a table of random numbers? Why?

12. Suppose a friend predicts that candidate Smith will win a local election, and the prediction is based on the opinions expressed by his or her friends and neighbors. What would you say to help your friend understand that this method of sampling is unsound?

For Students Who Are Planning Research

13. Will you use sampling to obtain participants for your research? If yes, do you plan to use random sampling, systematic sampling, or some other method of sampling? Explain.

14. Do you think that the method of sampling you plan to use might create a bias? Explain.

As indicated in the previous two topics, simple random sampling gives each member of a population an equal chance of being included in a sample. The resulting sample is, by definition, *unbiased*, yet still may contain *sampling errors*, which are errors created by chance (i.e., created by the random sampling process). The technical term for discussing the magnitude of sampling errors is **precision**. Results are more precise when researchers reduce sampling errors. The two major ways to reduce sampling errors are to increase sample size, which is discussed in Topics 25 and 26, and to use stratification in conjunction with random sampling, which is called **stratified random sampling**.

To obtain a stratified random sample, first divide a population into strata. For instance, researchers can easily divide a population into men and women because gender is easily identifiable. If a researcher draws separately at random from each stratum (i.e., separately from men and from women), the researcher will obtain a stratified random sample.

Note that researchers usually draw the same percentage of participants, not the same *number* of participants, from each stratum.[1] Thus, if there are 600 women and 400 men in a population and if a researcher wants a sample size of 100, the researcher would draw 10% of the women (i.e., 600 × .10 = 60) and 10% of the men (i.e., 400 × .10 = 40). Thus, the resulting sample consisting of 60 women and 40 men is representative in terms of gender (i.e., it accurately represents the gender composition of the population). Note that while this stratified random sample will be accurate in terms of its gender composition, the sample from each gender might not be representative of its respective group. For instance, the sample of 60 women drawn at random might be unrepresentative of the 600 women in the population due to errors created by random sampling (i.e., unrepresentative by the luck of the random draw). Nevertheless, for studies in which there might be differences associated with gender, it is better to assure that men and women are represented in the correct proportions by using stratified random sampling than to take a chance on misrepresentation of gender that might be obtained by using simple random sampling.

At first, some students think that men and women should have equal representation in the sample. To illustrate why this is wrong, suppose a researcher was trying to predict the outcome of a local election on a proposition requiring equal pricing of services such as dry cleaning for men and women. Because women are traditionally charged more than men, women might be more likely to vote in favor of the proposition than men. Thus, because there are more women voters in the population (600 women vs. 400 men), there should be more women voters in the sample (60 vs. 40).

Notice that if men and women do not differ in their opinions on a particular issue, stratification on the basis of gender will not increase the precision of the result. In other words, if men and women are the same in their opinions (perhaps 80% approve and 20% disapprove), it does not matter if a sample consists of all men, all women, or something in between because in any of these combinations, about 80% will say they approve. In other words, the stratification variable of gender is irrelevant if those in the various strata are the same in terms of what is being studied. Thus, stratification will improve precision only if the stratification is based on a variable that is relevant to the issue being studied.

Researchers can further increase precision (remember, this means reducing sampling errors) by using multiple strata in selecting a given sample. A researcher might, for instance, stratify on the basis of both gender and age by drawing separate random samples from each of the four subgroups shown here:

Women Ages 18–39	Men Ages 18–39
Women Ages 40+	Men Ages 40+

Of course, researchers are not confined to using just two variables for stratification: Having a larger number is better as long as they are relevant and *independent* of each other. To see what is meant by independence, suppose a researcher stratified on both age and number of years employed. Because older individuals have had more years in which to be employed, the two tend to be highly correlated. Thus, stratifying on age has probably already ac-

---

[1] If equal numbers are drawn, the responses from each stratum can be statistically weighted to make the statistical result reflect the population proportions.

counted to a great extent for years of employment (i.e., they are not independent of each other).

Keep in mind the primary purpose of stratification, which is to ensure that different subgroups are represented in the correct proportions. The goal in stratification is *not* to make comparisons across subgroups but to obtain a single sample that is representative in terms of the stratification variables.

EXERCISE ON TOPIC 22

1. What is the technical term for discussing the magnitude of sampling errors?

2. Is it possible for a random sample to contain sampling errors?

3. What is the first step in stratified random sampling?

4. Does a researcher usually draw the "same number" *or* "same percentage" from each stratum?

5. If the population of freshmen and the population of sophomores on a college campus are the same in their opinion on a particular issue on which a researcher will be conducting a survey, will it be to the researcher's advantage to stratify by drawing samples separately from each group?

6. What does stratification do to precision?

7. Is it possible to stratify on more than one variable?

8. Is the primary purpose of stratifying to be able to compare subgroups (such as comparing freshmen and sophomores in Question 5)?

Questions for Discussion

9. Think of an issue on which you might want to conduct a survey using the students at your college or university as the population. Name the issue and two variables you think would be relevant for stratification purposes when drawing a stratified random sample.

10. Students were given a test on a research article they read for class. (The article reported on the use of stratified random sampling.) One test question asked, "What type of sampling was used in the research?" Students who answered using only the term "random sampling" lost a point for the question. The instructor's comment was that the answer was ambiguous. Do you think the instructor was right in taking off the point? Why? Why not?

For Students Who Are Planning Research

11. If you planned to use simple random sampling (see Topic 21), do you now think your study would be improved if you used stratified random sampling instead? If yes, on what basis do you plan to stratify?

Simple random sampling, systematic sampling, and stratified random sampling are described in the previous three topics. In this topic, three additional methods are considered.

In **cluster sampling**, researchers draw groups (or clusters) of participants instead of drawing individuals. For instance, suppose a researcher wants to survey a sample of members of United Methodist churches throughout the United States. If the researcher obtains a membership list with addresses, the researcher might draw a simple or stratified random sample of individuals and mail questionnaires to them. However, mailed questionnaires are notorious for their low response rates. The researcher might get a better response rate if he or she draws a sample of clusters—in this case, a sample of congregations—and contacts the ministers of the congregations to request that they personally distribute the questionnaires to their church members, collect the completed questionnaires, and mail them back to the researcher. If the ministers are convinced that the survey is appropriate and important, they might use their influence to help obtain responses from the members of their congregations (i.e., the clusters). Of course, for cluster sampling to be unbiased, a researcher must draw the clusters *at random*. This could be done by assigning a number to each congregation and using a table of random numbers to select a sample of the congregations. (See Topic 21 for a description of how to use a table of random numbers.)

A major drawback to cluster sampling results from the fact that each cluster tends to be more homogeneous in a variety of ways than the population as a whole. Suppose, for instance, that church members in the South tend to be more conservative than members in the North. Then, members of any one cluster in the South are unlikely to reflect accurately the attitudes of all members nationally. If a researcher draws only five clusters (i.e., congregations) at random, the researcher might obtain a large number of participants, especially if one or two congregations have very large memberships. However, by drawing only five clusters, the researcher could easily obtain a sample in which most of the churches are in the South *or* most are in the North, potentially creating much sampling error. To avoid this problem, the researcher should draw a large

number of clusters.[1] To help increase precision, the researcher could also stratify on geography and draw a random sample of clusters from each stratum, which would assure, for instance, that the North and South are represented in the correct proportions.

Another method is **purposive sampling**. When researchers use this method, they purposively select individuals whom they believe will be good sources of information. For instance, a researcher might observe over a long period that several members of the academic senate at a university consistently vote on the winning side on controversial issues. The researcher might decide that rather than interviewing a random sample drawn from the whole membership of the senate, he or she will interview only these consistent winners to predict the outcome on a new issue before the senate. While this method is interesting and may be useful at times, it is dangerous—in this case because professors may change their orientations or a new issue may raise different kinds of concerns from those raised by earlier issues. Qualitative researchers frequently use purposive sampling. For more information on sampling in qualitative research, see Topics 64 and 65 in Part H of this book.

Snowball sampling can be useful when attempting to locate participants who are hard to find. For instance, suppose a researcher wants to study heroin addicts who have never had institutional contacts (e.g., had never sought treatment nor been arrested). How will the researcher find them? With the snowball technique, a researcher initially needs to find *only one*. If the researcher can convince this one individual that the research is important and that the data will remain confidential, this one participant might put the researcher in contact with several other potential participants. Each of these may help the researcher contact several more. This technique is based on trust. If the initial participants trust the researcher, they may identify and convince other potential participants to trust the researcher also. Of course, snowball samples should be presumed to be

---

[1] Sample size for quantitative research is discussed in Topic 25. Note that statisticians consider each cluster to be a single participant. Thus, if five clusters are drawn, the sample size is 5. A comparison of sample sizes in both qualitative and quantitative research is discussed in Topic 65.

biased because individuals are not drawn at random. However, without using snowball sampling, there are many special populations that researchers would be unable to study, such as successful criminals (i.e., criminals who have never been caught), homeless individuals with no institutional contacts, and others who are hard to identify and locate. Both quantitative and qualitative researchers use snowball sampling.

EXERCISE ON TOPIC 23

1. To conduct a survey on a campus, a researcher drew a random sample of 25 class sections and contacted the instructors who then administered the questionnaires in class. This researcher used what type of sampling?

2. Which type of sampling is based on trust between participants and a researcher?

3. What is a major drawback to cluster sampling?

4. Which type of sampling is especially useful when attempting to locate participants who are hard to find?

5. Briefly define purposive sampling.

6. What must researchers do in cluster sampling to obtain an unbiased sample of clusters?

7. Suppose a researcher identified an individual who has engaged in an illegal activity to be a participant in a research project, and then the researcher identifies others who have engaged in the same activity through the first individual's contacts. The researcher is using what type of sampling?

Questions for Discussion

8. To study a sample of all nurses employed by hospitals in a state, a researcher drew two hospitals (clusters) at random, both of which happened, by chance, to be large public hospitals, each with hundreds of nurses, yielding a large sample. Are you impressed with the sample size? Why? Why not?

9. Name a population (other than those mentioned in the topic) for which snowball sampling might be better than other types of sampling. Explain the reason(s) for your answer.

For Students Who Are Planning Research

10. In light of Topics 20, 21, 22, and this topic, what type of sample do you plan to draw? If you will be using a less-than-satisfactory sample, explain why it will be necessary to draw such a sample.

Demographics are the background characteristics of the participants in research such as gender, age, and income. Consider a research project conducted with participants at a local substance abuse counseling center. By collecting demographic information on the participants (age, gender, marital status, types of substances used, length of use, and so on), the researcher can provide readers of the research a "picture" of the types of individuals who constituted the sample for the study. This information allows readers to make informed judgments regarding the extent to which the results apply to their own settings. For instance, if the clients to whom a reader wants to generalize are similar in their demographics to the demographics of the participants in the study, the results are more likely to be generalizable.

Of course, certain demographic characteristics are more relevant for some studies than others. For instance, for a study on the use of a new method for teaching mathematics, grade level, age, and GPA are more relevant than political affiliation, religious affiliation, and weight.

Sometimes, the demographics of a particular population are known, and these data can be useful for analyzing and interpreting the results of a study. For instance, suppose that the population consists of all students enrolled at a college, and the college has data indicating that 20% of the students in the population are Asian American. If a researcher draws a sample of the population and obtains a sample in which only 10% of the respondents are Asian American, the researcher could make a statistical adjustment in the results, giving the Asian Americans in the sample more weight. For the example presented here, a researcher could count the responses of each Asian American in the sample *twice* when analyzing the results. This would boost the percentage of Asian Americans from 10% to 20% in the sample, yielding a sample with a correct percentage of Asian Americans in it.[1]

Even if a researcher does not make a statistical adjustment based on the difference between the demographics of a population and a sample, the researcher can warn readers that the sample differs from the population in terms of its demographics (e.g., Asian Americans are underrepresented in the sample).

When relying on voluntary participation in research, it is important to collect demographics that permit a comparison of volunteers with nonvolunteers whenever possible. Consider research on an after-school tutoring program in reading in which the program is offered to all students, but only 30% volunteer to participate. From school records, it may be possible to provide information on demographic differences between the volunteers and nonvolunteers such as previous grades in reading, gender differences, differences in age, and so on. Such information could be of value to a reader who is interested in the application of the program in their local settings.

Mailed surveys are notorious for low response rates (low rates of volunteering), which create a bias in sampling. The fact that most mail is marked with zip codes provides a unique opportunity for researchers to collect demographic information for comparing volunteers with nonvolunteers. Specifically, a researcher could keep track of the zip codes to which questionnaires were mailed as well as the zip codes from which completed questionnaires were received. If the zip codes from which the questionnaires were received tend to be from higher-socioeconomic (SES) neighborhoods than the zip codes to which they were mailed, the bias in favor of higher income respondents could be noted in the research report (or statistical adjustments could be made).[2]

In experiments, a special type of sampling bias results from what researchers call **mortality**. As indicated in Topic 2, experiments are studies in which researchers administer treatments in order to examine their effects on participants. Consider an experiment in which a new prescription drug is administered to an experimental group while the control group receives no special treatment. If some of the participants drop out of the experiment at mid-course, *mortality* is said to have oc-

---

[1] For technical reasons that are beyond the scope of this book, such an adjustment is sounder for adjusting the results for an unbiased sample than for adjusting the results for a biased sample.

[2] For instance, suppose 50% were mailed to a high SES zip code and 20% were returned from this zip code, while 50% were mailed to a low SES zip code and 10% were returned from this zip code. The bias in favor of the high SES zip code could be noted.

curred. Because mortality does not occur at random, the result is presumed to bias the sample. For instance, those in the experimental group who experience less relief from the drug may get discouraged and drop out of the experiment before it is completed. This would bias the results of the experiment in favor of those for whom the drug is effective.

Because of mortality, it is important for experimenters to mention in their research reports whether there was mortality and, if so, the number and percentage who dropped out from each group. In addition, information on the demographics of those who dropped out and those who completed the experiments should be reported. For instance, did those who dropped out have more severe symptoms to begin with? Did the dropouts tend to be older? Answers to these types of questions can help readers assess the severity of the effects of mortality on the outcome of experiments.

EXERCISE ON TOPIC 24

1. By collecting demographic information on the participants, a researcher can provide readers of the research with what?

2. Consider the demographic of "marital status." Is this demographic likely to be equally relevant in all studies?

3. A researcher can do what two things if the researcher compares the demographics of a sample with its population and finds that a subgroup is underrepresented?

4. According to this topic, is it important to compare the demographics of volunteers with the demographics of nonvolunteers?

5. What provides a unique opportunity for researchers who conduct mailed surveys to collect demographic information?

6. If some of the participants drop out of an experiment at mid-course, what is said to have occurred?

Question for Discussion

7. Consider a survey on campus services for freshmen. Name three demographic variables that might be especially relevant.

For Students Who Are Planning Research

8. Do you anticipate collecting demographics? If yes, do you anticipate using the demographic information in any of the ways mentioned in this topic? Explain.

In the previous topics in this part of the book, various methods of drawing samples are described,[1] with an emphasis on the importance of considering bias when evaluating the adequacy of a sample. **Sample size** is an important but secondary consideration. To understand why sample size is secondary to bias, consider this example: Suppose a student is conducting a survey on whether the main cafeteria on campus should remain open during evening hours. Being a commuter with only day classes, the student goes to the cafeteria at lunchtime and asks every tenth student who enters to participate in the survey. Of the 100 participants in the survey, 80% have no opinion and 20% want evening hours. After considering the results, the student decides that he or she should have used a larger sample, so the student obtains another 100 participants in the same way (asking every tenth student entering the cafeteria at lunchtime). This time, the student gets 85% with no opinion and 15% who want evening hours. Being very cautious, the student samples again, and this time obtains a 75%–25% split. Combining results from the three surveys, the student obtains the total results shown in the bottom row of this table:

	No Opinion	Want Evening Hours
Sample 1	80%	20%
Sample 2	85%	15%
Sample 3	75%	25%
Total	**80%**	**20%**

Notice that for all practical purposes the three results are the same. That is, only a small minority wants evening hours. With a total sample size of 300, the student might feel rather comfortable that he or she has pinned down an answer close to the truth. However, there is a serious problem in the method of sampling, which results from the fact that each time the student sampled, he or she sampled only from those entering the cafeteria at lunchtime. Thus, the sample is biased against those who are not on campus during lunch hours. Specifically, it is biased against evening students who are the members of the population most likely to want evening cafeteria hours. If the student continues to increase the sample size by sampling only at lunchtime, obtaining the responses of many more hundreds of students, the increase in sample size will be of no benefit in correcting the bias. Instead, the student would get much more accurate results by using an unbiased sample—even if the student studies only a small, unbiased sample. As a rule, then, small, unbiased samples tend to yield more accurate results than biased samples, even if the sizes of the biased samples are large and the sizes of the unbiased samples are small.

Increasing sample size is of benefit in research because it increases **precision**. When researchers say that they have highly precise results, they are saying that the results will vary by only a small amount from sample to sample, which is what will happen if each sample is large. Notice that in the cafeteria example, the results of the three samples were reasonably close, so a researcher could correctly say that there is a reasonable degree of precision. However, because of the bias in the method of sampling, it would be more accurate to say that the results are *precisely wrong* to the extent that the bias has consistently thrown the results off in the same direction each time a sample was drawn. Thus, researchers should strive first to obtain an unbiased sample and then seek a reasonably large number of participants.

If increasing the size of a sample increases precision, which is desirable, especially when using unbiased (random) sampling, then the larger the sample, the better—right? Yes, this is true, but researchers need to consider the principle of *diminishing returns* for each unit of increase in sample size. To understand this principle, consider the following two cases in which the sample size was increased by 50 participants.

	Original Sample Size	Increase	New Sample Size
Researcher A	50	+50	100
Researcher B	3,000	+50	3,050

Considering the data in the box immediately above, it is clear that Researcher A gets a much bigger payoff for increasing her sample size by 50 because she has doubled her sample size, which gives her a big boost in precision. Researcher B, on the

---

[1] The topics on sampling in this part of the book emphasize sampling in quantitative research. For sampling in qualitative research, see Topics 64 and 65.

other hand, gets a very little increase in precision because the addition of 50 to his original sample of 3,000 can have little influence on the results because the responses of the 50 additional participants will be overwhelmed by the responses of the first 3,000. Thus, at some point, the returns (in terms of an increase in precision) diminish to the point that further increases in sample size (such as adding 50 participants) are of very little benefit. Because of this principle, even the most important and prestigious national surveys are often conducted with only about 1,500 respondents.

EXERCISE ON TOPIC 25

1. Is sample size the primary consideration when judging the adequacy of a sample?

2. Does increasing sample size reduce bias?

3. Does increasing sample size increase precision?

4. Researcher A increased his sample size from 200 to 250, and Researcher B increased her sample size from 1,000 to 1,050. Which researcher will get a bigger payoff in increased precision by adding 50 participants?

5. If a researcher uses a very large sample, is it still possible for the results to be wrong?

6. Does each additional participant a researcher adds to a sample make an equal contribution to increasing precision?

7. According to the topic, prestigious national surveys are often conducted using about how many respondents?

Questions for Discussion

8. A magazine editor conducted a poll by printing a questionnaire in an issue of the magazine for readers to mail back. Several thousand readers returned completed questionnaires. Suppose a friend reads the results of this poll and is convinced that it reflects the views of all adults in the United States. What would you say to convince him that he might be wrong?

9. Consider the statement, "The larger the sample, the better." Explain why this statement might be misleading to a novice researcher.

For Students Who Are Planning Research

10. What is the anticipated sample size for your study? On what basis did you make your decision on sample size? (Note that you will be learning more about sample size in the next topic.)

One of the first questions students ask when planning their theses or classroom research projects is, "How many participants do I need?" Students often ask this question even before a discussion of the purposes of the research and the procedures that will be used. Without considering these matters, however, it is impossible to make informed decisions on sample size.

The following are the major factors that influence researchers' decisions on how large samples should be.[1]

First, researchers frequently conduct **pilot studies**, which are studies designed to obtain preliminary information on how new treatments and instruments work. For instance, when studying a new drug, a researcher might conduct a pilot study on the route of administration and the maximum tolerable dose. Also, a researcher might try out a new instrument such as a new questionnaire to determine if there are ambiguous questions, questions that participants refuse to answer, and so on. Pilot studies are usually conducted on small samples, such as 10 to 100. Based on the results, treatments and instruments can be modified for use in more definitive future studies with larger samples.

Second, some research procedures are so expensive and time-consuming that researchers must limit the sizes of their samples. For instance, when conducting qualitative research, researchers might plan to spend considerable time interacting with each participant and thus the researchers might have to be content with small samples.

Third, researchers might want to document the incidence of something rare, such as the incidence of heart attacks among men ages 18 to 30. If a researcher drew a small sample, such as 25 participants, and waited a year, he or she probably would not observe any heart attacks in such a small sample, but it would be a mistake to conclude that there are no heart attacks in this age group. For this type of research, if a researcher cannot afford to use very large samples, he or she should let another researcher with adequate resources do it because small samples are not useful for observing the incidence of rare events.

Fourth, researchers need to consider the variability in the population of interest. If there is very little variability (i.e., the population is homogeneous), researchers can obtain accurate results from a small sample. For instance, the population of small bags of Frito chips is homogeneous with respect to their weight because the manufacturer strives to be consistent in this respect. Studying a random sample of only 50 would give a researcher about the same information as studying a random sample of 1,000. In contrast, if a population is very heterogeneous, a researcher needs a large sample. Suppose, for instance, a researcher wants to study the rate of reading literacy among adults in a large metropolitan area. There undoubtedly is great variability, ranging from the totally illiterate to the exceptionally literate. If the researcher draws a small sample of 50 individuals from such a diverse population, the researcher might obtain a result with major errors such as not having a single illiterate individual in the sample. Using a larger sample, however, the researcher would be more likely to capture the diversity of the entire population.

Fifth, if researchers are looking for small differences, they need to use large samples. For instance, suppose the population of women voters is just slightly more in favor of a ballot proposition than the population of men voters. In small random samples of these voters, the random sampling errors could easily overwhelm the small difference and might even produce a result in which it appears that the men are slightly more in favor of the proposition than women. Using large samples in this case is necessary if a researcher wants to identify the correct direction and size of such a small difference.

So what is large and what is small? The answer is relative to what is being studied and the traditional sample sizes used in various types of research. A national public opinion poll with a few hundred respondents, for instance, would be considered to have a small sample because survey researchers have learned over the years that it takes about 1,500 respondents to get highly precise results at the national level. On the other hand, an experiment in which clients are given a new form of psychotherapy for several years might be considered to have a very large sample if the sample size were a few hundred because it is traditional in this type of research to use small numbers of participants. Thus, it is important to read many instances

---

[1] The topics on sampling in this part of the book emphasize sampling in quantitative research. For sampling in qualitative research, see Topics 64 and 65.

of the type of research being planned in order to learn about the various research traditions—including traditional sample sizes—researchers use.

When a small population is of interest, Table 2 near the end of this book is helpful for estimating a sample size for survey research. Using the sample size (n) recommended in the table that corresponds to the population size (N) will usually hold the error down to about 5%. That is, the true percentage in the whole population should fall within 5% of the percentage obtained from the sample. For instance, the table indicates that for a population of 200, a researcher needs a sample size of 132 (more than half of the population), but for a population of 400, a researcher needs a sample size of only 196 (less than half of the population), illustrating a practical application of the principle of diminishing returns discussed in the previous topic.

EXERCISE ON TOPIC 26

1. What are pilot studies?

2. Do researchers usually use "small" *or* "large" samples in pilot studies?

3. If a researcher suspects that a trait is rare in a population, should the researcher use a "small" *or* "large" sample to identify the incidence of the trait?

4. In what type of research might a researcher spend considerable amounts of time interacting with participants, and what effect might this have on sample size?

5. Suppose a researcher suspects that there is only a very small difference in the math abilities of boys and girls at the sixth-grade level. Should the researcher use a "small" *or* "large" sample to measure this difference?

6. Suppose the population consists of church members in the Southern Baptist Convention. If a researcher believes the members of this population are very homogeneous in their belief in an afterlife, would it be acceptable to use a small sample to identify the percentage who hold such a belief?

7. According to Table 2 on page 191, if there is a population of 1,900 students in a school, what is the recommended sample size?

8. According to Table 2, if there are 130 nurses in a hospital, what is the recommended sample size?

9. What is the symbol for population size in Table 2?

Question for Discussion

10. Some research articles based on small samples in academic journals are characterized by their authors as being pilot studies. Do you think the publication of pilot studies is justifiable? Why? Why not?

For Students Who Are Planning Research

11. In light of the information in this topic and in the previous topic, what is your anticipated sample size? Explain the basis for your decision. (Note that your decision may hinge, in part, on practical matters such as the availability of participants and your financial resources.)

PART D

INSTRUMENTATION

In this part, the essentials of measurement, with an emphasis on how to assess the validity of tests and measures, are examined. Reliability, which is closely linked to validity, is also explored in detail. In addition, how norm groups help in the interpretation of scores as well as how to interpret scores that are not based on norm groups are considered. Finally, the distinguishing features of measures of optimum performance and measures of typical performance are explored.

This part of the book emphasizes instrumentation in quantitative research. For information on instrumentation in qualitative research, see Part H of this book.

NOTES

The generic term for any type of measurement device (e.g., test, questionnaire, interview schedule, or personality scale) is **instrument**. Thus, for instance, one might ask the question: "What type of *instrument* did the researcher use to collect the data?" In formal research reports, **instrumentation** is the term used as the heading for the section of the report where the measurement devices used in the research are described. An important issue that is often addressed in this section of a research report is the **validity** of the instruments.

Researchers say that an instrument is **valid** to the extent that it measures what it is designed to measure and accurately performs the function(s) it is purported to perform. For instance, consider an achievement test that emphasizes knowledge of facts on the westward movement in the United States. It will be only *modestly valid* when administered to students whose instruction emphasized more than just the memorization of facts (such as critical appraisal of historical evidence on that period in history). Likewise, a typing test used by an employer is likely to be only *partially valid* if it is administered to applicants who are applying for a job that includes filing in addition to typing.

It is important to note that validity is *relative* to the purpose of testing. If the purpose is to measure achievement of students exposed to instruction on critical thinking, a test that measures only factual knowledge will be largely lacking in validity. For the purpose of measuring the achievement of students exposed to instruction in which the acquisition of factual knowledge was emphasized, the same test will be much more valid. Thus, before researchers can assess the validity of a particular instrument, the purpose for testing must be clearly identified.

Also, note that validity is a *matter of degree*. Therefore, it is appropriate to discuss *how valid* a test is—not *whether* it is valid. Given the imperfect state of measurement practice, it is safe to say that no test is perfectly valid.

Consider some reasons why perfect validity is elusive. First, almost all tests tap only a *sample* of the behavior underlying the constructs being measured. Consider the construct of aptitude for college (i.e., having the abilities to succeed in college). College aptitude tests emphasize verbal and mathematical skills and leave untapped other skills that relate to success in college, such as ability to use a personal computer to do homework, knowledge of how to use an academic library, command of effective study skills, and having the maturity to persist in the face of difficulty in a course of instruction. Even within the domains that are tapped by a college aptitude test, only a small sample of verbal and mathematical problems can be presented within a test of reasonable length. Just as when researchers sample participants from a population (see Part C of this book), some samples of material and skills covered by tests are better than others, and all samples are subject to error.

Another reason why perfect validity is elusive is that some traits researchers want to measure are inherently difficult to measure. Consider the trait of cheerfulness. Almost everyone has known individuals whose cheerfulness is contagious. However, even though it is known when it is seen, how can researchers measure this trait in a systematic way in order to study it? Researchers could, for instance, ask a series of questions on how participants interact with other individuals in various types of contexts, how they view adversity, etc. On the other hand, researchers might observe participants and rate them on the cheerfulness they exhibit in their interactions with others (e.g., Do they smile? Is the tone of their voice upbeat? and so on). While these procedures probably tap certain aspects of cheerfulness, they fail to capture the *full essence* of the trait. This illustrates the old principle that often the whole is greater than the sum of its parts. To compound the problem, researchers often examine only some of the parts when they measure a given trait (e.g., researchers look at only certain behaviors that indicate cheerfulness and do this in only certain specific settings).

The problem of elusiveness, at first glance, seems to plague those with a quantitative orientation more than those with a qualitative orientation because quantitative researchers seek to reduce elusive constructs, such as cheerfulness, to numerical scores. Qualitative researchers, on the other hand, tend to measure in ways (such as unstructured interviews) that yield words to describe the extent to which traits are present. Yet, unless qualitative researchers refer to specific behaviors and events in their reports, they will fail to describe results in enough detail so readers can picture the meanings that have been attached to a construct such as cheerfulness. While qualitative researchers' descriptions (including quoting participants' words), are less artificial than the numerical scores obtained by quantitative researchers, qualitative researchers can find it difficult to describe the essence of a trait, such as the feelings a genuinely cheerful individual creates when interacting with others.

The next three topics explore the major methods researchers use to assess the extent to which instruments are valid.

EXERCISE ON TOPIC 27

1. What is the generic term for any type of measurement device?

2. An instrument is said to be valid to the extent that it does what?

3. Suppose a researcher purchases a commercial reading test that is highly valid for students who receive reading instruction that emphasizes phonics. Is it possible that the test is of limited validity for students who are taught with a method that does not emphasize phonics?

4. According to this topic, is it safe to say that no test is perfectly valid?

5. Tapping only a sample of the behaviors underlying the constructs a researcher wants to measure has what effect on validity?

6. If a trait is elusive, is it "easy" *or* "difficult" to measure it with a high degree of validity?

Questions for Discussion

7. Have you ever taken an achievement test in school that was seriously flawed in its validity? If so, describe the test and state why you believe it was seriously flawed. In your discussion, mention the purpose for testing.

8. Name a trait you think is *elusive* and thus may be difficult to measure with great validity. Be prepared to defend your answer.

For Students Who Are Planning Research

9. What types of instruments (e.g., tests, questionnaires, interview schedules, or personality scales) do you plan to use in your research?

10. Will the instruments and measurement procedures you named in response to Question 9 measure a *sample* of the behavior underlying the construct? Have you considered how to draw the sample? Explain.

11. Measuring the ability to add one-digit numbers is *not* very elusive. Are the traits you plan to measure inherently more *elusive* than measuring this mathematics skill? Explain.

To determine the **content validity** of an instrument, researchers make judgments on the appropriateness of its contents. For achievement tests, this type of validity is essential.

Suppose a researcher wants to build an achievement test on the material in this book through Topic 27. What steps could the researcher take to maximize the content validity of the test? First, the researcher would need to consider the amount of testing time and the types of test items to be used. For instance, the researcher could ask many more multiple-choice items than essay items in a given amount of testing time. Assume the researcher decided to write 35 multiple-choice items to be administered in a 50-minute period. The researcher could write one item on each of the 25 topics, assuring that a broad sample of the material was covered. Then, the researcher could allocate the remaining 10 items to those topics he or she deemed to be most important. Then, the researcher would need to decide which types of skills to measure. The researcher could test primarily for facts and definitions (e.g., "Which of the following is the definition of validity?") or for higher-level skills (e.g., "Which one of the following statements from a test manual indicates something about the content validity of a test?").

Although the above example has been simplified, it illustrates three principles for writing achievement tests with high content validity. First, a broad sample of content is usually better than a narrow one. Second, important material should be emphasized. Third, questions should be written to measure the appropriate skills, such as knowledge of facts and definitions, application of definitions to new situations, drawing inferences, making critical appraisals, and so on. Of course, the skills should be those covered in instruction. Keeping these principles in mind, researchers can make *judgments* of the content validity of achievement tests.

Although content validity is most closely associated with achievement testing, it is sometimes applied when evaluating other types of instruments. For instance, if a researcher wants to measure the broad construct called *self-concept* with a series of questions, the researcher could consider sampling from each of the narrower constructs that constitute it, such as physical self-concept, academic self-concept, social self-concept, and so on, assuring that a broad sample has been covered. If the re-searcher believes one type of self-concept is more important than others for his or her research purpose (e.g., academic self-concept for a study in a school setting), the researcher might emphasize one type over the others by asking more questions about it. Finally, the researcher will need to write the questions in such a way that they elicit common, shared meanings from the examinees. To do this, the researcher should consider the participants' educational levels and the meanings they are likely to attach to particular words in the questions. Will the participants find some words too difficult to understand? Are some terms ambiguous in their meaning? Careful consideration of these points regarding the contents of instruments helps improve their validity.

Researchers also make judgments when they consider **face validity**. In this approach to validity, judgments are made on whether an instrument appears to be valid *on the face of it*. In other words, on superficial inspection, does the instrument appear to measure what it purports to measure? For instance, one might use a spatial relations test for selecting individuals for pilot training school. A test that uses drawings of geometric shapes moving in space would have less face validity than one that uses drawings of miniature airplanes moving in space. That is, the second one has more face validity in terms of its appearance, even though both tests might be equally valid for measuring the underlying ability to visualize objects moving in space. Thus, face validity is primarily a public relations concern. Note that researchers usually prefer to use tests that *look like* they are related to their purpose because this promotes public acceptance of testing and motivates examinees to do their best.

It is possible for a test to have high face validity for a certain purpose while having low content validity. An extreme example makes the point clear: A test consisting of math items such as a drawing of one airplane followed by a plus sign and two more airplanes might have some face validity for pilot selection (because of the drawings of airplanes) but would have essentially no content validity because the skill being tested (adding one-digit numbers) is not appropriate for selecting adults who are likely to be successful in pilot training.

Occasionally, researchers deliberately use instruments with *low face validity*. For instance, in a recent survey on the drug Viagra (which is a potentially sensitive topic), the pollsters asked about a variety of drugs even though they were concerned only with attitudes toward Viagra. The face validity of the survey questions was deliberately diluted with questions about other drugs in the hope of re-ducing the potential sensitivity of the questions on the drug of interest. In general, low face validity is desirable when researchers want to disguise the true purpose of the research from the respondents. This can, of course, raise ethical issues (see Topic 12).

EXERCISE ON TOPIC 28

1. For which type of instrument is content validity essential?

2. Should researchers consider the types of skills required by achievement test items when judging content validity?

3. "To improve content validity, it is usually desirable to cover only a narrow sample of content from the broad content area to be covered by an achievement test." Is this statement "true" or "false"?

4. Is content validity relevant only to achievement tests?

5. Which type of validity is based on superficial inspection?

6. Which two types of validity rely on judgments?

7. Is it possible for a test to have high face validity but low content validity?

8. When might a researcher deliberately use an instrument with low face validity?

Questions for Discussion

9. Suppose an instructor fails to tell students the types of items (e.g., multiple-choice or essay) that will be on a midterm examination. Could this affect the validity of the results? Explain.

10. Have you ever taken an achievement test in which the content emphasized was different from the content you concentrated on while studying for the test? If so, describe the discrepancy, and speculate on what caused it (e.g., Was there a miscommunication between you and the instructor?).

For Students Who Are Planning Research

11. Will you be evaluating the content validity of any instruments you will be using in your research? Explain.

12. Do you anticipate that your instrument(s) have high face validity? Explain.

In the empirical[1] approach to validity, researchers make planned comparisons to see if an instrument yields scores that relate to a **criterion**. To understand this approach to validity, consider Example 1.

Example 1

Nine applicants for the position of clerk–typist were administered an employment test, yielding scores from 15 to 35. Because there was a labor shortage, all nine were hired even though some had low test scores. After six months on the job, the employees were rated on their job performance by their supervisors on a scale from 10 (excellent performance) to 1 (poor performance). Here are their scores and ratings:

Employee	Test Score	Supervisors' Ratings	
Jose	35	9	
Jane	32	10	Top third on test.
Bob	29	8	
Fernando	27	8	
Sue	25	7	Middle third on test.
Debbie	22	8	
Milly	21	6	
Ling	18	4	Bottom third on test.
John	15	5	

Comparing the test scores with the supervisors' ratings provides information about the validity of the new employee test. The set of ratings is called the *criterion*, which is the standard by which the test is being judged. Because the purpose of an employment test is to *predict* success on the job, the most appropriate test of its validity is **predictive validity**, which poses this question: To what extent does the test predict the outcome it is supposed to predict?

So how valid is the employee test in Example 1? A researcher can begin to answer the question by examining the table. First, notice that those in the bottom third on the test are also in the bottom third in terms of ratings, suggesting that the test is highly valid for identifying those who will get low ratings on the job. Next, notice that the results for the top and middle thirds are more mixed. For instance, Bob, who is in the top third on the test with a score of 29, has a rating of 8, which is the same as the ratings of Fernando and Debbie, who are in the

middle third. Thus, while the test has some validity at these high levels, it is less than perfectly valid.

A researcher can obtain more information on the test's predictive validity by looking at the rank order of individuals on the test in comparison to their rank order on the ratings. In Example 1, the individuals are already ordered from high to low in terms of test scores. Notice that their order on ratings is to some extent similar but not the same. For instance, Jose has the highest test score, but only the second highest rating. Sue is higher than Debbie on the test, but Debbie is higher than Sue on the ratings. Despite exceptions such as these, the overall ordering of individuals by the test is similar to their ordering in terms of supervisors' ratings.

Another way to look at a test's predictive validity is to compute its **validity coefficient**. A validity coefficient is a *correlation coefficient* used to express validity. Correlation coefficients are described in detail in Topic 53. At this point, only some basic properties of validity coefficients will be considered. In practice, the coefficients range from 0.00 to 1.00.[2] At the upper limit, a 1.00 indicates perfect validity. For practical purposes, this can be thought of as indicating that the ranks on the test are identical to the ranks on the criterion. At the lower limit, 0.00 indicates that there is no relationship between the ranks on the test and the ranks on the criterion, which indicates that knowing the test scores is of no benefit when predicting the criterion. For the data in Example 1, the value of the validity coefficient is .89, indicating a very high degree of validity—higher than is usually found in validity studies of this type.

So how high should predictive validity coefficients be? Of course, higher is better. But how high are they in practice? For an employment test validated against supervisors' ratings, a researcher would be surprised to obtain a coefficient greater than about .60 and would not be at all surprised to obtain one as low as .20 or less, indicating poor validity. Why are employment tests only modestly to poorly valid? For two reasons: First, success on the job is a complex construct involving many traits such as interpersonal skills (e.g., getting along with coworkers), psychomotor skills (e.g., typing), work

---

[1] The definition of *empirical* that applies to this discussion is "relying or based on observation rather than theory."

[2] It is also possible to obtain negative coefficients, but they are very rare in validity studies. Negative correlation coefficients are discussed in Topic 53.

habits (e.g., being punctual), and so on. It is not reasonable to expect a single test (especially a paper-and-pencil test) to predict all these traits successfully. Second, coefficients are not higher because criteria such as supervisors' ratings are themselves less than perfectly reliable and valid. Thus, even if a test, in truth, were perfectly valid, the coefficient would be less than 1.00 if the supervisors failed to put the employees in the correct order. (Note that human judgments are subject to biases and other sources of errors.)

Sometimes, researchers determine the empirical validity of a test that is *not* designed to predict future behavior. For instance, a new, self-administered version of the Addiction Severity Index (ASI) was validated by correlating scores on it with scores obtained using the expensive and time-consuming original version, which involves a lengthy, structured clinical interview. The original version, which had been widely accepted as being highly valid, was the *criterion* (or "gold standard") by which the new version was judged. In this study, the Drug Domain subscale on the self-administered version of the ASI had a *validity coefficient* of .62,

which is moderately high, indicating that to a reasonable extent the less expensive version of the ASI provided information similar to the more expensive, original version.[3]

Another approach is to correlate scores on a test that is being validated with scores on a *different test* of the same trait. For instance, scores on the *Beck Depression Inventory* were correlated with scores on the *Revised Hamilton Psychiatric Rating Scale for Depression*, which resulted in a validity coefficient of .71. This relatively strong correlation indicates that to the extent that one of the measures is valid, the other one has a similar degree of validity.[4]

A validity coefficient that is obtained by administering the test and collecting the criterion data at about the same time is called a **concurrent validity coefficient** (as opposed to a **predictive validity coefficient**). The general term for both types of validity examined in this topic is **criterion-related validity**. Notice that in both predictive and concurrent validity, researchers validate by comparing scores with a criterion. The following table shows the relevant features of both.

Types of Criterion-Related Validity[1]	What is the **criterion**?	When is the **criterion** measured?
1. **Predictive Validity**	A measure of the outcome that the test is designed to predict.	After examinees have had a chance to exhibit the predicted behavior.
2. **Concurrent Validity**	An independent measure of the same trait that the test is designed to measure.	At about the same time that the test is administered.

[1]Both types of criterion-related validity employ the empirical approach. That is, they are based on data that have been collected (planned empirical data collection)—not subjective judgments or theory.

[3] Butler, S. F. et al. (2001). Initial validation of a computer-administered Addiction Severity Index: The ASI-MV. *Psychology of Addictive Behaviors, 15*, 4–12.
[4] Beck, A. T., Steer, R. A., & Brown, G. K. (1996). *Manual for the Beck Depression Inventory–Second Edition*. San Antonio: The Psychological Corporation.

Exercise on Topic 29

1. What is the term for the "standard" by which a test is judged?

2. How is *empirical* defined in this topic?

3. What question does predictive validity answer?

4. If a test is perfectly valid, what value will its validity coefficient have?

5. In light of this topic, should a researcher be surprised to get a validity coefficient of .95 for a paper-and-pencil employment test when validated against supervisors' job-performance ratings?

6. If a test has no validity whatsoever, what value will its validity coefficient have?

7. If a researcher collects the criterion data at about the same time the test is being administered, the researcher is examining what type of empirical validity?

Questions for Discussion

8. Suppose a researcher validated a new multiple-choice reading test by correlating the test scores with teachers' ratings of students' reading abilities (i.e., the scores on the test were correlated with the ratings made by teachers). What is your opinion on using teachers' ratings for this purpose? Could teachers' ratings themselves be less than perfectly valid? Explain.

9. Suppose a researcher wanted to validate a new measure of self-esteem. Name a criterion that might be used in a criterion-related validity study. Be prepared to justify its use.

10. The validity of an achievement test might be validated using either content validity (see Topic 28) or concurrent validity (such as correlating the scores with teachers' judgments of students' achievements). In your opinion, which approach to validity is more useful for achievement tests? Should both be used? Explain.

For Students Who Are Planning Research

11. Will you be evaluating the empirical validity of the instruments you will be using in your research? Explain. (Note that if you use a published instrument, information on empirical validity may already be available in the manual for the instrument or in a research report in which the instrument was used.)

NOTES

The type of validity that relies on subjective judgments *and* empirical data (i.e., data based on observations) is **construct validity**.

A **construct** stands for a collection of related behaviors that are associated in a meaningful way. For instance, "depression" is a construct that stands for a personality trait manifested by behaviors such as lethargy, flat affect when speaking, loss of appetite, loss of sexual drive, preoccupation with suicidal thoughts, difficulty in concentrating on tasks, and so on. Notice that each of these is an *indicator* of depression—the construct itself does not have a physical being outside of its indicators. That is, researchers infer its existence by observing the *collection* of related indicators. The emphasis on *collection* is important to notice because any one indicator may be associated with several constructs. For instance, although loss of appetite is an indicator of depression, it may also be an indicator of anxiety, fear, physical illness, and so on. Thus, loss of appetite is indicative of depression only when it is found in association with a number of other indicators of depression.

To determine the construct validity of an instrument, researchers begin by hypothesizing about how the construct the instrument is designed to measure should affect or relate to other variables. For instance, a researcher might hypothesize that students who are depressed will earn lower grades and be more likely to drop out of college than students who are not depressed. Note that this is a *hypothesis* (see Topic 7) because it *predicts* a relationship between depression and grades earned in college. Also, note that the researcher arrived at the hypothesis by making a subjective judgment regarding the likely effects of the indicators of depression on grades. If a researcher tests the hypothesis using empirical methods, he or she is conducting a construct validity study.

Consider how this works for a new, 50-question paper-and-pencil depression *scale*.[1] To determine its construct validity, the researcher could test the hypothesis stated above using a sample of college students as participants. First, suppose the researcher finds *no* relationship between the scores obtained on the depression scale and success in col-

lege. What does this mean? Either (1) the scale lacks validity for measuring depression (i.e., it measures something else that is not related to grades earned in college) or (2) the hypothesis is wrong. If the researcher holds firmly to his or her belief in the hypothesis, the researcher will have to conclude that the empirical evidence argues against the validity of the scale.

Next, suppose the researcher finds a relationship between scores obtained on the new depression scale and success in college. What does this mean? Either (1) the depression scale is, to some degree, valid for measuring depression or (2) the depression scale measures a variable other than depression that is also related to grades earned in college. This "other variable" could be many things. For instance, maybe the scale is heavily loaded with signs of depression that are also signs of anxiety so that it is more a measure of anxiety than depression. Because debilitating anxiety may lead to poor grades earned in college, the scores on the scale may relate to success in college because it measures anxiety, not depression.

At this point, it should be clear that determining construct validity is a complex matter that involves both judgment and empirical data. Also, it should be clear that this method offers only *indirect* evidence regarding the validity of a measure. Notice that direct evidence on the validity of a depression scale could be obtained by determining *criterion-related validity* (see Topic 29). For instance, this could be done by correlating scores obtained with the depression scale with clinical psychologists' judgments on how depressed each participant is. This is direct evidence because the researcher would be comparing scores from a depression scale with some other established measure of depression, not with an entirely different variable such as grades earned in college.

Consider another example: the construct called *dependence on others*. A researcher might hypothesize that younger children are, on the average, more dependent on adults than are older children. If the researcher tests the hypothesis and finds that the scores on a dependence scale fail to relate to age among children, this result would argue against the validity of the dependence scale. On the other hand, if the researcher finds the predicted relationship between the dependence scores and age, this em-

---

[1] Instruments that measure personality traits are often called *scales* to distinguish them from *tests* of cognitive skills, which have right and wrong answers.

pirical evidence would suggest that the scale might have validity.

Because the evidence generated by construct validity studies is indirect, researchers should be very cautious about declaring a measure to be valid based on a single study. Instead, researchers would hope to see a series of construct validity studies for a given measure—testing various hypotheses derived by considering how the construct should be related to other variables—before reaching firm conclusions.

From one perspective, the indirect nature of the evidence obtained in construct validity studies may be regarded as a weakness. However, when there are a series of construct validity studies on a given instrument, researchers gain insights into how meaningful the scores are in various contexts. This gives richness to researchers' understanding of how well an instrument works, which is a strength of this approach to validity.

Note that construct validity requires *judgments* about the nature of relationships as well as *empirical evidence* regarding whether an instrument provides scores consistent with the judgments. Hence, construct validity is classified as "judgmental-empirical" in this book.

Historically, construct validity has been most closely associated with personality scales. However, its proper application can yield useful information about all types of instruments.

It is often desirable to examine a given instrument in several different types of validity studies. The types of validity considered in Topics 28, 29, and this topic are summarized in Table 1.

Table 1
A Comparison of Major Approaches to Validity

Approaches to Validity	Types	How Determined
Judgmental	Content	Make expert judgments of the appropriateness of the content.
	Face	Make judgments based on superficial appearance.
Empirical	Predictive	Correlate test scores with criterion scores obtained after examinees have had a chance to achieve the outcome that is supposedly predicted by the test.
	Concurrent	Correlate test scores with criterion scores obtained at about the same time the test is administered.
Judgmental–Empirical	Construct	Hypothesize a relationship between the test scores and scores on another variable. Then, test the hypothesis.

EXERCISE ON TOPIC 30

1. How is the term *construct* defined in this topic?

2. Is "fear" a construct?

3. To determine construct validity, researchers begin by hypothesizing what?

4. Does confirming a hypothesis in a construct validity study offer "direct" *or* "indirect" evidence on the validity of a test?

5. In Table 1, which two types of validity are classified as solely "empirical"?

6. In Table 1, which two types of validity are classified as solely "judgmental"?

7. Why is construct validity identified as "judgmental-empirical" in this book?

Questions for Discussion

8. In your opinion, what are some of the physical indicators of (or behaviors associated with) the construct called *industriousness*?

9. To determine the construct validity of a paper-and-pencil industriousness scale, a researcher hypothesized that scores earned on it should be correlated with the number of promotions employees receive on the job. Do you think this is a good hypothesis for a construct validity study? Explain.

10. Consider the physical signs of *shyness*. Propose a hypothesis that might be tested in a construct validity study on an instrument designed to measure this construct.

For Students Who Are Planning Research

11. Will you be considering the construct validity of any instruments you will be using in your research? Explain.

NOTES

A test is said to be **reliable** if it yields *consistent* results. It is easy to see what this means by considering an extreme example. Suppose a professor writes a midterm exam on research methods that contains only four multiple-choice items. The items are on four different important concepts that were emphasized during instruction. Thus, the exam is valid in the sense that it covers appropriate content. Students who have thoroughly mastered the course content, however, should be concerned about taking such a test because it would be very easy to misinterpret a question or to miss a key term in it and get it wrong, yielding a score of 3 out of 4 right, or only 75% correct. On the other hand, students who have moved through the semester in a fog—not understanding even basic concepts—should be pleased at the prospect of taking this exam. With only four items, the odds of getting a few right by guessing and thus passing the test, are reasonably high.

Now suppose some students complain about their scores on the midterm, so the professor writes four new multiple-choice items, and again, the items are all on appropriate content. After administering the test at the next class meeting (without announcing there would be a second test, so students are not motivated to study again), should the professor expect to obtain the same scores as he or she did the first time? In all likelihood, no. Some students who were lucky in guessing the first time will have their luck wash out. Other students who misinterpreted a key term in a question will not do so on the new set of items. Examining the scores from the two tests provides the professor with information on the *consistency of results* or *reliability*. In this case, he or she would probably find that the scores are rather inconsistent from one test to the other.

What can the professor do to increase the reliability of the midterm? Obviously, the professor can increase the length of the test. This reduces the effects of the occasional ambiguous item and the effects of guessing. After realizing this principle, the professor instructs a graduate assistant to prepare a 100-item test overnight. The assistant, being pressed for time, takes the easy route and pulls a standardized test off the shelf. Although it has 100 items, they are on educational psychology, which includes some research concepts but also much material not covered in the research methods class. Administering this test should give highly reliable results because it contains a large number of test items. If the professor administers it twice, for instance, students who have a good command of educational psychology should do well on both tests. Also, those who have little knowledge of educational psychology will have little chance of getting a good grade by guessing on such a large number of items and, thus, do poorly on both administrations. However, the professor has a new problem: The test lacks **validity** because it covers the wrong content (see Topics 27 through 30 to review the concept of validity). This example illustrates an important principle: *A test with high reliability may have low validity*.

Here is another example of this principle: An employer wants to reward the best employees with end-of-year bonuses. The employer decides that to be perfectly fair, a completely objective method for determining who should get the bonuses should be used. To do this, the employer examines the employees' time cards, and selects those who were never late for work during the previous year to receive bonuses. Notice that this method of measurement is highly reliable because of its high level of objectivity. Thus, another individual could independently perform the same measurement procedure and, if careful, would identify exactly the same employees for bonuses, yielding consistent (reliable) results. But is the procedure valid? Probably only minimally so because the employer's measurement technique is limited to only one simple characteristic. Those who are outstanding in a number of other ways (such as identifying more effective ways to advertise products) but who were late to work even once are excluded from getting bonuses. Thus, the procedure is reliable, but it is of questionable validity.

This leads to the next principle: When evaluating instruments, *validity is more important than reliability*. This should be clear from considering the example of the employer basing bonuses on employees' time cards. A complex measure involving subjective judgments of employees' performances that taps a variety of important types of behavior and achievement on the job would be much more valid (even if it turned out to be only modestly reliable) than a highly reliable measure that considers only punctuality measured by examining time cards.

Finally, there is a third principle: *To be useful, an instrument must be both reasonably valid and reasonably reliable.*

To understand the complex relationship between reliability and validity, consider Figures 1 through 4 below.

In Figure 1, the gun is aimed in a valid direction (toward the target), and all the shots are consistently directed, indicating that they are reliable.

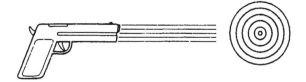

Figure 1. Reliable and valid.

In Figure 2, the gun is also aimed in the direction of the target, but the shots are widely scattered, indicating low consistency or reliability. The poor reliability makes it unlikely that most of the bullets will hit the target. Thus, poor reliability undermines the valid direction in which the gun is pointed.

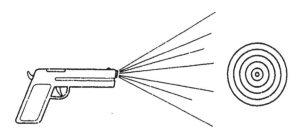

Figure 2. Unreliable, which undermines the valid aim of the gun. Less useful than Figure 1.

In Figure 3, the gun is not pointed at the target, making it invalid, but there is great consistency in the shots, indicating that it is reliable. (In a sense, it is very reliably invalid.)

Figure 3. Reliable but invalid. Not useful.

In Figure 4, the gun is not pointed at the target, making it invalid, and the lack of consistency in the direction of the shots indicates its poor reliability.

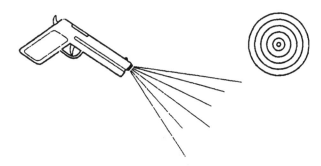

Figure 4. Unreliable and invalid. Not useful.

Of course, Figure 1 represents the ideal in measurement. For most measures in the social and behavioral sciences, however, researchers expect the direction of the gun to be off at least a small amount, indicating less-than-perfect validity. They also expect some scatter in the shots, indicating less-than-perfect reliability.[1] Clearly, the first priority should be to point the gun in the correct *general direction*, which promotes validity. Then, researchers should work on increasing reliability.

---

[1] Examination of the technical manuals for published tests indicates that professional test makers usually are more successful in achieving high reliability than in achieving high validity. This is because it is relatively easy to increase reliability by increasing the number of objective-type test items, while the tasks that need to be undertaken to increase validity vary greatly from construct to construct and may not be obvious.

Exercise on Topic 31

1. A test is said to be reliable if it yields what?

2. Should a researcher expect a very short multiple-choice test to be highly reliable?

3. Is it possible for a test with high reliability to have low validity?

4. Overall, is "validity" *or* "reliability" more important when evaluating an instrument?

5. If a test is highly reliable but highly invalid, is it useful?

6. In light of this topic, should a researcher expect most tests to be both perfectly reliable and perfectly valid?

7. "Professional test makers tend to be more successful in achieving high validity than in achieving high reliability." Is this statement "true" *or* "false"?

Questions for Discussion

8. Consider the example of the employer who was trying to identify the "best" employees using a measure of punctuality because it was reliable even though it was not especially valid. Name one or two other traits that might be examined in evaluating employees. Comment on whether you think each of your suggestions can be measured reliably. Also, comment on whether you think each is more valid than punctuality for determining which employees should receive bonuses.

9. Suppose you were offered a choice between two midterm examinations for your research methods class. The first one contains eight short essay questions, and the second contains 38 multiple-choice questions. Both are on appropriate content. Which would you prefer to take? Why? In your opinion, which one is likely to be more reliable?

For Students Who Are Planning Research

10. Will you be evaluating the reliability of any instruments you will be using in your research? Explain. (Note that reliability will be considered in more detail in the next topic.)

NOTES

How can a researcher determine reliability? The classic model is to measure twice and then check to see if the two sets of measurements are consistent with each other.

First, consider **interobserver reliability**. Suppose a researcher wants to test the hypothesis that tall individuals are waited on more quickly in retail stores than short individuals. To do this, the researcher could observe unobtrusively[1] to (1) classify each customer as tall, medium, or short, and (2) count the number of seconds from the time each customer enters the store to the time a salesperson greets the customer.

Because judgments of height made from a distance might not be reliable, the researcher could check their reliability by having two observers independently observe. The researcher could then determine the *percentage* of participants that were put in the same height category (tall, medium, or short) *by both observers*. How high should the percentage be? Although there is no standard answer to this question, it is clear that if the percentage gets too low (say less than 60% agreement), the researcher has a serious problem: either one or both of the observers. Such a lack of consistency in their judgments would cast serious doubt on the meaningfulness of the results of the study.

Measurements of the number of seconds also might be unreliable if, for instance, the observers are distracted by other events, are inattentive to the measurement task, and so on. To check on this possibility, the researcher could compare the measurements reported by the two observers. When there are two quantitative scores per participant (such as the number of seconds for each customer, as indicated by each of the two observers), the researcher can check on the degree of relationship by computing a correlation coefficient.[2] As indicated in the discussion of empirical validity (see Topic 29), a correlation coefficient may vary in value from 0.00 to 1.00.[3] A 1.00 indicates perfect reliability. That is,

the rank order of the customers based on the observations by one observer is the same as the rank order based on the observations made by the other observer. When researchers use *correlation coefficients* to describe reliability, they call them **reliability coefficients**. When researchers use reliability coefficients to describe the agreement between observers, they are usually called **interobserver reliability coefficients**.

Notice that when studying interobserver reliability, researchers usually obtain the two measurements *at the same time* (i.e., the two observers observe the same participants at the same time). In contrast, in **test–retest reliability**, researchers measure at *two different points in time*. For instance, suppose a researcher wants to know the reliability of a new test designed to assess the ability to learn college-level math. The researcher might administer the test one week and then readminister it two weeks later. Because the ability to learn college-level math should not change very much from week to week, the researcher would expect the scores from the two administrations to be consistent. Once again, for two sets of scores, the researcher would compute a correlation coefficient, which would indicate the *test–retest reliability* of the test.

Some published tests come in two parallel (or equivalent) forms that are designed to be interchangeable with each other; they have different items that cover the same content. When they are available, **parallel-forms reliability** should be determined. This is usually done by administering one form of the test to examinees and about a week or two later, administering the other form to the same examinees, thus yielding two scores per examinee. When the sets of scores are correlated, the result indicates the *parallel-forms reliability* of the test.

How high should a reliability coefficient be? Most published tests have reliability coefficients of .80 or higher, so researchers should strive to select or build instruments that have coefficients at least this high, especially if researchers plan to interpret the scores for *individuals*. For *group averages* based on groups of participants of about 25 or more, instruments with reliability coefficients as low as .50 can be serviceable. To understand why re-

---

[1] Researchers attempt to measure *unobtrusively* to avoid changing participants' behavior. For instance, if salespeople know that researchers are observing them, the salespeople might modify their normal behavior toward customers.

[2] See Topic 53 of this book for a detailed discussion of correlation.

[3] Correlation coefficients may also be negative, as discussed in Topic 53. In the unlikely event that a re-

---

searcher obtains a negative when studying reliability, it should be interpreted as representing no reliability.

searchers can tolerate rather low reliability coefficients in research in which they are examining averages, first keep in mind that reliability coefficients indicate the reliability of *individuals' scores*. Statistical theory indicates that averages are more reliable than the scores that underlie them because when computing an average, the negative errors tend to cancel out the positive errors. For instance, suppose a researcher wants to compare the average age of parents who read extensively with their sixth-grade children with the average age of parents who do not. Asking children their parents' ages is likely to be unreliable. However, a researcher might expect about half the children to overestimate the ages and half to underestimate them. To the extent that this is true, the averages may be reasonably accurate because the underestimates will cancel the overestimates.

EXERCISE ON TOPIC 32

1. Researchers need to use at least how many observers to determine interobserver reliability?

2. When there are two quantitative scores per participant, researchers can compute what statistic to describe reliability?

3. Do researchers usually measure at two different points in time to estimate interobserver reliability?

4. Do researchers usually measure at two different points in time to estimate test–retest reliability?

5. According to this topic, most published tests have reliability coefficients that are about how high?

6. According to this topic, serviceable reliability coefficients may be how low if researchers are measuring in order to examine group averages?

Questions for Discussion

7. In your opinion, which of the following variables mentioned in this topic would probably be easier to measure reliably: (1) height of customers based on observations made from a distance *or* (2) number of seconds from the time each customer enters a store until a salesperson greets him or her, also based on observations from a distance? Explain your choice.

8. For which of the following would test–retest reliability (with the instruments administered two weeks apart) probably be more appropriate: (1) a questionnaire on voters' opinions on the honesty of two presidential candidates *or* (2) a questionnaire on prejudice against minority groups? Explain your choice.

For Students Who Are Planning Research

9. Will you be considering the reliability of any instruments you will be using in your research? If so, which method(s) for examining reliability will you use? Explain.

TOPIC 33   INTERNAL CONSISTENCY AND RELIABILITY

Two methods for estimating the reliability of a test (such as an achievement test) or a scale (such as an attitude scale) are covered in the previous topic. They are test–retest reliability, in which a test[1] is administered twice, and parallel-forms reliability, in which two alternative forms of a test are administered. In both of these types of reliability, examinees must take a test twice, with a week or two intervening between the administrations. Thus, if a test is less than perfectly reliable (i.e., the scores are not perfectly consistent), which is usually the case, variables associated with time can be partly responsible. For instance, at the time of the first administration, an examinee might be emotionally upset and not do well on the test, while the same examinee might not be upset at the time of the second administration and perform much better. Such time-associated variables obviously reduce the consistency of the scores from one administration of the test to the other, reducing reliability (and the reliability coefficient).

A different approach to reliability is to use the scores from a single administration of a test to examine the consistency of test scores. One way to do this is to determine the **split-half reliability** of a test. To do so, a researcher administers a test but scores the items in the test as though they consisted of two separate tests. Typically, researchers do this by performing what is known as an odd-even split. Specifically, a researcher scores all the odd-numbered items and obtains a score for each examinee. Then, the researcher scores all the even-numbered items and obtains a second score for each examinee. This process results in two scores per examinee. Then, the researcher correlates the two sets of scores, yielding what is known as a *split-half reliability coefficient*. As with other types of reliability coefficients, these can range from 0.00, indicating a complete absence of reliability (i.e., the scores on the odd-numbered items have no relationship to the scores on the even-numbered items) to 1.00, indicating complete consistency in the ordering of the two sets of scores.[2]

Note that the split-half method checks on the consistency of scores *within the test itself* (not across two test administrations). Hence, the split-half method belongs to a class of reliability estimates known as estimates of **internal consistency**.

An alternative to the split-half method for estimating internal consistency is **Cronbach's alpha**, whose symbol is α. While the computation of alpha is complex, it is conceptually relatively easy to understand. Like the split-half method, it is based on a single administration of a test. After the test has been administered, mathematical procedures are used to obtain the equivalent of the average of all possible split-half reliability coefficients. For instance, an odd-even split could be used, yielding a split-half reliability coefficient. Then, the split could be the first half of the test versus the second half of the test, and a second split-half reliability coefficient could be obtained. Yet another split (maybe items 1–5 and items 11–15 for one half of a 20-item test versus the remaining items) could be used to obtain a third split-half reliability coefficient. After continuing in this way until all possible splits have been used, a researcher could average all the split-half reliabilities and obtain a value equivalent to Cronbach's alpha. Fortunately, the formula devised by Cronbach makes it possible to obtain this value without physically rescoring various splits over and over.

Because modern computer programs can be used to easily compute alpha, it has become much more commonly used than the split-half method, which depends on only a single split. Thus, the split-half method is reported primarily in older literature.[3]

Having high internal consistency is desirable when a researcher has developed a test designed to measure a single unitary variable, which is usually the case. For instance, if a researcher builds a test on the ability to sum one-digit numbers, students who score high on some of the items should score high on the other items and vice versa. Thus, the researcher should expect high internal consistency (i.e., a high value of α such as .80 or more). In con-

---

[1] In this topic, the term "test" is being used to refer to both tests and scales.
[2] As indicated in Topic 31, the larger the number of items in a test, the more reliable it tends to be. However, the split-half method estimates the reliability of a test only half as long as the full test. To correct for this un-

derestimate, a correction using the Kuder-Richardson Prophecy Formula should be made.
[3] Other older methods for estimating internal consistency are obtained by using Kuder-Richardson's Formulas 20 and 21. Like the split-half method, these have fallen by the wayside in favor of Cronbach's alpha.

trast, if the researcher builds a general achievement test with some math items, some social studies items, some vocabulary items, and so on, the researcher would expect less internal consistency (a lower value of α).

In review, test–retest reliability and parallel forms reliability measure the consistency of scores over time, while internal consistency methods (split-half and alpha) measure consistency among the items within a test at a single point in time.

EXERCISE ON TOPIC 33

1. Which two methods for estimating reliability require two testing sessions?

2. Does the split-half method require "one" *or* "two" administrations of a test?

3. What is meant by an "odd-even split"?

4. If a split-half reliability coefficient equals 0.00, what does this indicate?

5. What is the highest possible value for a split-half reliability coefficient?

6. To obtain alpha, mathematical procedures are used to obtain the equivalent of what?

7. Does alpha estimate the consistency of scores over time?

Question for Discussion

8. Suppose a researcher prepares a poorly written test in which some items are ambiguous. Speculate on the effect of the ambiguous items on split-half reliability.

For Students Who Are Planning Research

9. Will you be considering the internal consistency of any instruments you will be using in your research? If so, which method (split-half or alpha) will you use? Explain.

TOPIC 34 NORM- AND CRITERION-REFERENCED TESTS

Tests designed to facilitate a comparison of an individual's performance with that of a norm group are called **norm-referenced tests (NRTs)**.[1] For instance, if an examinee takes a test and earns a *percentile rank* of 64, the examinee knows that he or she scored higher[2] than 64% of the individuals in the norm group. Often, the norm group is a national sample of examinees, but it also may be an entire local population (such as all seniors in a school district) or a sample of a local population (such as a random sample of all seniors in a state).

In contrast, tests designed to measure the extent to which individual examinees have met performance standards (i.e., specific criteria) are called **criterion-referenced tests (CRTs)**.[3] For instance, suppose a researcher wants to test student nurses on their ability to administer an injection. The researcher might draw up a list of 10 behaviors that must be performed correctly for a student to pass the test, such as measuring the correct amount of medication, using a sterile needle, and so on. In this case, performing all the behaviors correctly is the criterion (i.e., performance standard).[4] Notice that the interpretation of an examinee's test score is independent of how other students perform. For instance, an examinee might be the best in a group with nine items right, but he or she along with everyone else will have failed the test because the standard is to perform all ten behaviors correctly. Thus, being higher or lower than others who take the same criterion-referenced test is irrelevant to the interpretation.

Researchers who build norm-referenced tests approach the task differently from those who build criterion-referenced tests. NRTs are intentionally built to be of medium difficulty. Specifically, items that are answered correctly by about 50% of the examinees in tryouts during test development are favored in the selection of items for the final versions of the tests. It is essential that an NRT be of medium difficulty because this level of difficulty facilitates the comparison of an individual with a group. This can be seen most easily at the extremes. For instance, if a researcher foolishly built an NRT that was so easy that all participants in the norm group got every item right, the researcher could not interpret scores in terms of who has a higher or lower score than other examinees because everyone would have the same score. The same problem would occur if a researcher built an NRT that was so difficult that all the examinees got all the items wrong.

In contrast, when building CRTs, item difficulty typically is of little concern. Instead, expert judgment is used to determine the desired level of performance and how to test for it. These judgments are influenced very little by how "difficult" a task is. Certainly, this approach is often appropriate. For instance, it would be inappropriate for the professors at a nursing school to drop a test item on measuring the correct amount of medication before injecting it simply because it is too difficult for their students. Because of its importance, the item should be retained regardless of its difficulty.

The need to have items of medium difficulty in NRTs is the basis of a major criticism of this type of test. Specifically, the criticism is that building NRTs is primarily driven by statistical considerations (i.e., item difficulty) and not by content considerations. Of course, those who build NRTs do consider carefully the content that a test should cover, but essential content may be deleted if the items that measure it are very easy or very difficult in try-outs of the items.

Which type of test should be favored in research? The answer depends on the research purpose. Here are two general guidelines:

---

[1] Some individuals use the terms *norm-referenced tests* and *standardized tests* interchangeably. However, it is better to reserve the term *standardized* to describe tests that come with standard directions for administration and interpretation. Both *norm-referenced tests* and *criterion-referenced tests* may be standardized.

[2] Strictly speaking, a percentile rank indicates the percentage of those in a norm group that an examinee scored *as high as or higher than*.

[3] The term *criterion-related validity* is used in Topic 29. Note that the word *criterion* is being used here and in Topic 29 to mean a *standard*. In Topic 29, using a standard for validating tests is discussed. Here, the discussion concerns using a standard to interpret the scores of individuals. These are, of course, separate matters, even though the same adjective is used in both cases.

[4] Performance standards are established by expert judgments and may be less than 100% correct, depending on the trait being measured. For instance, on a typing test, a test administrator might require only 95% accuracy. Of course, performance standards are not always expressed as a percentage. Instead, descriptive labels such as "expert," "novice," and so on can be used.

Guideline 1:

If the purpose is to describe specifically what examinees know and can do, criterion-referenced tests should be used.

Example: To what extent voters can understand a ballot proposition.

Example: Have students mastered the essentials of simple addition?

Guideline 2:

If the purpose is to examine how a local group differs from a larger norm group, norm-referenced tests should be used.[5]

Example: How well are students in New York doing in reading in comparison with the national average?

EXERCISE ON TOPIC 34

1. A norm-referenced test is designed to facilitate a comparison of an individual's performance with what?

2. Are norm groups always national samples?

3. What is the definition of a criterion-referenced test?

4. In which type of test are items answered correctly by about 50% of the participants favored in item selection?

5. In which type of test are items typically selected based on the content they cover without regard to item difficulty?

6. Which type of test should be used in research where the purpose is to describe specifically what examinees can and cannot do?

Questions for Discussion

7. Assume you are a parent and your child's second-grade teacher offers to provide you with *either* scores on a "norm-referenced test" *or* a "criterion-referenced test" of your child's basic math ability. Which would you choose? Why?

8. For research on the percentage of students whose swimming skills are good enough for them to save themselves if they jump into the deep end of a pool, which type of test would you choose? Explain.

For Students Who Are Planning Research

9. Will you be using norm-referenced tests in your research? Criterion-referenced tests? Explain.

---

[5] To make predictions, researchers need tests that differentiate among participants. For instance, if all examinees earn the same score on a college admissions test, the scores cannot be used to predict who will and who will not succeed in college. Because norm-referenced tests are specifically built to make differentiations by being of medium difficulty, they are also useful in prediction studies.

When researchers measure achievement, aptitude, and intelligence, they want examinees to strive to do their best—to perform at their optimum.

An **achievement test** measures *knowledge and skills individuals have acquired*. When researchers conduct research on the effectiveness of direct, planned instruction, they should use achievement tests designed to measure the objectives of that instruction. To the extent that the tests do that, they are *valid* (i.e., they measure what they should).

Multiple-choice tests of achievement are frequently used by researchers because of the ease with which such tests can be administered and scored. Indeed, multiple-choice are often appropriate when a researcher wants a quick snapshot of participants' achievement. Researchers can also measure achievement by having participants write answers to open-ended questions (e.g., essay questions), by evaluating participants' overt performances (e.g., a musical performance), or by assessing products (e.g., a portfolio of watercolor paintings). Scoring of the latter types is more time-consuming than scoring multiple-choice tests and may be *unreliable* unless researchers make sure that the scorers know specifically what characteristics of the essays, performances, or products they are to consider and how much weight to give to each characteristic in arriving at the scores. For instance, to evaluate the ability of a student nurse to give an injection, a researcher could develop a list of desirable characteristics, such as "measures the appropriate amount of medication," "checks the patient's armband," etc. These can be the basis for a *checklist* (a list of desirable characteristics of a product or performance, each of which is awarded a point) or a *rating scale* (e.g., "excellent," "above average," "average," "below average," "poor," which are applied in evaluating each characteristic).

An **aptitude test** is designed to *predict some specific type of achievement*. An example is the College Board's *Scholastic Aptitude Test* (*SAT*), which is used to predict success in college. The validity of an aptitude test is determined by correlating the scores participants earn (such as *SAT* scores determined while participants are in high school) with a measure of achievement obtained at a later date (such as freshman GPA in college). Other widely used aptitude tests are reading readiness tests (designed to predict reading achievement in the first grade by measuring whether examinees can discriminate among shapes, have basic concepts such as color names, etc.) and algebra prognosis tests (designed to predict achievement in algebra by measuring basic math skills that are used in algebra).

The most widely used aptitude tests are developed by commercial test publishers. Typically, they have low to modest validity (with validity coefficients of about .20 to .60). The modest predictive validity of aptitude tests is understandable because they measure only some of the skills needed for achievement in a particular area. For instance, many other skills such as persistence in the face of difficulty, study habits, as well as physical characteristics such as being chronically ill can affect achievement, but are not measured by aptitude tests. Published aptitude tests, however, usually have high reliability (with reliability coefficients of .80 or higher).

An **intelligence test** is designed to *predict achievement in general*, not any one specific type. The most popular intelligence tests (1) are culturally loaded and (2) measure knowledge and skills that can be acquired with instruction (with questions such as, "How far is it from New York to Los Angeles?"). The arguable assumption underlying intelligence tests is that all individuals are exposed to such information and more intelligent individuals are more likely to retain the information. Almost all contemporary experts on measurement, however, reject the notion that such tests measure innate (inborn) intelligence. At best, intelligence tests measure skills that have been acquired in some specific cultural milieu. Commercially available intelligence tests of this type have low to modest validity for predicting achievement in school—a degree of validity that can be achieved with less controversial aptitude tests.

Extensive efforts have been made to develop culture-free intelligence tests. Typical efforts in this area have concentrated on nonverbal tasks because of the high cultural load of language usage. These tests are usually less predictive of subsequent achievement than the more traditional intelligence tests, possibly because achievement is accomplished in a cultural context in which language is critical.

Research on intelligence can be controversial when, for instance, researchers assume that intelligence tests measure innate ability or that they measure all important aspects of intelligence. Issues such as racial and ethnic differences in innate intelligence, if worthy of study at all, cannot be satisfactorily investigated with the instruments available at this time.

Because of increasing awareness of widespread misinterpretations of intelligence test scores and the structural limitations of intelligence tests (e.g., arguable assumptions underlying them), intelligence tests are used in research much less frequently now than they were several decades ago.

EXERCISE ON TOPIC 35

1. Which type of test is designed to predict achievement *in general*?

2. An algebra prognosis test is an example of what type of test?

3. A test designed to measure how much students learn in a particular course in school is what type of test?

4. A test designed to predict success in learning a new set of skills is what type of test?

5. A list of desirable characteristics of a product or performance is known as what?

6. How can researchers increase the reliability of scoring essays, products, and performances?

7. According to this topic, are intelligence tests good measures of innate ability?

8. According to this topic, how valid are commercially published aptitude tests?

Questions for Discussion

9. Did you ever take an achievement test on which you did not perform up to your optimum? If yes, briefly describe why. Was the test maker or test administrator responsible for your less-than-optimum performance? Were you responsible? Explain.

10. Name a specific type of achievement for which you think scores obtained by using a checklist or rating scale applied in the measurement of overt behaviors would be more valid than scores obtained by using a multiple-choice test.

For Students Who Are Planning Research

11. Will you be using an achievement test in your research? Have you selected it yet? Explain.

12. Will you be using an aptitude test? What will it be designed to predict? Explain.

13. Will you be using an intelligence test? Will it be one designed to be "culture-free"? If yes, do you believe it is fully "culture-free"? Explain.

TOPIC 36 MEASURES OF TYPICAL PERFORMANCE

As indicated in the previous topic, when researchers measure achievement, aptitude, and intelligence, they encourage examinees to perform their best. In contrast, when researchers measure personality traits such as attitudes, interests, dispositions, as well as deep-seated personality traits, researchers want to determine participants' *typical* levels of performance. For instance, when selecting employees to work as salespeople, a employer might want to know how assertive each applicant typically is, not just how assertive they claim to be in their responses to an assertiveness scale (a series of questions that are scored to get an overall assertiveness score). When measuring such traits, a major concern is that applicants might indicate what is *socially desirable* rather than indicate their true level of assertiveness in order to increase their chances of employment.

Individuals are often hesitant to reveal they have *socially undesirable* traits even when they have nothing directly to gain by being deceitful. Thus, the responses of participants in research projects may frequently be influenced by social desirability. To the extent that researchers can reduce the influence of social desirability, they increase the validity of personality measures.

There are three basic approaches to reducing social desirability in participants' responses in order to measure without the influence of social desirability. First, by administering personality measures anonymously, researchers may reduce this tendency. Another approach is to observe behavior unobtrusively (without the participants' awareness—to the extent this is ethically possible) and rate selected characteristics such as aggressiveness.

A third approach is to use *projective techniques*. These provide loosely structured or ambiguous stimuli such as ink blots. As participants respond to these stimuli, such as by telling what they see, they are presumed to be projecting their feelings and beliefs and revealing them in their responses. For instance, a test administator might infer that participants whose responses to ink blots contain numerous references to aggressiveness are themselves aggressive. To the extent that participants are unaware of the specific traits an investigator is looking for, the tendency to give socially desirable responses is reduced.

The literature on the validity and reliability of popular projective techniques is quite mixed, with some studies showing that they are remarkably deficient in these respects. Thus, they are best used only by those who have had formal training in their administration and scoring. Furthermore, they are seldom used in personality research because (1) they are time-consuming to administer and score, (2) they do not naturally lend themselves to numerical results; instead, the interpretations are usually in terms of words, and (3) their validity is highly suspect. Instead, researchers usually use objective-type personality measures in which participants respond to statements or questions with restricted choices such as true–false, Strongly agree to Strongly disagree, and checklists in which respondents check off the characteristics they believe are true of themselves.

Scales that have choices from "Strongly Agree" to "Strongly Disagree" are known as **Likert-type scales**.[1] Each statement in a Likert-type scale should present a clear statement on a single topic. For instance, to measure attitudes toward school, a researcher might use statements such as, "In the mornings, I look forward to going to school" and "I get along well with my teacher." To reduce response bias (such as marking "Strongly agree" to all items without considering the individual items), it is a good idea to provide some positive and some negative statements and score them according to whether the associated statements are positive or negative. For instance, if five points are awarded for strongly agreeing to a positive statement toward school, a researcher would award five points for strongly disagreeing with a negative statement toward school. Researchers call this process **reverse scoring**.

Of course, the statements in a Likert-type scale should be derived from an analysis of the possible components of the attitude. For attitude toward school, a researcher might have several statements concerning attitudes in each of these areas: (1) learning in academic areas, (2) relationships with classmates, (3) relationships with teachers and staff, (4) participation in extracurricular activities, and so on. Such an analysis helps to assure that the contents of the attitude scale are comprehensive, which will contribute to its content validity (see Topic 28).

In short, when researchers measure personality traits, they want respondents to indicate what they

---

[1] Named for Rensis Likert, who popularized the format.

are typically like, not how well they can make themselves look. This is quite different from measurement of cognitive skills with achievement, aptitude, and intelligence tests on which researchers want respondents to show their best.

Exercise on Topic 36

1. Do researchers usually want participants to show their best when measuring personality traits?

2. In this topic, what is the main reason for administering personality measures anonymously?

3. What do researchers reduce by observing behavior unobtrusively?

4. Loosely structured stimuli are used in which type of personality measure?

5. According to this topic, which type of personality measure is seldom used in personality research?

6. What is the range of choice in a Likert-type scale?

7. Is content validity a relevant concern when assessing the validity of a Likert-type scale for measuring attitudes?

Questions for Discussion

8. Have you ever given a socially desirable response that was not true of you when being interviewed or answering a questionnaire? If yes, briefly describe why. Is there anything the interviewer or questionnaire writer could have done to increase the odds that you would be more forthright?

9. Write three statements that could be used with a Likert-type scale to measure attitudes toward your research methods class. Each should be on a different aspect of the class, such as the textbook, the instructor, and so on. Two should be positive statements and one should be negative. Explain how they would be scored.

For Students Who Are Planning Research

10. Will you be using a measure of typical performance in your research? If so, to what extent might it be subject to the influence of social desirability? Explain.

11. Will you be measuring attitudes? If yes, will you use a Likert-type scale? Explain.

PART E

EXPERIMENTAL DESIGN

In experiments, researchers give treatments in order to observe their effects on participants' behavior. In this part of the book, various designs for experiments are described. Specifically, designs for true experiments, pre-experiments, and quasi-experiments are explained and illustrated. The external validity of experiments (which answers the question, "Can a researcher generalize beyond the experimental setting?") as well as their internal validity (which answers the question, "Did the treatments, in fact, cause the observed differences?") are considered.[1]

---

[1] This part highlights some of the main ideas in the classic work of Campbell, D. T., & Stanley, J. C. (1963). *Experimental and quasi-experimental designs for research*. Chicago: Rand McNally.

NOTES

Topic 37   True Experimental Designs

As indicated in earlier topics, the purpose of an experiment is to explore cause-and-effect relationships. In this discussion, the terminology and symbols first suggested by Campbell and Stanley are used.[1]

First, consider a classic design for exploring cause-and-effect relationships:

Design 1:

Assign participants at random to groups.	Group A: (Experimental Group)	Pretest	Experimental Treatment	Posttest
	Group B: (Control Group)	Pretest	Control Condition	Posttest

Design 1 is the **pretest-posttest randomized control group design**. By assigning participants at random to groups, researchers are assured that there are no biases in the assignment.[2] That is, the two groups of participants are equal except for random differences.

In Design 1, if the experimental group makes greater gains from pretest to posttest than the control group *and* if the two groups have been treated the same in all respects except for the experimental treatment, the difference is attributable to only one of two causes: (1) the treatment or (2) random errors. As indicated in Part F of this book, researchers can use inferential statistics to assess the role of random errors in creating any observed differences. Thus, researchers can tolerate random errors because the results can be interpreted in light of their possible effects. There are no generalizable statistical techniques for assessing the influence of bias. Hence, researchers prefer to avoid bias in the assignment to the two conditions (i.e., experimental and control conditions) by using random assignment.

Researchers can simplify the representation of Design 1 by using symbols suggested by Campbell and Stanley: R (which stands for random assignment to groups), O (which stands for observation or

measurement, whether pretest or posttest), and X (which stands for experimental treatment). There is no symbol for "control condition," so it is represented by a blank. Note that a control condition may include some type of treatment (in education, it might be a traditional form of instruction; in medicine, it might be a placebo—a sugar pill). Thus, the control condition is the standard by which the effectiveness of the experimental treatment is judged. Using symbols, Design 1 looks like this:

$$R \quad O \quad X \quad O$$
$$R \quad O \qquad O$$

The advantage of using a pretest is that it permits researchers to determine how much each group has *gained*, not just whether they are different at the end of the experiment. However, sometimes having a pretest causes a problem because it can sensitize participants to the experimental treatment and in effect become part of the treatment. For instance, by taking a pretest at the beginning of an experimental course of instruction, participants can gain an overview of what will be covered, in how much depth the material will be covered, and so on. Thus, changes observed in the experimental group may be the result of a *combination of the pretest and the treatment*. This problem is called **pretest sensitization** (also called the **reactive effect of testing**). It can be overcome by conducting an experiment without a pretest, as is shown in Design 2, which is the **posttest-only randomized control group design**.

Design 2:

$$R \quad X \quad O$$
$$R \qquad O$$

At first, the lack of a pretest may seem to be a flaw, but remember that the comparability of the two groups in Design 1 was achieved by assigning participants at random to the two groups. This initial comparability is also achieved in Design 2 by this random assignment. In other words, it is not the pretest that makes the two groups comparable. Rather, it is the random assignment that does this.

Researchers can have the best of both designs by using the **Solomon randomized four-group design**, which is a combination of Designs 1 and 2. Solomon's design is shown in Design 3. Because it has four rows of symbols, it has four groups. The first two rows are the same as Design 1, while the

---

[1] Campbell, D. T., & Stanley, J. C. (1963). *Experimental and quasi-experimental designs for research*. Chicago: Rand McNally.
[2] See Topic 21 for a discussion of how to select participants at random. If half of them are selected at random to be the experimental group and the rest are designed as the control group, the researcher has used random assignment to groups.

bottom two rows are the same as Design 2. In effect, the Solomon design is two experiments conducted at the same time.

Design 3:

R O X O
R O   O
R   X O
R   O

The advantage of Design 3 is that researchers can compare the first two groups to determine how much gain is made and can also compare the last two groups to determine whether the treatment is more effective than the control condition in the absence of a pretest (without pretest sensitization). The only potential drawback to Design 3 is that a researcher must begin with a reasonably large pool of participants so that when they are divided into four groups, each of the groups will have a suffi-

cient number to yield reliable results. How many is enough? The answer is complex, but generally speaking, it probably would be unwise to use the four-group design instead of a two-group design if the total pool of participants is less than 48.

All three of the above designs are called **true experimental designs**. True experimental designs are easy to spot because they all are characterized by random assignment to treatments.

Note that sometimes it is not possible to assign participants at random. For instance, for ethical and legal reasons, a researcher might not be able to withhold a particular treatment from individuals. In such a case, the researcher might treat an entire group with a treatment mandated by law and use another group that is not required to have the treatment as the control group. Because the participants were *not* assigned at random to treatments, such experiments are *not* true experiments.

EXERCISE ON TOPIC 37

1. What is the purpose of an experiment?

2. How can researchers ensure that there are no biases in the assignment of participants to groups in an experiment?

3. In a diagram for an experimental design, the symbol "O" stands for what?

4. In a diagram for an experimental design, the symbol "X" stands for what?

5. What is the name of the potential problem caused by the pretest in the pretest-posttest randomized control group design?

6. What is the name of the true experimental design that has no pretests?

7. What is a potential drawback to the Solomon randomized four-group design?

8. True experimental designs are easy to spot because they all are characterized by what?

Question for Discussion

9. Briefly describe an experimental problem for which a researcher probably would not be able to assign participants at random to conditions.

For Students Who Are Planning Research

10. Will you be conducting an experiment? If so, will you be using a true experimental design? Explain.

Suppose a researcher observes major changes in participants' behavior in an experiment. Is it reasonable to attribute these changes to the effects of the treatment(s)? Depending on the design of the experiment, there may be explanations for the changes other than the treatment. These alternative explanations are called **threats to internal validity**. It is easiest to understand them in the context of a poor experiment with no control group (specifically, one in which a researcher pretests, treats, and then posttests one group of participants). Using the symbols described in the previous topic, the design looks like this:

$$O \quad X \quad O$$

Suppose the treatment (X) was designed to improve participants' self-concept, and the researcher observed an average gain of 9 points in self-concept from pretest (the first O) to posttest (the second O). Of course, the treatment could be responsible for the increase. Another possibility is the internal threat called **history** (i.e., other environmental influences on the participants between the pretest and posttest). For instance, perhaps some of the participants read a new self-help book that improved their self-concepts during the same period of time that the treatment was being administered. Thus, the gain could have resulted from reading the book and not from the treatment.

Another threat in this design is **maturation**. Perhaps the participants matured during the period between the pretest and posttest, and the increase is due to maturation and not the treatment.

Instrumentation is another threat. This refers to possible changes in the instrument (measurement procedure) from the time it was used as a pretest to the time it was used as a posttest. For instance, the particular observers who made the pretest observations may have been less astute at noticing signs of good self-concept than the observers who made the posttest observations.

Another threat is **testing**, which is defined as the effects of the pretest on the performance exhibited on the posttest. For instance, while taking the pretest self-concept scale, the participants may have learned how to interpret the questions. Their posttest performance might be affected by this learning experience that occurred while taking the pretest.

Statistical regression is another threat that occurs only if participants are selected on the basis of their extreme scores. For instance, perhaps a large group of students was administered a self-concept scale, and those in the lowest 20% were selected for treatment in the experiment. A fundamental principle of measurement is that those who are extremely low on a screening test will, on the average, tend to have a higher score when tested again, purely because of the nature of random errors created by the less-than-perfect reliability of the measures researchers use—whether or not the treatment is effective.[1]

The next threat to internal validity can occur when researchers use two comparison groups that are *not* formed at random. Suppose for instance a researcher uses the students in one school as the experimental group and those in another as the control group. Because students are not assigned to schools at random, the researcher is using **intact groups** (i.e., previously existing groups). This is diagrammed by putting a dashed line between the symbols for the groups, which indicates that the groups were intact, as shown here:

$$\begin{array}{ccc} O & X & O \\ \hline O & & O \end{array}$$

Notice that when researchers do not assign participants to the two groups at random, there is a very strong possibility that the two groups are not initially the same in all important respects, which is the threat called **selection**. Selection can *interact* with all the other threats to internal validity. For instance, consider **selection–history interaction**. Because the selection of participants for the two groups was not at random, they may be systematically subjected to different life experiences. For instance, it may be that the teachers in the school with the experimental group took a self-concept workshop, which was not part of the treatment, and applied what they learned to their students. Thus, the improvement in self-concepts may be the result of the teachers' efforts and not of the treatment. Another example is **selection–maturation interac-**

---

[1] Statistical regression is difficult to grasp without a solid background in measurement theory. However, some students may recall the principle of "regression toward the mean" from their study in other sciences Those who are very low will, on the average, tend to be higher on retesting (closer to the mean—an average), and those who are very high will tend to be lower on retesting.

tion. Perhaps the two groups, on the average, were at somewhat different developmental stages at the time of the pretest, which would have led to different rates of maturation in the two groups, which could affect self-concept.

Selection can also interact with a threat called **mortality** (i.e., differential loss of participants from the groups to be compared). For instance, those in an experimental school may have a higher dropout rate than those in a control school. If those who drop out have lower self-concepts, the posttest mean for the experimental group will be higher than the pretest mean, resulting in a statistical change in the average that is not the result of the treatment. At the same time, the control group will not exhibit as much change because it has a lower dropout rate.

All threats to internal validity can be overcome by using a **true experimental design** (see Topic 37), in which participants are assigned at random to experimental and control conditions. Because random assignment has no bias (or favorites), both the experimental and control groups are equally likely to experience the same environmental events (have the same history), mature at the same rates, drop out at the same rates, and so on.

Exercise on Topic 38

1. What is the name of the threat that indicates that taking a pretest may affect performance on a posttest?

2. Suppose an experimental group is being taught letters of the alphabet as a treatment. At about the same time, the students are watching an educational program on television, from which they learn the names of the letters. What is the name of the threat that this problem illustrates?

3. If observers are more tired and less astute when making posttest observations than when making pretest observations, what threat is operating?

4. What is the name of the threat posed by nonrandom assignment of participants to experimental and control groups?

5. If infants naturally improve in visual acuity and thus perform better at the end of an experiment than at the beginning, what threat is operating?

6. Under what circumstance will statistical regression operate?

7. How can researchers overcome all the threats to internal validity?

Question for Discussion

8. Suppose a researcher gave a series of wellness workshops over a six-month period and then determined that five of the employees had quit smoking during the six-month period. The researcher's interpretation was that the workshops caused the decrease in smoking. Is this interpretation flawed? Explain.

For Students Who Are Planning Research

9. If you will be conducting an experiment, which threats, if any, will it be subject to? Explain.

TOPIC 39   THREATS TO EXTERNAL VALIDITY

Consider this example: A researcher drew a sample from a population and divided it into an experimental group and a control group. To conduct the experiment, the researcher administered the experimental treatment and control condition in a laboratory on a college campus. Suppose the results of the experiment showed that the experimental group improved significantly more than the control group. Can the researcher accurately **generalize** from the sample to the population (i.e., is it accurate to assume that the treatment administered to the experimental group will work as well in the population as it did in the sample)? Also, will the treatment be as effective in the population's natural setting as it was in the artificial laboratory setting? The answers depend on the extent to which the experiment is subject to what researchers call **threats to external validity**.

The first threat is **selection bias** and its interaction with the experimental (independent) variable. As indicated in Part C of this book, if a sample is biased, a researcher's ability to generalize to a population is greatly limited. In a strict, scientific sense, no generalizations should be made when this is the case. This threat reminds researchers that if a biased sample of participants is used in an experiment (such as using the students who happen to be in one professor's class), a researcher will not know whether the effects of the treatment (observed in that class) can be expected if the treatment is administered to the entire population. Of course, the way to control this threat is to select the participants for an experiment at random from a population because a random sample is, by definition, unbiased.

Another threat is the **reactive effects of experimental arrangements**. This threat reminds researchers that if the experimental setting is different from the natural setting in which the population usually operates, the effects that are observed in the experimental setting may not generalize to the natural setting. For instance, if a treatment is administered in a laboratory to fifth-graders, the responsiveness of the students may be different from the responsiveness of the population of fifth-graders when the treatment is used in public school classroom settings. In other words, it can be risky to generalize from an experimental setting to a natural setting. The way to control this threat is to conduct experiments under natural conditions, when possible.

The possible **reactive effect of testing** (also called **pretest sensitization**) is another threat. This threat refers to the possibility that the pretest might influence how the participants respond to the experimental treatment. For instance, if a researcher gives a pretest on racial prejudice and then administers a treatment designed to lessen prejudice, participants' responses to the treatment may be affected by the experience of taking the pretest. That is, having to think about prejudice (while taking the pretest) might change participants' sensitivity to the treatment. This is a problem when researchers want to generalize about how well the treatment will work in the population *if* the population will not be given a pretest. As indicated in Topic 37, researchers can conduct true experiments without pretests, thereby eliminating this threat.

Multiple-treatment interference is a threat that occurs when a group of participants is given more than one treatment. For instance, at first a researcher might give participants no praise for correct answers, then start giving them moderate amounts of praise, and finally give them large amounts of praise. Suppose the researcher finds that large amounts of praise work best. Will it work in the same way in the population? The generalization will be risky if those in the population will *not* first be given the no-praise condition, then the moderate-praise condition, and finally, large amounts of praise. In other words, the fact that these participants first received small and then moderate amounts of praise might make their responses to large amounts of praise different from the responses of a population that will receive *only* large amounts of praise. In other words, treatment(s) given earlier in an experiment might affect the effectiveness of treatments given later to the same participants.

Take care to distinguish between **internal validity** (see Topic 38) and **external validity**. As indicated in this topic, the external validity of an experiment is concerned with "To whom and under what circumstances can the results be generalized?" Internal validity is concerned with the question, "Is the treatment, *in this particular case*, responsible for the observed change(s)?" Thus, threats to internal validity are potential explanations for the observed changes. That is, they are possible explanations that become confounded with the treatment as an explanation for any observed changes. Threats to internal validity are controlled by using *true experimental designs* (see Topic 37).

Note that internal and external validity are separate considerations. Even if an experiment has excellent internal validity, it may not be appropriate to generalize the results to other populations because of the threats to external validity discussed in this topic. Likewise, a study with high external validity might have poor internal validity because the threats to internal validity have confounded a researcher's understanding of what caused the observed changes. Thus, each one of these two types of threats should be considered and evaluated independently.

EXERCISE ON TOPIC 39

1. Which type of validity deals with the question of whether a researcher can generalize with confidence to a larger population in a natural setting?

2. Which type of validity deals with whether the treatment is directly responsible for any changes observed in the experimental setting?

3. What is the name of the threat that warns researchers to be careful in generalizing the results to a population when an experiment is conducted on a nonrandom sample?

4. Suppose a random sample of workers in a factory is exposed to five different reward systems, with each system being used for one month. What is the name of the threat that reminds researchers that the results may not generalize to the population of workers if the population is to be exposed to only the last reward system tried in the experiment?

5. Suppose an experimental classroom has research observers present at all times. What is the name of the threat that reminds researchers that the results may not generalize to other classrooms without observers?

6. If a pretest causes a change in participants' sensitivity to a treatment, what threat is operating?

Question for Discussion

7. Briefly describe a hypothetical experiment that has high internal validity but low external validity.

For Students Who Are Planning Research

8. If you will be conducting an experiment, which threats to external validity, if any, will it be subject to? Explain.

The three designs discussed in this topic are of very limited value for investigating cause-and-effect relationships because of their poor internal validity. Thus, they are called **pre-experimental designs**. One of the designs was introduced in Topic 38: the **one-group pretest–posttest design**. Its diagram is shown here as Design 4.[1]

Design 4:

O   X   O

As indicated in Topic 38, changes from pretest to posttest in Design 4 may be attributable to *history*, *maturation*, *instrumentation*, *testing*, and, if the participants were selected on the basis of extreme scores, *statistical regression*[2] (see Topic 38 for a discussion of these threats to internal validity). These threats are possible explanations for any changes observed from the pretest to the posttest. Of course, researchers want to determine what changes, if any, the treatment (X) caused. Thus, the interpretation of pretest to posttest change is *confounded* by multiple explanations.

Design 5 is called the **one-shot case study**. In it, one group is given a treatment (X) followed by a test (O). This is its diagram:

Design 5:

X   O

If a teacher provides instruction on a unit of material and follows it with an achievement test, he or she is using Design 5. For instructional purposes, there is nothing wrong with this design. For instance, the posttest will help the teacher determine what grades to assign for students' achievement on the unit of instruction. However, if a teacher wants to know whether the instruction *caused* whatever achievement is seen on the test, the design is of no value because it fails to make comparisons. The teacher cannot determine whether the students

achieved anything as a result of the instruction without a pretest (or a randomly selected control group). In other words, it is quite possible that the achievement the students display on the posttest is at the same level they might have displayed on a pretest, if there had been one.[3]

Design 6, the **static-group comparison design**, has two groups, but participants are not assigned to the groups at random. The dashed line between the two groups indicates they are **intact groups** (i.e., previously existing groups that were not formed at random).

Design 6:

X   O

O

The obvious problem with Design 6 is the threat to internal validity called *selection* (the selection of the two groups was not made in such a way that a researcher can have confidence that they are initially the same in all important respects).[4] Furthermore, without a pretest, a researcher does not have a basis for knowing whether the two groups were similar at the beginning of the experiment. For instance, the treatment might have been totally ineffective, but the experimental group might have been superior to the control group at the beginning of the experiment and retained the same amount of superiority throughout the experiment. This initial superiority would produce a difference in favor of the experimental group in the posttest results, which might lead to the risky assumption that the treatment caused the difference.[5]

Because of their weaknesses, the three pre-experimental designs are of very limited value in exploring cause-and-effect relationships. However, they are sometimes useful in *preliminary pilot stud-*

---

[1] Each of the designs in this part is given a number for reference in class discussions. The numbering system is not a universal one. Thus, in discussions outside of class, refer to the names of the designs given in boldfaced type, not to the design numbers.

[2] Campbell and Stanley (1963) note that this design is also subject to the *interaction of selection with history, maturation*, etc. See Campbell, D. T., & Stanley, J. C. (1963). *Experimental and quasi-experimental designs for research*. Chicago: Rand McNally.

[3] Campbell and Stanley (1963) note that this design is subject to the internal threats of history, maturation, selection, and mortality.

[4] Campbell and Stanley (1963) note that this design is also subject to the internal threats of mortality and the interaction of selection with history, maturation, etc.

[5] As indicated in Topic 37, a pretest is not essential in a two-group design *if* the participants are assigned at random to the groups. This is because the random assignment assures that the two groups are initially the same *except for random differences*, which can be assessed with inferential statistics. See the discussion of Design 2 in Topic 37.

ies in which a researcher's goal is to try out potential treatments and measuring tools to learn more about their acceptability and accuracy, not to obtain definitive information on causal relationships. For instance, a researcher might administer a new drug to a small group of participants in order to observe for side effects, to determine the maximum tolerable dosage, to explore different routes of administration, and so on. The results could be used in planning a subsequent true experiment on the effects of the drug, using a design that has a randomized control group (see Topic 37).

EXERCISE ON TOPIC 40

1. Are pre-experimental designs valuable for identifying cause-and-effect relationships?

2. Suppose a researcher administered a new program to all students in a school. At the end of the school year, the researcher administered a standardized test to the students in the school as well as to students in another school who were serving as a control group. Is the comparison of the average scores for the two groups of students useful for determining the effects of the program?

3. What is the name of the pre-experimental design used in Question 2?

4. If a researcher gives a pretest on knowledge of child abuse to a group of social workers, then gives them a series of seminars on child abuse followed by a posttest, what is the name of the pre-experimental design the researcher used?

5. Is the design used in Question 4 useful for determining cause-and-effect relationships?

Questions for Discussion

6. Suppose a researcher selected participants at random from a population and then used the one-group pretest–posttest design. Would random selection make this design good for exploring cause-and-effect relationships?

7. Have you ever used a pre-experimental design in any of your professional or everyday activities (e.g., tried doing something in a new way and observing for its effects without a control group)? If so, briefly describe it. Discuss whether your activity shed light on a cause-and-effect relationship.

For Students Who Are Planning Research

8. If you will be conducting an experiment, will you be using a pre-experimental design? If yes, explain why you will be using such a design given that it has serious weaknesses.

TOPIC 41 QUASI-EXPERIMENTAL DESIGNS

As indicated in Topic 37, true experimental designs, which involve random assignment to treatment conditions, are excellent for exploring cause-and-effect relationships. Often, however, it is not possible to assign participants at random. When this is the case, pre-experimental designs (see Topic 40) should be avoided. Instead, **quasi-experimental designs**, which are of intermediate value for exploring cause-and-effect, should be used.[1]

Design 7, which is diagrammed again immediately below, was first discussed in Topic 38, where threats to internal validity were discussed. It is a widely used quasi-experimental design that has two intact groups (not assigned at random as indicated by the dashed line). This is the **nonequivalent control group design**.

Design 7:

$$O \quad X \quad O$$
$$\overline{}$$
$$O \qquad\quad O$$

As indicated in Topic 38, this design is subject to the threats of *mortality*, *selection*, and *interaction of selection* with other threats such as *history*. Thus, it is far from ideal but is superior to the pre-experimental designs, which are not directly interpretable in terms of causal effects. When random assignment to groups is not possible, Design 7 may provide useful results.

Even though participants are not assigned at random to the two groups in Design 7, researchers often use some form of matching to increase the internal validity of the results. For instance, in studying the effects of patients' satisfaction with their experiences in hospitals, the patients in one hospital that is undergoing organizational change might be designated as the "experimental group" while the patients in another hospital that is not undergoing organizational change might be designated as the "control group." To form matched groups, a researcher might select a sample from the first hospital and determine their status on these demographics: medical condition, age, gender, and socioeconomic status. Then, the researcher could handpick participants from the other hospital who are similar in terms of the same demographics. Although this is better than using unmatched samples from both hospitals, there is still the danger that the two groups may not have been matched on all relevant variables. For instance, in this example, the researcher has not taken into account whether the patients have insurance or not. Those with insurance and those without insurance may be fundamentally different in their views of patient satisfaction. Obviously, assigning participants at random to the two conditions (using a true experimental design) would be vastly superior because the random assignment would assure the researcher that the two groups were initially the same on *all variables* except for random differences, whose effects can be assessed with inferential statistics, a topic that is considered in detail in Part F of this book.

Design 8, which is known as the **equivalent time-samples design**, has only one group (or possibly only one participant). Treatment conditions are alternated (preferably on a random basis), as indicated in the diagram by alternating X_1 (an experimental treatment) with X_o (a control condition or comparison treatment).

Design 8:

$$X_oO \quad X_1O \quad X_oO \quad X_1O$$

The participants in Design 8 are, in effect, serving as both the control participants (when they are receiving X_o) and the experimental participants (when they are receiving X_1). This is a major advantage because researchers know the experimental participants and control participants (who are actually the same individuals) are identical in their genetic characteristics, income level, attitudes, beliefs—in fact, in all ways—at the beginning of the experiment. A major disadvantage of this design is the strong possibility of *multiple-treatment interference*. In this case, the second time the participants receive X_1, they have already been exposed to and possibly changed by the earlier exposure to X_1O.

Notice that giving the treatments repeatedly in Design 8 strengthens internal validity because it is unlikely that the threats to internal validity are operating only at the times when X_1 is given but not when X_o is given. For instance, it is unlikely that participants mature only at X_1 and not at X_o. Similarly, it is unlikely that *history* confounds the interpretation by causing changes only when X_1 is given.

---

[1] Only the two most widely used quasi-experimental designs are presented in this topic. For a discussion of others, see Campbell, D. T., & Stanley, J. C. (1963). *Experimental and quasi-experimental designs for research*. Chicago: Rand McNally.

In psychology, a single-group design in which treatments are alternated is often called an ABAB design, where A and B indicate alternating treatments. Typically, when this design is used, there are multiple initial observations before any treatment is given. These initial observations constitute the **baseline**, which determines the typical variation in the behavior of participants over time before any intervention. For instance, perhaps a researcher plans to give rewards for in-seat behavior in a classroom to a hyperactive child. The researcher could measure the amount of out-of-seat behavior on a daily basis for a number of days to determine the natural amount of variation from day to day without treatment. Then, when the researcher introduces the rewards, any changes observed during treatment can be evaluated in terms of the natural variation before treatment. In other words, the researcher would ask: Is the decrease in out-of-seat behavior after treatment greater than the natural day-to-day decreases (and increases) observed during the baseline?

EXERCISE ON TOPIC 41

1. What is the name of the design diagrammed immediately below?

$$\frac{O \quad X \quad O}{O \qquad O}$$

2. In the design shown in Question 1, what indicates that the participants were not assigned at random to the groups?

3. If a researcher uses matching to form the two groups in the design in Question 1, would the resulting experiment be superior to a true experiment?

4. What is a major advantage of the equivalent time-samples design?

5. What is a major disadvantage of the equivalent time-samples design?

6. In psychology, what is an ABAB design?

Question for Discussion

7. Suppose a researcher observed two classes for baseline data on calling-out behavior (i.e., calling out in class when it is inappropriate). In Class A, the researcher observed much variation in the amount of calling out from day to day. In Class B, there is little variation (i.e., there is about the same amount from one day to the next). In your opinion, for which class would it be desirable to have a longer baseline? Why?

For Students Who Are Planning Research

8. If you will be conducting an experiment, will you be using a quasi-experimental design? If yes, which one? Why are you using a quasi-experimental design instead of a true experimental one? (See Topic 37.)

TOPIC 42 CONFOUNDING IN EXPERIMENTS

In experimental research, a **confound** is a source of confusion regarding the explanation for a given difference. Suppose, for instance, a researcher gave an experimental group instruction in algebra using a new software program, and, at the same time, a student teacher taught the same algebra skills to the participants using manipulative devices. Furthermore, suppose the control group received no algebra instruction. If the experimental group outperformed the control group, the results would be said to be confounded because there would be no way to sort out the relative influence of the software versus the manipulatives. Unfortunately, not all sources of confounding are as obvious as the one in this example.

An important source of confounding is the **Hawthorne effect**, which can be thought of as the "attention effect." This source was discovered in a series of industrial psychology studies at the Hawthorne Plant of Western Electric. In the studies, worker productivity went up when the lighting was increased. Oddly, however, when the lighting was decreased, productivity also went up. This was interpreted to mean that participants were responding to the attention they were receiving from the researchers (knowing they were being observed in an experiment) in addition to (or in spite of) the treatments with varying illumination. Thus, there were two intertwined explanations for the differences observed (i.e., the amount of illumination and the amount of attention participants received).

To control for the Hawthorne effect, some researchers use three groups: (a) an experimental group, (b) a control group that receives attention, and (c) a control group that receives no special attention. For instance, an experimental group could be shown a film containing aggressive behaviors to determine whether students' aggressiveness on the playground increased after seeing the film. The "attention-control" group could be shown a film with no aggression (thus, giving attention to this control group), while the "no-attention control group" could be shown no film. Comparing the aggressiveness of the three groups on a playground would yield information on how much "attention" contributed to any changes as well as how much the film with aggressive behaviors contributed.

A related confound is the **John Henry effect**. This effect refers to the possibility that the control group might become aware of its "inferior" status

and respond by trying to outperform the experimental group. Thus, researchers should try to conceal the control group's knowledge of their status whenever possible. For ethical reasons, participants usually need to be informed that they will be participating in an experiment, but it is often sufficient to inform them that they may be in either the experimental or control group, without revealing the group to which they were assigned.

Researchers who study the effectiveness of medications usually are concerned with the potentially confounding effects of the **placebo effect**. The placebo effect refers to the tendency of individuals to improve (or at least feel that they are improving) simply because they know they are being treated. Suppose, for instance, a new drug was given to a group of individuals suffering from a certain condition. Because of the placebo effect, some individuals might report that they feel better (or might have real improvement) even if the drug was totally ineffective.

To control for the placebo effect, researchers use a control group that is given a **placebo**. In drug studies, for instance, a placebo could be a "pill" that contains only inert ingredients (e.g., a "sugar pill"), which provides a "treatment" for the control group. Comparing the experimental group with a placebo-control group indicates how much more effective the new medication is than "treatment" with an inactive substance.

When administering a placebo, researchers say they are using a **blind** procedure when they do not disclose to the participants whether they are receiving an active or inactive substance. (For ethical reasons, participants are told that they will be receiving *either* an active or inactive drug.) In a **double-blind** experiment, neither the participants nor the individual dispensing the drug know which is the active drug and which is the placebo. This is done to prevent the possibility that the individual dispensing the drug will subtly communicate to the participants their status as being either "control" or "experimental" participants.[1] For instance, the packaging of the drug and placebo could be color-coded; the individual who is dispensing might only know that the blue

---

[1] Note that those who dispense the drugs in these experiments might also subconsciously communicate their *expectations* (i.e., that those receiving the active drug will improve).

package should be dispensed to a random half while the yellow package should be dispensed to the other half, without knowing which color package contains the active drug.

Demand characteristics can also be a source of confounding. A demand characteristic is a cue that lets participants know the expected outcome of an experiment. This can be a problem if participants attempt to "please" the experimenter by reporting or acting in a way they believe is expected. To the extent possible, researchers should try to conceal their expectations from the participants regarding the researchers' expectations (i.e., the researchers' hypotheses).

EXERCISE ON TOPIC 42

1. A confound is a source of confusion regarding what?

2. What is the name of the effect that refers to the possibility the control group might become aware of its "inferior" status and respond by trying to outperform the experimental group?

3. What is the formal name of what is characterized as the "attention effect" in this topic?

4. In addition to an experimental and a traditional control group (with no treatment) what other group can be used to control for the Hawthorne effect?

5. The term "placebo effect" refers to what tendency?

6. In what type of experiment do neither the participants nor the individuals dispensing the drug know which is the active drug and which is the placebo?

7. A "demand characteristic" is a cue that lets participants know what?

Question for Discussion

8. If you were a participant in an experiment, did you try to guess what the researcher's hypothesis was? If yes, do you think that your guess(es) influenced your behavior in the experiment? Explain.

For Students Who Are Planning Research

9. If you will be conducting an experiment, will you be taking measures to try to prevent any of the potential sources of confounding discussed in this topic?

PART F

UNDERSTANDING STATISTICS

This part of the book begins by examining the differences between the two major branches of statistics: (1) *descriptive statistics*, which help summarize and describe data that have been collected, and (2) *inferential statistics*, which help in making inferences from samples to the populations from which the samples were drawn. Then, the use of statistical techniques for analyzing the results of research are described.

Because this part of the book is designed to prepare readers to comprehend statistics reported in research reports, the emphasis is on understanding their meanings—not on computations.

Important Note

The topics in this part are highly interrelated. Therefore, students are strongly advised to read the topics in this part of the book in the order presented.

NOTES

TOPIC 43 DESCRIPTIVE AND INFERENTIAL STATISTICS

Descriptive statistics summarize data so they can easily be comprehended. For instance, suppose a researcher administered a test to all 362 freshmen enrolled in a university. It would be difficult to see even the major trends in an unordered list of such a large number of scores. However, if the researcher prepares a **frequency distribution** such as the one in Table 1, the researcher can easily see how the scores are distributed. For instance, the frequency distribution clearly indicates that a majority of the freshmen had scores from 14 through 16, with a scattering above and below these levels.

Table 1
Frequency Distribution with Percentages

Score (X)	Frequency (f)	Percentage
20	5	1.4
19	9	2.5
18	24	6.6
17	35	9.7
16	61	16.9
15	99	27.3
14	68	18.8
13	29	8.0
12	21	5.8
11	11	3.0
Total	362	100.0%

The **frequencies** in Table 1 are descriptive statistics. They describe how many students earned each score. The **percentages** in the table are also descriptive. They describe how many students *per one hundred* had each score. For instance, 3.0% had a score of 11. This means that for each 100 freshmen, three of them have a score of 11. These and other descriptive statistics, such as averages, are described in this part of the book.

Now, suppose that in order to economize, a researcher sampled at random (by drawing names out of a hat) only 100 freshmen to be tested (instead of testing all 362). Would the researcher obtain exactly the same results as he or she would if the researcher tested all freshmen? The answer is: in all likelihood, *no*. As indicated in Topics 20 through 23, random sampling produces random errors that statisticians call *sampling errors*. The purpose of **inferential statistics** is to help researchers draw inferences about the effects of sampling errors on the results that are described with descriptive statistics. More specifically, inferential statistics help researchers make generalizations about the characteristics of populations based on data obtained by studying samples.

An inferential statistic widely reported in the mass media is a **margin of error**. When reporting the results of public opinion polls for instance, reporters frequently cite margins of error to help readers interpret results in light of sampling error. For instance, a recent poll indicated that approval of the president was at 45%, with a margin of error of ±2 (i.e., plus/minus 2) percentage points. This indicates that readers can be highly confident that the level of approval in the population is between 43% and 47% (i.e., within two points of the 45% observed in the sample).

An important family of inferential statistics consists of *significance tests*, which help researchers decide whether the differences in descriptive statistics they identify (such as differences in the reading achievement between samples of boys and girls) are reliable. In the next topic, the general purpose of significance testing is considered in more detail, and in later sections, three popular tests of significance are considered.

Because inferential statistics help researchers evaluate results in light of sampling errors, it follows that if researchers do *not* sample, they do *not* need inferential statistics. For instance, if a researcher conducts a *census* (a study in which all members of a population are included), the descriptive statistics the researcher obtains (such as percentages) are values that are free of sampling errors. Because margins of error, for instance, are designed to help interpret results in light of sampling errors and because there are no sampling errors in the results obtained in a census, margins of error are not needed to assist in interpreting the results.

Researchers distinguish between values obtained from a sample and values obtained from a census by using the terms **parameters** (for values from a census) and **statistics** (for values from studies in which samples were examined). Thus, statistical values are referred to as parameters when they are derived from a census, but they are classified as statistics when they are based on the results obtained from a sample. As a mnemonic device, remember the first letters shown here in italics:

Samples yield *Statistics*, and
Populations yield *Parameters*.

EXERCISE ON TOPIC 43

1. Which branch of statistics ("inferential" *or* "descriptive") helps researchers summarize data so they can be easily comprehended?

2. According to Table 1 in this topic, how many participants had a score of 19?

3. What is the name of the statistic that describes how many participants per 100 have a certain characteristic?

4. Which branch of statistics helps researchers draw inferences about the effects of sampling errors on their results?

5. If a researcher tests a random sample instead of all members of a population, is it likely that the sample results will be the same as the results the researcher would have obtained by testing the population?

6. Is a margin of error a "descriptive" *or* an "inferential" statistic?

7. Are significance tests associated with "descriptive" *or* "inferential" statistics?

8. By studying populations, do researchers obtain "statistics" *or* "parameters"?

9. By studying samples, do researchers obtain "statistics" *or* "parameters"?

Question for Discussion

10. Keep your eye out for a report of a poll in which a margin of error is reported. Copy it and bring it to class for discussion.

For Students Who Are Planning Research

11. Will you be reporting descriptive statistics? (Note that statistics often are not reported in qualitative research. See Topics 9 and 10.) Explain.

12. Will you be reporting inferential statistics? Explain.

TOPIC 44   INTRODUCTION TO THE NULL HYPOTHESIS

Suppose a researcher drew random samples of engineers and psychologists, administered a self-report measure of sociability, and computed the mean (the most commonly used average) for each group. Furthermore, suppose the mean for engineers is 65.00 and the mean for psychologists is 70.00. Where did the five-point difference come from? There are three possible explanations:

1. Perhaps the population of psychologists is truly more sociable than the population of engineers, and the samples correctly identified the difference. (In fact, the *research hypothesis* may have been that psychologists are more sociable than engineers, which now appears to be supported by the data the researcher collected.)

2. Perhaps there was a bias in procedures. By using random sampling, the researcher has ruled out sampling bias, but other procedures, such as measurement, may be biased. For instance, maybe the psychologists were contacted during December, when many social events take place, and the engineers were contacted during a gloomy February. The only way to rule out bias as an explanation for the difference between the two means is to take *physical steps* to prevent it. In this case, the researcher would want to make sure that the sociability of both groups was measured in the same way at the same time.

3. Perhaps the populations of psychologists and engineers are the same in their sociability, but the samples are unrepresentative of the populations because of random sampling errors. For instance, the random draw may have provided a sample of psychologists who are more sociable, on the average, than their population purely by chance (at random).

The third explanation has a name: the **null hypothesis**. The general form in which it is stated varies from researcher to researcher. Here are three versions, all of which are consistent with each other:

Version A of the null hypothesis:

The observed difference was created by sampling error. (Note that the term *sampling error* refers only to *random errors*, not errors created by a bias. Note that there is no bias in sampling in the example because the researcher sampled at random.)

Version B of the null hypothesis:

There is no true difference between the two groups. (The term *true difference* refers to the difference a researcher would find in a census of the two populations. That is, the *true difference* is the difference a researcher would find if there were no sampling errors.)

Version C of the null hypothesis:

The true difference between the two groups is zero.

Significance tests determine the probability that the null hypothesis is true. (The use of specific significance tests is covered in Topics 47–48 and 54–56.) Suppose the researcher in the example being considered conducted a significance test and found that the probability that the null hypothesis is a correct hypothesis is less than 5 in 100. This would be stated as $p < .05$, where p stands for the word *probability*. If the odds that something is true are less than 5 in 100, it seems likely that it is *not* true. Thus, the researcher would *reject the null hypothesis*, leaving the researcher with only the first two explanations listed earlier in this topic.

There is no rule of nature that dictates at what probability level the null hypothesis should be rejected. However, conventional wisdom suggests that .05 or less (such as .01 or .001) is reasonable because they are low probabilities. Of course, researchers should state in their reports the probability level they used to determine whether to reject the null hypothesis.

Note that when researchers fail to reject the null hypothesis because the probability is greater than .05, they do just that: They "fail to reject" the null hypothesis, and it remains on the list of possible explanations for the difference. Note that it is *not* possible to "accept" the null hypothesis as the only explanation for a difference based on inferential statistics because there are three possible explanations for a difference. In other words, failing to reject one possible explanation (the null hypothesis) does *not* mean researchers are accepting it as the only explanation (because there are two additional explanations on the list).

An alternative way to say that a researcher has rejected the null hypothesis is to state that the difference is **statistically significant**. Thus, if a researcher states that a difference is statistically significant at the .05 level (meaning .05 or less), it is equivalent to stating that the null hypothesis has been rejected at that level.

In research reports in academic journals, the null hypothesis is seldom stated by researchers, who assume that readers know the sole purpose of a significance test is to test the null hypothesis. Instead, researchers report which differences were tested for significance, which significance test they used, and which differences were found to be statistically significant. It is more common to find null hypotheses stated in theses and dissertations because committee members may want to make sure the students they are supervising understand the reason they have conducted a significance test.

The most commonly used significance tests are described later in this part of the book.

EXERCISE ON TOPIC 44

1. How many explanations were there for the difference between psychologists and engineers in the example in this topic?

2. What does the null hypothesis say about sampling error?

3. Does the term *sampling error* refer to "random errors" *or* to "bias"?

4. The null hypothesis says the true difference equals what numerical value?

5. Significance tests are designed to determine the probabilities regarding the truth of what hypothesis?

6. The expression $p < .05$ stands for what words?

7. Do researchers reject the null hypothesis when the probability of its truth is "high" *or* when the probability is "low"?

8. What do researchers do if the probability is greater than .05?

9. What is an alternative way of saying a researcher has rejected the null hypothesis?

10. Are null hypotheses more likely to be explicitly stated in a "journal article" *or* in a "dissertation"?

Question for Discussion

11. All individuals use probabilities in everyday activities to make decisions. For instance, when deciding whether to cross a street with traffic, individuals estimate the odds that they will get across the street safely before beginning to cross. Briefly describe one other specific use of probabilities in everyday decision-making.

For Students Who Are Planning Research

12. Will you be testing the null hypothesis in your research? Explain.

There are four scales (or levels) at which researchers measure. The lowest level is the **nominal** level (also called the *nominal scale*). This may be thought of as the "naming" level. For instance, when researchers ask participants to name their marital status, participants will respond with *words*—not numbers—such as "married," "single," "divorced," and so on. Notice that nominal data do not put participants in any particular mathematical order. There is no logical basis for saying that one category, such as "single," is higher or lower mathematically than any other category.

The next level is **ordinal**. At this level, the measurements place participants in order from high to low. For instance, an employer might rank applicants for a job on their professional appearance. Traditionally, researchers give a rank of 1 to the participant who is highest, 2 to the next highest, and so on. It is important to note that ranks do not indicate the amount by which participants differ. If a researcher knows that Janet has a rank of 1 and Frank has a rank of 2, the researcher does not know if Janet's appearance is greatly superior to Frank's or only slightly superior. To measure the *amount* of difference among participants, researchers use the next two levels of measurement.

Measurements at the **interval** and **ratio** levels have equal distances among the scores they yield. For instance, when researchers say that Jill weighs 120 pounds and Sally weighs 130 pounds, they know by *how much* the two participants differ. Also, note that a 10-pound difference represents the same amount regardless of where participants are on the scale. For instance, the difference between 120 and 130 pounds is the same as the difference between 220 and 230 pounds.

The ratio scale is at a higher level than the interval scale because the ratio scale has an absolute zero point that researchers know how to measure. Thus, *weight* is an example of the ratio scale because it has an absolute zero.

The interval scale, while having equal intervals like the ratio scale, does not have an absolute zero. The most common examples of interval scales are scores obtained using objective instruments such as attitude scales and multiple-choice tests of achievement. For achievement tests, it is widely assumed that each multiple-choice test item measures a single point's worth of the trait being measured and that all points are equal to all other points, making it

an interval scale (just as all pounds are equal to all other pounds of weight). However, such tests do not measure at the ratio level because the zero on such tests is arbitrary, not absolute. To see this, consider someone who gets a zero on a multiple-choice final examination. Does the zero mean that the student has absolutely no knowledge of or skills in the subject area? Probably not. He or she probably has some knowledge of simple facts, definitions, and concepts, but the test was not designed to measure at the low skill level at which the student is operating. Thus, a score of zero indicates only that the student knows nothing *on that test*, not that the student has zero knowledge of the content domain. Thus, the scores are at the interval level, not the ratio level.

Here is a summary of the levels:

Lowest Level	Scale	Characteristic
	Nominal	*naming*
	Ordinal	*ordering*
⇩	**Interval**	*equal interval without an absolute zero*
	Ratio	*equal interval with an absolute zero*
Highest Level		

For those who like to use mnemonics, remember this environmentally friendly phrase:

No Oil In Rivers

The first letters—**NOIR**—are the first letters of the scales in order from lowest to highest.

At which level should researchers measure? There is no simple answer. First, some variables are inherently nominal in nature. For instance, when researchers need to know participants' gender or state of residence, nominal data are the natural choice. Second, many novice researchers overuse the ordinal scale. For instance, if a researcher wants to measure reading ability, it would usually be much better to use a carefully constructed standardized test (which measures at the interval level) than having teachers rank students in terms of their reading ability. Remember, measuring at the interval level provides more information than measuring at the ordinal level because the interval-level measurements indicate the amount by which participants differ. Thus, when possible, researchers prefer to measure at the interval or ratio levels instead of the ordinal level.

The choice between interval and ratio depends solely on whether it is possible to measure with an absolute zero. When it is possible, researchers usually do so. For the purposes of applied statistical analyses, however, interval and ratio data are treated in the same way.

The level at which researchers measure has important implications for data analysis, so there are references to scales of measurement throughout the discussion of statistics in subsequent topics in this part of the book.

EXERCISE ON TOPIC 45

1. If a researcher asks participants to name the country in which they were born, the researcher is using which scale of measurement?

2. Which two scales of measurement have equal distances among the scores they yield?

3. If a researcher has a teacher rank students according to their oral language skills, the researcher is using which scale of measurement?

4. Which scale of measurement has an absolute zero?

5. Which scale of measurement is at the lowest level?

6. Objective, multiple-choice achievement tests are usually assumed to measure at what level?

7. If a researcher measures in such a way that the researcher finds out which participant is most honest, which is the next most honest, and so on (without measuring to determine how much honesty each one has), the researcher is measuring with what scale of measurement?

8. The number of minutes of overtime work that employees perform is an example of which scale of measurement?

9. Weight measured in pounds is an example of which scale of measurement?

Question for Discussion

10. Name a trait that inherently lends itself to nominal measurement. Explain your answer.

For Students Who Are Planning Research

11. List the measures you will be using in your research, and name the scale of measurement for each one.

TOPIC 46 DESCRIPTIONS OF NOMINAL DATA

As indicated in the previous topic, researchers obtain *nominal data* when they classify participants according to names (words) instead of quantities. For instance, suppose a researcher asked each member of a population of 540 teachers which candidate he or she prefers for a school board vacancy and found that 258 preferred Smith and 282 preferred Jones. (Since "Smith" and "Jones" are names, the data are at the nominal level.) The 258 and 282 are *frequencies*, whose symbol is *f*. Researchers sometimes also refer to them as **numbers of cases**, whose symbol is *N*.

The numbers of cases can be converted into *percentages* by dividing the number who prefer each candidate by the number in the population and multiplying by 100. Thus, for Smith, the calculations are:

$$258 \div 540 = 0.478 \times 100 = 47.8\%$$

When reporting percentages, it is desirable to also report the underlying numbers of cases, which is done in Table 1.

Table 1
Teachers' Preferences

Candidate	Percentage
Jones	52.2% (N = 282)
Smith	47.8% (N = 258)
Total	100.0% (N = 540)

Table 1 is an example of what is called a **univariate analysis**. The researcher is analyzing how participants *vary* (hence, researchers use the root *variate*) on only *one* variable (hence, researchers use the prefix *uni-*).

Researchers can examine a relationship between two nominal variables by conducting a **bivariate analysis**. Perhaps a researcher wants to know whether there is a relationship between teachers' gender and their preferences for candidates. Table 2 shows the results of a bivariate analysis of these variables.

The data in Table 2 clearly indicate that there is a relationship between gender and the preferences for the two candidates because a larger percentage of males than females prefers Jones, but a larger percentage of females than males prefers Smith. In general, teachers' gender is predictive of their preferences. For instance, by knowing a teacher is male, a researcher would predict that the teacher is more likely to vote for Jones than to vote for Smith.

Table 2
Teachers' Preferences by Gender

Gender	Jones	Smith	Total
Male	66.4% (N = 85)	33.6% (N = 43)	100.0% (N = 128)
Female	47.8% (N = 197)	52.2% (N = 215)	100.0% (N = 412)

Note that in this population of teachers, there are many more female teachers than male teachers. When this is the case, examining only the numbers of cases (e.g., 85 males for Jones versus 197 females for Jones) can be misleading. For instance, in Table 2, a *majority* of the population of males (the smaller population) is in favor of Jones, but only a *minority* of the larger population of females is in favor of him. With percentages, legitimate comparisons of groups of unequal size are possible. This is because percentages convert numbers of cases to a common scale, with a base of 100. (The percentage of 66.4% of males for Jones indicates that *for every 100 males*, 66.4 of them are in favor of Jones, while the percentage of 47.8% of females for Jones indicates that *for every 100 females*, only 47.8 of them are in favor of Jones.)

In academic writing, some researchers report **proportions** instead of *percentages*. For instance, a percentage of 47.8% in favor of Smith in Table 1 corresponds to a proportion of 0.478 or 0.48. (Proportions are calculated in the same way percentages are except that the multiplication by 100 is not performed. For instance, $258 \div 540 = 0.478 = 0.48$.) Because a proportion has a base of 1, a proportion of 0.48 means that for every *one* participant, 48 hundredths of each participant favors Smith. Clearly, proportions are harder to comprehend than percentages. When consumers of research encounter proportions in reports, it is a good idea to convert them mentally to percentages. That is, think of the proportion of 0.48 as 48% (i.e., the percentage obtained by multiplying 0.48 by 100).

In the next topic, a method for analyzing univariate nominal data in studies in which researchers have sampled at random and need to take account of random sampling errors is considered. In Topic

48, the analysis of bivariate nominal data in light of sampling errors is described.

Note that researchers use an uppercase N when they study an entire population, as in the example in this topic. They use a lowercase n when they study only a sample, as in the example in the next topic.

EXERCISE ON TOPIC 46

1. If 600 individuals in a population of 1,000 are Democrats, what is the corresponding percentage of Democrats?

2. When reporting a percentage, is it a good idea to also report the underlying number of cases?

3. Do researchers use "univariate" *or* "bivariate" analyses to examine relationships between two nominal variables?

4. Percentages for different groups are expressed on a common scale with what base?

5. What is the base for a proportion?

6. Are "percentages" *or* "proportions" easier for most individuals to comprehend?

7. When consumers of research encounter proportions in research reports, it is a good idea to do what?

Question for Discussion

8. Try to locate a report in the popular press in which percentages are reported. Bring a copy to class. Be prepared to discuss whether the frequencies are also reported and whether the analysis is univariate *or* bivariate.

For Students Who Are Planning Research

9. Will you be measuring one or more variables at the nominal level? Explain.

10. Will you be reporting percentages?

11. Will you do a univariate analysis? A bivariate analysis? Explain.

TOPIC 47   INTRODUCTION TO THE CHI-SQUARE TEST

Suppose a researcher drew at random a sample of 200 members of an association of sociologists and asked them whether they were in favor of a proposed change to their bylaws. The results are shown in Table 1. Note that these *observed results* are not necessarily the *true results*[1] that the researcher would have obtained if the researcher had questioned the entire population. Remember that the null hypothesis (see Topic 44) asserts that any observed difference was created by random sampling errors (i.e., in the population, the true difference is zero). Put another way, the null hypothesis states that the observed difference ($n = 120$ vs. $n = 80$) is an *illusion* created by random errors created by random sampling (i.e., created by sampling errors).

Table 1
Members' Approval of a Change in Bylaws

Response	Percentage
Yes	60.0%
	($n = 120$)
No	40.0%
	($n = 80$)
Total	100.0%
	($n = 200$)

The usual test of the null hypothesis for differences between frequencies (i.e., number of cases or *n*) is **chi-square**, whose symbol is:

$$\chi^2$$

After doing some computations for the data in Table 1 (which are beyond the scope of this book), the results are:

$$\chi^2 = 4.00, \, df = 1, \, p < .05$$

What does this mean for a consumer of research who sees this in a report? The values of chi-square and degrees of freedom (*df*) were calculated solely to obtain the probability that the null hypothesis is correct. In other words, chi-square and degrees of freedom are *not* descriptive statistics that a typical consumer of research should attempt to interpret. Rather, they should be thought of as sub-steps in the mathematical procedure for obtaining the value of

p. Thus, a consumer of research should concentrate on the fact that *p* is *less than* .05. As indicated in Topic 44, when the probability (*p*) that the null hypothesis is correct is .05 or less, researchers reject the null hypothesis. (Remember, when the probability that something is true is less than 5 in 100, which is a low probability, conventional wisdom suggests it should be rejected.) Thus, the difference observed in Table 1 was probably not created by random sampling errors. Therefore, a researcher can say that the difference is *statistically significant* at the .05 level.

At this point, the conclusion has been reached that the difference observed in the sample was *probably not* created by sampling errors. So where did the difference come from? These two possibilities remain:

1. Perhaps there was a bias in procedures, such as the interviewer asking the question in the survey leading the respondents by talking enthusiastically about the proposed change in the bylaws. Thus, the sample would no longer be representative of the population because the interviewer biased the respondents.

    If consumers of research are convinced that adequate measures were taken to prevent procedural bias, they are left only with the next possibility as a viable explanation.

2. Perhaps the *population* of sociologists is, in fact, in favor of the proposed change, and this fact has been correctly identified by studying the random sample.

Now, consider some results from a survey in which the null hypothesis was *not* rejected. Table 2 shows the numbers and percentages of participants in a random sample from a population of teachers who prefer each of three methods for teaching reading.

Table 2
Teachers' Preferences for Methods

Method A	Method B	Method C
$n = 30$	$n = 27$	$n = 22$
(37.97%)	(34.18%)	(27.85%)

In Table 2, there are three differences: **(1)** 30 preferring A versus 27 preferring B, **(2)** 30 preferring A versus 22 preferring C, and **(3)** 27 preferring B versus 22 preferring C. The null hypothesis states

---

[1] The term *true results* stands for the results that would be obtained by conducting a census of the entire population. The results of a census are *true* in the sense that they are free of *sampling errors*.

that this *set of three differences* was created by random sampling errors. In other words, it says that there is no true difference in the population—that a difference has been observed only because of sampling errors. The results of the chi-square test for the data in Table 2 are:

$$\chi^2 = 1.241, df = 2, p > .05$$

Note that *p* is *greater than* (>) .05. Using the decision rule that *p* must be equal to or less than .05 to reject the null hypothesis, the null hypothesis should *not* be rejected (i.e., "fail to reject"), which is called a *statistically insignificant* result. In other words, the null hypothesis must remain on the list as a viable explanation for the set of differences observed by studying a sample. Put another way, the probability that sampling error created the difference is too great for it to be rejected as a possible explanation for the differences.

In this topic, the use of chi-square in a *univariate analysis* in which each participant is classified in only one way (such as which candidate each prefers) has been considered. In the next topic, the use of chi-square in a *bivariate analysis* (in which each participant is classified in two ways such as which candidate each prefers *and* the gender of each) is considered.

EXERCISE ON TOPIC 47

1. When researchers study a sample, are the results called the "true results" *or* the "observed results"?

2. According to the null hypothesis, what created the difference in Table 1 in this topic?

3. What is the name of the test of the null hypothesis used in this topic?

4. According to this topic, should the typical consumer try to interpret the value of *df*?

5. What is the symbol for *probability*?

6. If a researcher found that a chi-square test of a difference yielded a *p* of less than 5 in 100, on the basis of conventional wisdom, what should the researcher conclude about the null hypothesis?

7. Does "*p* < .05" *or* "*p* > .05" usually lead a researcher to declare a difference to be statistically significant?

8. If a researcher fails to reject a null hypothesis, is the difference in question statistically significant?

9. If a researcher has a statistically significant result, should the null hypothesis remain on the list of viable explanations for an observed difference?

Question for Discussion

10. Briefly describe a hypothetical study in which it would be appropriate to conduct a chi-square test for univariate data.

For Students Who Are Planning Research

11. Will you be conducting a univariate chi-square test in your research? Explain.

Topic 48   A Closer Look at the Chi-Square Test

This topic concerns the use of the chi-square test in a *bivariate analysis* (i.e., an analysis in which each participant is classified in terms of two variables in order to examine the relationship between them). Consider an example. Suppose a researcher conducted an experiment in which three methods of job training were tried with welfare recipients. Random samples of recipients were drawn for each method, and the number who obtained jobs by the end of the training sessions was determined. The resulting data are shown in Table 1.

Table 1
Training Methods and Job Placement

Job?	Method A	Method B	Method C
Yes	$n = 20$ (66.7%)	$n = 15$ (51.7%)	$n = 9$ (31.0%)
No	$n = 10$ (33.3%)	$n = 14$ (48.3%)	$n = 20$ (69.0%)

Clearly, the statistics in Table 1 suggest there is a relationship between the method of job training and the outcome (whether or not participants got jobs). Specifically, the researcher has observed that Method A is superior to Methods B and C and that Method B is superior to Method C. A stumbling block in the interpretation of these results is the *null hypothesis*, which states there is no true difference (i.e., if all members of the population had been studied, the researcher would have found no differences among the three methods). For instance, quite by the luck of the random draw, recipients who were more employable to begin with (before treatment) were assigned to Method A, while the less employable were assigned by chance to the other two methods. A researcher can test this null hypothesis by using the chi-square test.

For the data shown in Table 1, this result would be shown in a report on the experiment:

$$\chi^2 = 7.54, df = 2, p < .05$$

As indicated in previous topics in this part of the book, the null hypothesis is rejected when the odds that it is true are equal to or less than .05 (i.e., $p < .05$). Thus, for these data, the researcher should reject the null hypothesis and declare the result to be significant at the .05 level. In other words, the researcher should conclude that the observed differences are too great to be attributed to random errors (i.e., sampling errors). Thus, it is unlikely that the

observed relationship is merely a result of random sampling errors.

Now consider more carefully what is meant by the term "the .05 level." When a researcher rejects the null hypothesis at exactly the .05 level (i.e., $p = .05$), there are 5 chances in 100 that the null hypothesis is correct. Thus, the researcher is taking 5 chances in 100 of being *wrong* by rejecting the null hypothesis at this level. Note that a researcher can never be certain that he or she has made the correct decision when rejecting the null hypothesis. It is always possible that the null hypothesis is true (in this case, there are 5 in 100 chances that it is true). The possibility that a null hypothesis is rejected when it is, in fact, a correct hypothesis is called a **Type I Error**. When researchers use the .05 level, the odds of making a Type I Error are 5 in 100; when they use the .01 level, the odds of making this type of error are 1 in 100; and when they use the .001 level, the odds of making it are 1 in 1,000.

When researchers fail to reject the null hypothesis, as in Topic 47 for the data in Table 2, they are also taking a chance of making an incorrect decision. That is, perhaps the null hypothesis should have been rejected, but the significance test failed to lead the researchers to the correct decision. This mistake is called a **Type II Error**.

In review, these are the two types of errors that researchers can make:

Type I Error: Rejecting the null hypothesis when it is in fact a correct hypothesis.

Type II Error: Failing to reject the null hypothesis when it is in fact an incorrect hypothesis.

At first, this discussion of errors may make significance tests such as chi-square seem weak because a researcher can be wrong regardless of the decision made. However, the usefulness is clear in light of the full context. Specifically, having decided to sample at random (the desirable way to sample because it is free from bias), it is likely that random error will affect the results—at least to some extent. In light of this, researchers can never be *certain* about decisions based on the observed differences. Instead, researchers must use *probabilities* to make decisions. Researchers use probabilities in such a way that the researchers *minimize* the probabilities that erroneous decisions are being made. To do this, researchers usually emphasize minimizing the probability of a Type I error by using a low probability such as .05 or less. By using a low probability, researchers will infrequently be in error when rejecting the null hypothesis.

EXERCISE ON TOPIC 48

1. What is the name of the type of analysis in which each participant is classified in terms of two variables in order to examine the relationship between the two variables?

2. What decision should researchers make about the null hypothesis if a chi-square test leads to the conclusion that the observed differences are unlikely to be due to random errors?

3. If $p = .05$ for a chi-square test, chances are how many in 100 that the null hypothesis is true?

4. When a researcher uses the .01 level, what are the odds of making a Type I Error?

5. What is the name of the error researchers make when they fail to reject the null hypothesis when, in fact, it is an incorrect hypothesis?

6. What is the name of the error researchers make when they reject the null hypothesis when, in fact, it is a correct hypothesis?

7. Why is random sampling desirable even though it creates errors?

Questions for Discussion

8. Are both variables in Table 1 in this topic nominal? Explain.

9. Briefly describe a hypothetical study in which it would be appropriate to conduct a chi-square test on bivariate data.

For Students Who Are Planning Research

10. Will you be using a chi-square test in a bivariate analysis? Explain.

TOPIC 49 SHAPES OF DISTRIBUTIONS

One way to describe quantitative data is to prepare a *frequency distribution* such as the one shown in Topic 43. It is easier to see the shape of a distribution if the data in a frequency distribution are used to construct a figure called a **frequency polygon**. Figure 1 is a frequency polygon for the data in Topic 43.

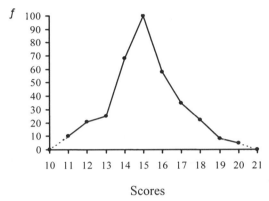

Figure 1. Frequency polygon for data on page 103.

A frequency polygon is easy to read. For instance, a score of 20 has a frequency (f) of 5, which is why the curve is low at a score of 20. A score of 15 has a frequency of 99, which is why the curve is high at 15.

Notice that the curve in Figure 1 is fairly symmetrical, with a high point in the middle and dropping off on the right and left. When very large samples are used, the curve often takes on an even smoother shape, such as the one shown in Figure 2.

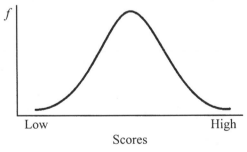

Figure 2. The normal curve.

The smooth, bell-shaped curve in Figure 2 has a special name: the **normal curve**. Many variables in nature are normally distributed, such as the weights of grains of sand on a beach, the heights of women (or men), the annual amounts of rainfall in most areas, and so on. The list is almost limitless. Many social and behavioral scientists also believe that mental traits of humans are also normally distributed.[1]

Some distributions are **skewed** (i.e., they have a tail on one side and not the other). Figure 3 shows a distribution that is *skewed to the right* (i.e., the tail is to the right), which is called a **positive skew**. An example of a distribution with a positive skew is income. Most individuals earn relatively small amounts, so the curve is high on the left. Small numbers of rich and very rich individuals create a tail to the right.

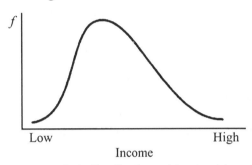

Figure 3. A distribution with a positive skew.

Figure 4 is *skewed to the left*; it has a **negative skew**. A researcher would get a negative skew, for instance, if the researcher administered a test of basic math skills to a large sample of college seniors. Almost all would do very well and get almost perfect scores, but a small scattering would get lower scores for a variety of reasons, such as misunderstanding the directions for marking their answers, not feeling well the day the test was administered, and so on.

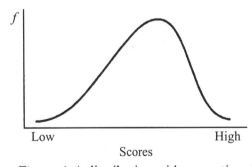

Figure 4. A distribution with a negative skew.

While there are other shapes, the three shown here are the most common ones. Whether a distri-

---

[1] Because measures of mental traits are far from perfect, it is not possible to show conclusively that mental traits are normally distributed.

bution is normal (or close to normal) *or* skewed affects how quantitative data at the interval and ratio levels are analyzed (see Topic 45). This issue is considered in the next topic.

To make the proper associations with the names "positive skew" and "negative skew," consider a number line on which zero is in the middle. The negative values are to the left of zero. Thus, when the tail of a curve points to the left, researchers say it has a *negative skew*. Because the positive values on a number line are to the right, when the tail points to the right, researchers say the curve has a *positive skew*. Sometimes, researchers merely say "skewed to the left" to indicate a "negative skew" and "skewed to the right" to indicate a "positive skew."

EXERCISE ON TOPIC 49

1. According to Figure 1, about how many participants had a score of 16?

2. In Figure 1, are the frequencies on the "vertical" *or* "horizontal" axis?

3. What is the name of the curve that is symmetrical?

4. If a distribution has some extreme scores on the right (but not on the left), it is said to have what type of skew?

5. If a distribution is skewed to the left, does it have a "positive" *or* "negative" skew?

6. In most populations, income has what type of skew?

7. Does a distribution with a tail to the right have a "positive" *or* "negative" skew?

Question for Discussion

8. Name a population and a variable you think might have a positive skew.

For Students Who Are Planning Research

9. Do you anticipate that any of your distributions will be highly skewed? Explain.

Topic 50 The Mean, Median, and Mode

The most frequently used average is the **mean**, which is the *balance point* in a distribution. Its computation is simple: Sum (add up) the scores and divide by the number of scores. The most common symbols for the mean in academic journals are M (for the mean of a population) and m (for the mean of a sample). The symbol preferred by statisticians is

$\overline{X}$, which is pronounced "X-bar."

Consider the formal definition of the mean: It is *the value around which the deviations sum to zero*. This definition is illustrated in Table 1, in which the mean of the scores is 4.0. When the mean is subtracted from each of the other scores, the *deviations* (whose symbol is lowercase x) are obtained. Notice that the sum of the deviations equals zero, as shown in the last column of Table 1.

Table 1
Scores and Deviation Scores

X	minus	M	equals	x
1	–	4.0	=	–3.0
1	–	4.0	=	–3.0
1	–	4.0	=	–3.0
2	–	4.0	=	–2.0
2	–	4.0	=	–2.0
4	–	4.0	=	0.0
6	–	4.0	=	2.0
7	–	4.0	=	3.0
8	–	4.0	=	4.0
8	–	4.0	=	4.0
Sum of the deviations (x) = 0.0				

Note that for *any set of scores*, if the steps in Table 1 are followed, the sum of the deviations will equal zero.[1] In other words, the mean always has this defining characteristic. If the deviations do not sum to zero, the statistic is not the mean (or a mistake was made in the computation of the mean).

Considering the formal definition, it is possible to see why the mean is also informally defined as the *balance point* in a distribution. This is because the positive and negative deviations *balance* each other out, causing the deviations to "balance out" to zero.

A major drawback of the mean is that it is drawn in the direction of extreme scores (i.e., in the direc-

tion of the skew). Consider the following two sets of scores and their means.

Scores for Group A: 1, 1, 1, 2, 3, 6, 7, 8, 8
$M = 4.11$

Scores for Group B: 1, 2, 2, 3, 4, 7, 9, 25, 32
$M = 9.44$

Notice that there are nine scores in both sets of scores, and the two distributions are very similar except for the scores of 25 and 32 in Group B, which are much higher than the others and thus create a skewed distribution. (To review skewed distributions, see Topic 49.) Also, notice that the two very high scores (i.e., 25 and 32) have greatly pulled up the mean for Group B. In fact, the mean for Group B is more than twice as high as the mean for Group A because of just the two high scores. Because seven of the nine scores for Group B are 9 or less, a mean of 9.44 is not a good descriptor of the typical or "center score."

While the mean is the most frequently used average, when a distribution is highly skewed, researchers use a different average: the **median**. The median is defined as the *middle score*. To get an *approximate median*, put the scores in order from low to high as they are for Groups A and B above (from low on the left to high on the right), and then count to the middle. Because there are nine scores in Group A, the median (middle score) is 3 (five scores up from the bottom). For Group B, the median (middle score) is 4 (also five scores up from the bottom). For Group B, an average of 4 is more representative of the center of this skewed distribution than the mean, which is 9.44. Thus, an important use of the median is to describe the averages of skewed distributions. Another use is to describe the average of ordinal data, which will be explored in Topic 52.

A third average, the **mode**, is the *most frequently occurring score*. For Group B, there are more scores of 2 (i.e., two 2s) than any other score. Thus, 2 is the mode. The mode is sometimes used in informal reporting but is very seldom reported in formal reports of research. Note that the mode does not always have a unique value. For instance, if one individual with a score of 3 joined Group B, there would be two modes: (a) 2 because there are two 2s and (b) 3 because there would also be two 3s. Note that the mean and median, unlike the mode, always

---

[1] It might be slightly off from zero if a rounded mean such as using 20.33 is used instead of its precise value such as 20.3333333333.

have only one value for a given set of scores (i.e., they have unique values).

Because there is more than one type of average, it is vague to make a statement such as, "The *average* is 4.11." Instead, researchers indicate the specific type of average being reported with statements such as, "The *mean* is 4.11."

A synonym for the term **averages** is **measures of central tendency**. Although this term is seldom used in reports of scientific research, it is often used in research and statistics textbooks when averages are discussed.

EXERCISE ON TOPIC 50

1. Which average is defined as the *most frequently occurring score*?

2. Which average is defined as the *balance point* in a distribution?

3. Which average is defined as the *middle score*?

4. What is the formal definition of the mean?

5. How is the mean calculated?

6. Should the mean be used for highly skewed distributions?

7. Should the median be used for highly skewed distributions?

8. Which one of the three averages is very seldom reported in formal reports of research?

9. What is a synonym for the term *averages*?

Question for Discussion

10. Suppose a fellow student gave a report in class and said, "The average is 25.88." For what additional information should you ask? Why?

For Students Who Are Planning Research

11. Do you anticipate calculating measures of central tendency? If so, name the one(s) you expect to report. Explain your choice(s).

TOPIC 51   THE MEAN AND STANDARD DEVIATION

Often, a set of scores is described with only two statistics: the **mean** to describe its *average* and the **standard deviation** (whose symbol is S or SD for a population, and s or sd for a sample) to describe its *variability*. The term "variability" refers to the amount by which participants *vary* or differ from each other. Consider what this means by considering the scores of three groups, all of which have the same mean but different standard deviations.

Group A: 0, 5, 10, 15, 20, 25, 30
$M = 15.00, S = 10.00$

Group B: 14, 14, 14, 15, 16, 16, 16
$M = 15.00, S = 0.93$

Group C: 15, 15, 15, 15, 15, 15, 15
$M = 15.00, S = 0.00$

Although Groups A, B, and C are the same on the average, as indicated by the mean, they are very different in terms of variability. Notice that the differences among the scores of Group A (a score of 0 vs. a score of 5 vs. a score of 10 vs. a score of 15, and so on) are much greater than the differences among the scores of Group B (a score of 14 vs. a score of 14 vs. a score of 14 vs. a score of 15, and so on). At the extreme, when all the scores are the same, as in Group C, there is no variability. As a result, the standard deviation equals zero. Thus, as a rule, the smaller the variability is, the smaller the standard deviation is.[1]

The standard deviation has a special relationship to the normal curve (see Topic 49). *If a distribution is normal, 68% of the participants in the distribution lie within one standard-deviation unit of the mean.*[2] For example, if a consumer of research reads in a report that $M = 70$ and $S = 10$ for a normal distribution, the consumer would know that 68% of the participants have scores between 60 and 80 (i.e., $70 - 10 = 60$ and $70 + 10 = 80$). This is illustrated in Figure 1.

In Figure 2, the mean is also 70, but the standard deviation is only 5. The smaller standard deviation in Figure 2 is reflected by the fact that the curve is narrower than in Figure 1. Yet in both distributions,

68% of the cases lies within one standard deviation unit of the mean because they are both normal.

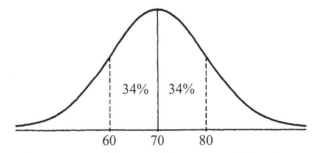

Figure 1. Normal curve with a mean of 70 and a standard deviation of 10.

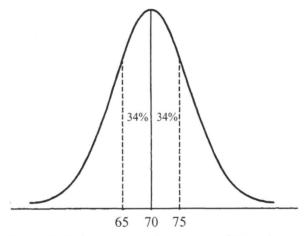

Figure 2. Normal curve with a mean of 70 and a standard deviation of 5.

Note that the middle area of Figure 2 is narrower *but taller* than the middle area of Figure 1. This additional height in Figure 2 makes it possible for it to have the same percentage (68%) of cases as the middle area of Figure 1 has.

At first, it may seem contradictory that, regardless of the value of the standard deviation, 68% of the cases lie within one standard-deviation unit of the mean in a normal curve. Actually, it is not a contradiction but a property of the normal curve. When a researcher is calculating the standard deviation, he or she is actually calculating the number of points that one must go out from the mean to capture 68% of the cases.

Note that the 68% rule-of-thumb does *not* strictly apply if the distribution is *not* normal. The less normal it is, the less accurate the rule is. Put another way, if the middle area of a distribution

---

[1] The computation of the standard deviation is illustrated in Appendix D. Considering the method of computation provides a more precise indication of its meaning.
[2] Note that *within* means on *both sides of the mean* (i.e., the mean plus/minus the standard deviation).

does not contain approximately 68% of the cases, the distribution is not normal.

Note that the normal curve (see Topic 49) is not an invention of statisticians. Instead, it is a curve that has been observed with great frequency in nature. Statisticians derived the standard deviation in order to have a standardized method for describing the variability of normal distributions.

EXERCISE ON TOPIC 51

1. Which average is usually reported when the standard deviation is reported?

2. What is meant by the term *variability*?

3. Is it possible for two groups to have the same mean but different standard deviations?

4. If all individuals in a group have the same score, what is the value of the standard deviation for the scores?

5. What percentage of the participants lies within one standard-deviation unit of the mean (i.e., on both sides of the mean) in a normal distribution?

6. The middle 68% of the participants in a normal distribution have scores between what two values if the mean equals 100 and the standard deviation equals 15?

7. If the mean of a normal distribution equals 50 and the standard deviation equals 5, what percentage of the participants have scores between 45 and 50?

8. Does the 68% rule strictly apply if a distribution is *not* normal?

9. If the standard deviation for Group X is 14.55 and the standard deviation for Group Y is 20.99, which group has less variability in their scores?

10. Refer to Question 9. Does "Group X" *or* "Group Y" have a narrower curve?

Question for Discussion

11. Locate a journal article in which the researcher reports a mean and standard deviation. Does the researcher indicate whether the underlying distribution being described is normal in shape? Do you think the 68% rule strictly applies? Explain.

For Students Who Are Planning Research

12. Will you be reporting means and standard deviations? Explain.

TOPIC 52   THE MEDIAN AND INTERQUARTILE RANGE

As indicated in Topic 50, the **median** is the *middle score* in a distribution. Being in the middle, it always has 50% of the scores above it and 50% of the scores below it. For the scores in Figure 1, the median is 6.5 (halfway between the middle two scores of 6 and 7).

1, 1, 1, 2, 3, 4, 5, 6, 7, 8, 8, 9, 10, 11, 11, 12

⇧

6.5

Figure 1. Scores for Group A and their median.

The median is used instead of the mean when a distribution is highly skewed (see Topic 49). It also is used to describe the average when the data are *ordinal* (i.e., data that put participants in *order* from high to low but do not have equal intervals among them; see Topic 45).[1]

When the **median** is reported as the average, it is customary to report the **range** or **interquartile range** as a measure of variability. As indicated in Topic 51, *variability* refers to the amount by which participants *vary* or differ from each other.

The *range* is simply the highest score minus the lowest score. For the scores shown above, it is 12 – 1 = 11. Thus, the range is 11, or a researcher might state that the scores *range from* 1 *to* 12. For reasons that are beyond the scope of this discussion, measurement theory indicates that the more extreme the score, the more unreliable it is. In other words, the more extreme the score is, the more likely that it has errors in it. (This is true in the natural sciences as well as the social and behavioral sciences.) Because the range is based on the two most extreme scores, it is an unreliable statistic. To get around this problem, researchers often use a modified version of the range, which is called the *interquartile range*. Because *inter-* means *between* and *-quartile* refers to *quarters*, *interquartile range* refers to the *range between quarters*. Specifically, it is the range of the middle two quarters. To calculate it, first divide the distribution into quarters, as shown in Figure 2 (e.g., the first quarter consists of scores 1, 1,

1, and 2). Thus, the middle 50% of the participants are between the values of 2.5 and 9.5. Because the formal definition of the *interquartile range* (*IQR*) is the *range of the middle 50% of the participants*, it is calculated as follows: 9.5 – 2.5 = 7.0. Thus, *IQR* = 7.0.[2]

1, 1, 1, 2, 3, 4, 5, 6, 7, 8, 8, 9, 10, 11, 11, 12

⇧   ⇧   ⇧

2.5   6.5   9.5

Figure 2. Scores for Group A divided into quarters.

To see how the *IQR* helps describe the variability in sets of data, compare Figure 2 (for Group A) with Figure 3 (for Group B). In Figure 3, the median is 43.0 and the interquartile range is 71.0 (i.e., 83.5 – 12.5 = 71.0). The larger interquartile range for Group B indicates greater variability.

0, 5, 7, 10, 15, 22, 30, 41, 45, 57, 67, 78, 89, 92, 95, 99

⇧   ⇧   ⇧

12.5   43.0   83.5

Figure 3. Scores for Group B divided into quarters.

Thus, for Groups A and B, the findings might be presented in a research report as illustrated in Table 1.

Table 1
Medians and Interquartile Range for Two Groups

Group	Median	Interquartile Range
A	6.5	7.0
B	43.0	71.0

Table 1 indicates two things. First, Group A has a lower average than Group B (as indicated by the median of 6.5 for Group A vs. the median of 43.0 for Group B). Second, Group A has less variability (as indicated by an interquartile range of 7.0 for Group A vs. 71.0 for Group B). Consideration of the scores shown in Figures 2 and 3 indicates that these results make sense. The middle score for Group A is much lower than the middle score for

---

[1] It is inappropriate to use the *mean* to describe ordinal data because the mean is the point around which the differences sum to zero. If the differences are unequal in size (as they are with ordinal data), it makes no sense to use a statistic based on the values of the differences. See Topics 45 and 50.

[2] Some researchers report the value of the *semi-interquartile range*. Because "semi-" means "half," the semi-interquartile range is half of the interquartile range. In this example, the semi-interquartile range for Group A equals half of 7.0 (i.e., 7.0/2 = 3.5).

Group B, and the differences among the scores for Group A (1 vs. 1 vs. 1 vs. 2 vs. 3, etc.) are much smaller than the differences among the scores for Group B (0 vs. 5 vs. 7 vs. 10 vs. 15, and so on), indicating less variability in Group A than Group B.

In summary, the median describes the average (i.e., the central tendency) of a set of scores while the interquartile range describes their variability. When the median is reported as the average (or measure of central tendency), it is customary to report the interquartile range as the measure of variability.

EXERCISE ON TOPIC 52

1. If the median for a group of participants is 25.00, what percentage of the participants has scores above a score of 25.00?

2. Should the "mean" or the "median" be used with ordinal data?

3. How is the range of a set of scores calculated?

4. Is the "range" or the "interquartile range" a more reliable statistic?

5. The interquartile range is the range of what?

6. Suppose a researcher reported that for Group X, the median equals 55.1 and the IQR equals 30.0, while for Group Y, the median equals 62.9 and the IQR equals 25.0. Which group has the higher average score?

7. Based on the information in Question 6, the scores for which group are more variable?

8. Which statistics discussed in this topic are measures of variability?

9. Which two statistics mentioned in this topic are averages (i.e., measures of central tendency)?

10. When the median is reported as the measure of central tendency, it is customary to report which measure of variability?

Question for Discussion

11. Name two circumstances under which the median is preferable to the mean.

For Students Who Are Planning Research

12. Do you anticipate reporting medians and interquartile ranges? Explain.

TOPIC 53 THE PEARSON CORRELATION COEFFICIENT

When researchers want to examine the relationship between two quantitative sets of scores (at the interval or ratio levels; see Topic 45), they compute a correlation coefficient. The most widely used coefficient is the **Pearson product-moment correlation coefficient**, whose symbol is r (usually called the **Pearson r**).

Consider the scores in Table 1. Note that the employment test scores put participants in *roughly* the same order as the ratings by supervisors. In other words, those who have high employment test scores (e.g., Joe and Jane) have high supervisors' ratings, *and* those who have low test scores (e.g., John and Jake) have low supervisors' ratings. This illustrates what is meant by a **direct relationship** (also called a **positive relationship**).

Table 1
Direct Relationship; $r = .89$

Employee	Employment Test Scores	Supervisors' Ratings
Joe	35	9
Jane	32	10
Bob	29	8
June	27	8
Leslie	25	7
Homer	22	8
Milly	21	6
Jake	18	4
John	15	5

Notice that the relationship in Table 1 is not perfect. For instance, although Joe has a higher employment test score than Jane, Jane has a higher supervisors' rating than Joe. If the relationship were perfect, the value of the Pearson r would be 1.00. Being less than perfect, its actual value is .89. As indicated in Figure 1, this value indicates a strong, direct relationship.

In an **inverse relationship** (also called a **negative relationship**), those who are high on one variable are low on the other. Such a relationship exists between the two sets of scores in Table 2. Individuals who are high on self-concept (such as Joe and Jane) are low on depression while those who are low on self-concept (such as Jake and John) are high on depression. However, the relationship is not perfect. The value of the Pearson r for the relationship in Table 2 is –.85.

Table 2
Inverse Relationship; $r = -.85$

Employee	Self-Concept Scores	Depression Scores
Joe	10	2
Jane	8	1
Bob	9	0
June	7	5
Leslie	7	6
Homer	6	8
Milly	4	8
Jake	1	9
John	0	9

The relationships in Tables 1 and 2 are strong because they are near 1.00 and –1.00, but in each case, there are exceptions, which make the Pearson rs less than 1.00 and –1.00. As the number and size of the exceptions increase, the values of the Pearson r become closer to 0.00. A value of 0.00 indicates the complete absence of a relationship. (See Figure 1 below.)

It is important to note that a Pearson r is *not* a proportion and *cannot* be multiplied by 100 to get a percentage. For instance, a Pearson r of .50 does not correspond to 50% of any characteristic of the data. To think about correlation in terms of percentages, values of Pearson r need to be converted to another statistic called the **coefficient of determination**, whose symbol is r^2, which indicates how to compute it: simply square r. Thus, for an r of .50, r^2 equals .25. Multiplying .25 by 100%, the result is 25%. What does this mean? Simply this: A Pearson r of .50 is 25% better than a Pearson r of 0.00. Table 3 on the next page shows selected values of r, r^2, and the corresponding percentages that should be considered when interpreting a value of r.[1]

–1.00	INVERSE RELATIONSHIP			0.00	DIRECT RELATIONSHIP			1.00
⇧	⇧	⇧	⇧	⇧	⇧	⇧	⇧	⇧
perfect	strong	moderate	weak	none	weak	moderate	strong	perfect

Figure 1. Values of the Pearson r.

---

[1] Note that the procedure for computing a Pearson r is beyond the scope of this book.

Table 3
Selected Values of r and r²

r	r²	Percentage better than zero[1]
.90	.81	81%
.50	.25	25%
.25	.06	6%
−.25	.06	6%
−.50	.25	25%
−.90	.81	81%

[1]Also called *percentage of variance accounted for* or *percentage of explained variance.*

EXERCISE ON TOPIC 53

1. "Pearson *r*" stands for what words?

2. When the relationship between two variables is perfect and inverse, what is the value of *r*?

3. Is it possible for a negative relationship to be strong?

4. Is an *r* of −.90 stronger than an *r* of .50?

5. Is an *r* of .75 stronger than an *r* of −.35?

6. Is a relationship "direct" *or* "inverse" when those with high scores on one variable have high scores on the other *and* those with low scores on one variable have low scores on the other?

7. What does an *r* of 1.00 indicate?

8. For a Pearson *r* of .60, what is the value of the coefficient of determination?

9. What must be done in order to convert a coefficient of determination into a percentage?

10. A Pearson *r* of .70 is what percentage better than a Pearson *r* of 0.00?

Question for Discussion

11. Name two variables between which you would expect to get a strong, positive value of *r*.

For Students Who Are Planning Research

12. Will you be reporting Pearson *r*s? If so, name the two variables that will be correlated for each value of *r*.

TOPIC 54 THE *t* TEST

Suppose a researcher had a *research hypothesis* that says "homicide investigators who take a short course on the causes of HIV will be less fearful of the disease than investigators who do not take the course." The researcher tested the hypothesis by conducting an experiment in which a random sample of investigators was assigned to take the course and another random sample was designated as the control group that did not take the course.[1] At the end of the experiment, the experimental group had a mean of 16.61 on a fear-of-HIV scale and the control group had a mean of 29.67 (where the higher the score, the greater the fear of HIV). These means support the research hypothesis. However, can the researcher be certain that the research hypothesis is correct? The answer is "no" because of the *null hypothesis*, which says that there is no *true* difference between the means. In other words, it says the difference was created merely by the chance errors created by random sampling. (These errors are known simply as *sampling errors*.) Put another way, unrepresentative groups may have been assigned to the two conditions quite at random, creating the difference between the two means.

The *t* **test** is often used to test the null hypothesis regarding the observed difference between two means.[2] For the example being considered, a series of computations, which are beyond the scope of this book, would be performed to obtain a value of *t* (in this case, it is 5.38) and a value of degrees of freedom (which, in this case, is $df = 179$). The values of *t* and *df* are not of any special interest to typical consumers of research because they are only sub-steps in the mathematical procedure used to get the *probability* (*p*) that the null hypothesis is true. In this particular case, *p* is less than .05. Thus, in a research report, the following statement could be made:

The difference between the means is statistically significant ($t = 5.38$, $df = 179$, $p < .05$).[3]

---

[1] Random sampling is preferred because (1) it precludes any bias in the assignment of participants to the groups and (2) the effect of random errors produced by random sampling can be assessed with significance tests.

[2] To test the null hypothesis between two *medians*, the *median test* is used. It is a specialized form of the chi-square test, which was covered in Topics 47 and 48.

[3] Sometimes, researchers leave out the abbreviation *df* and present the result as $t(179) = 5.38$, $p < .05$.

As indicated in Topic 44, the term *statistically significant* indicates that the null hypothesis has been rejected. When the probability that the null hypothesis is true is .05 or less (such as .01 or .001), the null hypothesis is rejected. (When something is unlikely to be true because it has a low probability of being true, it is rejected.)

Having rejected the null hypothesis, the researcher is in a position to assert that the research hypothesis is probably true (assuming no procedural bias was allowed to affect the results, such as testing the control group immediately after a major news story on a famous individual with AIDS while testing the experimental group at an earlier time).

What causes a *t* test to yield a low probability? Three interrelated factors:

1. *Sample size.* The larger the sample, the less likely that an observed difference is due to sampling errors. (As indicated in the previous topics on sampling, larger samples provide more precise data.) Thus, other things being equal, the larger the sample, the lower the value of *p*.

2. *The size of the difference between means.* The larger the difference, the less likely the difference is due to sampling errors. Thus, other things being equal, the larger the difference between the two means, the lower the value of *p*.

3. *The amount of variation in the population.* As indicated in Topic 26 when a population is very homogeneous (has little variability), there is less potential for sampling error. Thus, other things being equal, the smaller the variability (as indicated by the standard deviations of the samples), the lower the value of *p*.

A special type of *t* test is also applied to correlation coefficients. Suppose a researcher drew a random sample of 50 students and correlated their hand size with their GPAs and got an *r* of 0.19 on the Pearson *r* scale with possible values ranging from 1.00 to –1.00. The null hypothesis says that the *true* correlation in the population is 0.00. In other words, it says that a value of 0.19 was obtained merely as the result of sampling errors. For this example, the *t* test indicates that $p > .05$. Because the probability that the null hypothesis is true is greater than 5 in 100, the researcher would *not* reject the null hypothesis. In other words, the researcher would have a statistically insignificant correlation coefficient because the *t* test indicated that for *n* = 50, an *r* of 0.19 is not significantly different from an *r* of 0.00. When reporting the results of the *t* test for the significance of a correlation coefficient, it is conventional *not* to mention the value of *t*. Rather, researchers usually indicate only whether or not the correlation is significant at a given probability level.

EXERCISE ON TOPIC 54

1. What does the null hypothesis say about the difference between two sample means?

2. Are the values of *t* and *df* of any special interest to typical consumers of research?

3. Suppose you read that $t = 2.000$, $df = 20$, $p > .05$ for the difference between two means. Using conventional standards, should you conclude that the null hypothesis should be rejected?

4. Suppose you read that $t = 2.859$, $df = 40$, $p < .01$ for the difference between two means. Using conventional standards, should you conclude that the null hypothesis should be rejected?

5. Based on the information in Question 4, should you conclude that the difference between the means is statistically significant?

6. When a researcher uses a large sample, is the researcher "more" *or* "less" likely to reject the null hypothesis than when a researcher uses a small sample?

7. When the size of the difference between means is large, is a researcher "more" *or* "less" likely to reject the null hypothesis than when the size of the difference is small?

8. If a researcher found that for a sample of 92 participants, $r = .41$, $p < .001$, would the researcher reject the null hypothesis?

9. Is the value of *r* in Question 8 statistically significant?

Question for Discussion

10. Of the three factors that lead to a low probability when *t* tests are conducted, which one is most directly under the control of a researcher?

For Students Who Are Planning Research

11. Will you be conducting *t* tests? Explain.

TOPIC 55 ONE-WAY ANALYSIS OF VARIANCE

In the previous topic, the use of the t test for testing the null hypothesis for the observed difference between two sample means was covered. An alternative test for this problem is **analysis of variance** (often called **ANOVA**).[1] Instead of t, it yields a statistic called F, as well as degrees of freedom (df), sum of squares, mean square, and a p value, which indicates the probability that the null hypothesis is correct. As with the t test, the only value of interest to the typical consumer of research is the value of p. By convention, when p equals .05 or less (such as .01 or .001), researchers reject the null hypothesis and declare the result to be *statistically significant*.

Because the t test and ANOVA are based on the same theory and assumptions, when two means are compared, both tests yield exactly the same value of p and, hence, lead to the same conclusion regarding significance. Thus, for two means, both tests are equivalent. Note, however, that a single t test can compare only two means, but a single ANOVA can compare a number of means, which is a great advantage.

Suppose, for example, a researcher administered three drugs designed to treat depression in an experiment and obtain the means in Table 1.

Table 1
Posttest Means: Depression Scores for Three Drugs

Group X Drug A	Group Y Drug B	Group Z Drug C
$M = 6.00$	$M = 5.50$	$M = 2.33$

Note that the higher the score, the greater the depression. Inspection of the means shows that there are three observed differences:

1. Drug C is superior to Drug A.
2. Drug C is superior to Drug B.
3. Drug B is superior to Drug A.

The null hypothesis asserts that this *entire set* of three differences was created by sampling error. Through a series of computations that are beyond the scope of this book, an ANOVA for these data was conducted and this is the result: $F = 10.837$, $df = 2, 15$, $p < .05$. This result might be stated in a sentence or presented in a table such as Table 2, which is called an ANOVA table.

Table 2
ANOVA for Data in Table 1

Source of Variation	df	Sum of Squares	Mean Square	F
Between Groups	2	47.445	23.722	10.837*
Within Groups	15	32.833	2.189	
Total	17	80.278		

$* p < .05$

While Table 2 contains many values, which were used to arrive at the probability in the footnote to the table, the typical consumer of research is only interested in the end result, which is the value of p. As indicated in previous topics, when the probability is .05 or less (as it is here), researchers reject the null hypothesis. This means that the *entire set* of differences is statistically significant at the .05 level. Note that the ANOVA does *not* indicate which of the three differences are significant. It could be that only one, only two, *or* all three are significant. This needs to be explored with additional tests known as *multiple comparisons tests*. There are a number of such tests based on different assumptions, which usually yield the same result. (There is still some controversy over which multiple comparisons test is most appropriate.) For the data being considered, application of Scheffé's test (a popular multiple comparisons test) yields these probabilities:

1. for Drug C vs. A, $p < .05$
2. for Drug C vs. B, $p < .05$
3. for Drug B vs. A, $p > .05$

Thus, the multiple comparisons test has indicated that Drug C is significantly better than Drugs A and B because the probabilities are less than .05, but that Drugs B and A are not significantly different from each other because the probability is greater than .05.

In review, an ANOVA indicates whether a set of differences is significant *overall*. If so, researchers can use a multiple comparisons test to determine which individual pairs of means are significantly different from each other.

In this topic, the **one-way ANOVA** (also known as a **single-factor ANOVA**) has been considered. An ANOVA is called "one-way" when the participants have been classified in only one way. In this case, they were classified only in terms of which

---

[1] Because it yields a value of F, it is sometimes called an F test.

drug they took (A, B, or C). In the next topic, the two-way ANOVA is considered.

EXERCISE ON TOPIC 55

1. ANOVA stands for what words?

2. If a researcher compares two means for significance, will ANOVA and the *t* test yield the same probability?

3. If an ANOVA yields $p < .05$, should the null hypothesis be rejected?

4. If an ANOVA yields $p > .05$, is/are the difference(s) statistically significant?

5. If a researcher has four means on an achievement test for samples of students in four states, can the researcher determine whether the set of differences, overall, is statistically significant by using a *t* test? Explain.

6. For the information in Question 5, could a researcher use an ANOVA for the same purpose?

7. Should the typical consumer of research be concerned with the values of the degrees of freedom?

8. In an ANOVA table, which statistic is of the greatest interest to the typical consumer of research?

9. If an overall ANOVA for three or more means is significant, it can be followed up with what type of test to determine the significance of the differences among the individual pairs of means?

Questions for Discussion

10. Very briefly describe a hypothetical study in which it would be appropriate to conduct a one-way ANOVA but it would *not* be appropriate to conduct a *t* test.

11. If there are means for four groups (named A, B, C, and D), there are how many individual pairs of means to be compared with a multiple comparisons test?

For Students Who Are Planning Research

12. Will you be conducting a one-way ANOVA? Explain.

TOPIC 56 TWO-WAY ANALYSIS OF VARIANCE

In the previous topic, the use of **ANOVA** to test for the overall significance of a set of means when participants have been classified in only one way was considered. Often, however, researchers use a two-way classification, such as (1) which drug was taken and (2) how long participants have been depressed. Table 1 shows the means for such a study.[1] Because higher depression scores indicate more depression, a low mean is desirable.

Table 1
Means for a Study of Depression: Drugs and Length of Depression Comparisons

Length of Depression	Drug A	Drug B	Row Mean
Long Term	$M = 8.11$	$M = 8.32$	**$M = 8.22$**
Short Term	$M = 4.67$	$M = 8.45$	**$M = 6.56$**
Col. Mean	**$M = 6.39$**	**$M = 8.38$**	

Although the participants are classified in two ways, the statistics in the table answer *three* questions. First, by comparing the column means of 6.39 and 8.38, a researcher can see that overall, those who took Drug A are less depressed than those who took Drug B. It is important to notice that the mean of 6.39 for Drug A is based on both those who have long-term *and* those who have short-term depression. The same is true of the column mean of 8.38 for Drug B. Thus, by comparing the column means, a researcher is answering this question: Which drug is more effective *in general without regard to how long participants have been depressed*? In a two-way analysis of variance, this is known as a **main effect**.

Each way in which participants are classified yields a main effect in analysis of variance. Thus, because participants were also classified in terms of their length of depression, there is a main effect for short-term vs. long-term depression, which can be seen by examining the row means of 8.22 and 6.56. This main effect indicates that overall, those with short-term depression were less depressed at the end of the experiment than those with long-term depression.

In this example, the most interesting question is the question of an **interaction**. This is the interaction question: Is the effectiveness of the drugs dependent, in part, on the length of depression? By examining the individual cell means (those *not* in bold in Table 1), it becomes clear that the answer is "yes." Drug A is more effective for short-term than long-term depression (4.67 vs. 8.11) while Drug B is about equally effective for both types of depression (8.32 vs. 8.45). What is the practical implication of this interaction? The overall effectiveness of Drug A is almost entirely attributable to its effectiveness for short-term depression. In other words, if an individual has short-term depression, Drug A is indicated, but if an individual has long-term depression, either drug is likely to be about equally effective. Thus, the two classification variables *interact*: The best drug to take is dependent on the length of the depression.

For the data in Table 1, it turns out that $p < .05$ for both main effects and the interaction. Thus, the researcher can reject the null hypothesis that asserts that the differences are the result of random errors. Of course, it does not always turn out this way. It is possible for one or two of the main effects to be significant but the interaction to be not significant. It is also possible for neither main effect to be significant while the interaction is significant, which is the case for the data in Table 2.

Table 2
Means for a Study of Depression: Drugs and Gender Comparisons

Gender	Drug C	Drug D	Row Mean
Female	$M = 8.00$	$M = 5.00$	**$M = 6.50$**
Male	$M = 5.00$	$M = 8.00$	**$M = 6.50$**
Col. Mean	**$M = 6.50$**	**$M = 6.50$**	

In Table 2, notice that the column means (6.50 vs. 6.50) indicate no main effect for Drug C vs. Drug D. Likewise, the row means (6.50 vs. 6.50) indicate no main effect for gender. However, there is one very interesting finding: There is an interaction of drug type and gender, which indicates that for females, Drug D is superior, while Drug C is superior for males. (Keep in mind that higher scores indicate more depression.) Note that if the researcher had compared the two drugs in a one-way ANOVA without also classifying the participants according to gender (as was done here in a two-way ANOVA), the researcher would have missed this important interaction. By examining interactions

---

[1] For instructional purposes, only two types of drugs are shown. However, ANOVA may be used when there are more than two.

using ANOVA, researchers are one step closer to examining the effects of various traits in complex ways (not just one at a time).

EXERCISE ON TOPIC 56

1. Suppose a researcher drew random samples of urban, suburban, and rural children, tested them for creativity, and obtained three means. Should the researcher use a "one-way" or "two-way" ANOVA to test for significance? Explain.

2. Do the following means on a performance test indicate an interaction between type of reward and age?

Age Level	Praise Reward	Monetary Reward	Row Mean
Young Adults	$M = 50.00$	$M = 60.00$	$M = 55.00$
Older Adults	$M = 60.00$	$M = 50.00$	$M = 55.00$
Col. Mean	$M = 55.00$	$M = 55.00$	

3. Do the means for Question 2 indicate a main effect for type of reward?

4. Do the following means on an achievement test indicate an interaction between the method of instruction (A vs. B) and the aptitude of the students (high vs. low)?

Aptitude	Method A	Method B	Row Mean
High Aptitude	$M = 100.00$	$M = 85.00$	$M = 92.50$
Low Aptitude	$M = 100.00$	$M = 85.00$	$M = 92.50$
Col. Mean	$M = 100.00$	$M = 85.00$	

5. Do the means for Question 4 indicate a main effect for method of instruction?

6. Do the means for Question 4 indicate a main effect for aptitude?

7. If $p > .05$ for an interaction in an analysis of variance, should the researcher reject the null hypothesis?

Question for Discussion

8. Very briefly describe a hypothetical study in which it would be appropriate to conduct a two-way ANOVA but it would *not* be appropriate to conduct a one-way ANOVA.

For Students Who Are Planning Research

9. Will you be conducting a two-way ANOVA? Explain.

As indicated in previous topics, **statistical significance** deals with the question of whether a difference is reliable in light of random errors. Assume, for instance, that a researcher assigned students at random to two groups: one that was taught a mathematics lesson with new instructional software (the experimental group) and one that was taught using a traditional lecture/textbook approach (the control group). Furthermore, assume that use of the instructional software *in truth* is very slightly superior to the lecture/textbook approach (i.e., it really produces a superior outcome in math achievement, but the superiority is quite small). With a very large sample, randomization should yield experimental and control groups that are very similar at the beginning of the experiment (i.e., on the pretest). Because larger samples have less sampling error than smaller ones, a significance test such as a *t* test for the difference between the two posttest means may be able to detect the reliability of the small difference and allow the researcher to declare it to be *statistically significant* at some probability level such as $p < .05$. This illustrates an important principle: Even a small difference can be a statistically significant difference.[1] This is true because statistical significance determines only the likelihood that a difference is due to random errors, not whether it is a large difference.

While determining the statistical significance of a difference is the first step, determining the **practical significance** is the next step. Determining practical significance involves five considerations.

The first consideration is the cost in relation to the benefit, which is often referred to as a **cost-benefit analysis**. While there are mechanical, statistical means for conducting such an analysis, for most purposes, common sense and good judgment can give a good answer to the question of whether the results are of practical significance in terms of cost. Consider the example above. Suppose all students already have access to computers for their math lessons and the software is being donated (or is highly subsidized by some foundation). In this case, the low cost might make the small difference of practical significance. On the other hand, if expensive computers and software would need to be purchased and the teachers would need extensive (and, therefore, expensive) training in its use, educators might forgo using the experimental method in everyday instruction because the small increase in performance would come at a high cost.

The example being considered illustrates that even a small difference can be of both statistical and practical significance if the cost is low. In addition, a small, statistically significant difference can be of practical significance—even if it is costly—if it is **a crucial difference** (*the second consideration*). A crucial difference is one that results in a crucial increase or decrease. Consider an extreme example. Suppose an experiment in which very expensive computerized simulations that teach how to conduct a delicate form of surgery reduces the death rate from such surgery from 2 in 100,000 to 1.8 in 100,000. In this case, a surgeon might decide that even this small difference is worth the high cost because saving even a very small number of lives during surgery is crucial. The following is a less extreme example: If a school needs just a few points' increase (on the average) to cross a crucial threshold such as having the average student score at or above the 50th percentile rank on a standardized math test in order to obtain substantial increases in state funding for instruction, crossing this threshold might be considered crucial by teachers, parents, and students.

The third consideration in determining practical significance is **client acceptability**. In school settings, students are clients. If students greatly dislike a statistically superior computerized technique for improving math achievement, using the technique might cause students to develop negative attitudes toward math. If so, the statistically significant difference might be of little practical significance because of the *negative side effect* (i.e., development of negative attitudes).

The fourth consideration is **public and political acceptability**. For instance, studies suggest that stem cell research might be fruitful in curing a number of debilitating and deadly diseases. Yet some segments of the public (at the time of this

---

[1] As indicated in Topic 54, the *t* test is more likely to lead to significance if the difference between the two means is large. However, if there is little variation among the participants and if a large enough sample is used, even small differences can be reliably detected and declared statistically significant. Note that in some circumstances, a small difference can be of great practical importance. For instance, in a national election, having only one vote more than the competing candidate out of millions of votes can lead to victory.

writing) are opposed to it, calling into question its practical significance as a line of research that scientists should continue to pursue.

Fifth, the **ethical and legal implications** of statistically significant results should be considered. No matter how much benefit and no matter how low the cost, some treatments that have been shown to produce statistically superior results may violate the ethical standards of a profession or impinge on legal requirements such as the laws that govern the operation of schools and other institutions.

It should be clear that determining practical significance should not be done mechanically. If there is any question as to the practical significance of the results of a study, representative groups of potential providers of the treatments (such as teachers or psychologists, their clients, the public, and politicians) may need to be consulted. In addition, legal counsel may be needed to help in the determination of practical significance.

EXERCISE ON TOPIC 57

1. Is it possible for a small difference to be statistically significant?

2. This topic describes *how many* types of considerations for determining practical significance?

3. If the cost is very low, might a very small statistically significant difference be of practical significance?

4. Does a crucial difference need to be numerically large to be of practical significance?

5. According to this topic, should the acceptability of a treatment to the clients be considered when determining practical significance?

6. "According to this topic, ethical considerations should play no role in the interpretation of the results of a study." Is this statement "true" *or* "false"?

7. Should the determination of the practical significance of the results of a study be a mechanical process?

Questions for Discussion

8. In addition to the three examples in this topic, name a hypothetical result that you would favor implementing even if it were costly because it might make a *crucial difference*.

9. Consider the last research report you read that had statistically significant results. Did the researcher who wrote the article discuss the practical significance of his or her results? Explain.

For Students Who Are Planning Research

10. Can you anticipate any considerations that might limit the practical significance of the results you hope to obtain in your study? Explain.

PART G

EFFECT SIZE AND META-ANALYSIS

In this part of the book, a statistical tool called effect size, which helps in the evaluation of the size of a difference, such as the difference between two means, is described. In addition, a statistical technique named meta-analysis, which is used to combine results across diverse studies on a given topic, is considered.

NOTES

TOPIC 58   INTRODUCTION TO EFFECT SIZE (d)

To understand the need to consider the **effect size** of a difference, consider a practical problem in interpreting research. Suppose that Experimenter A administered a new treatment for depression (Treatment X) to an experimental group while the control group received a standard treatment. Furthermore, suppose that Experimenter A used a 20-item true–false depression scale (with possible raw scores from 0 to 20) and obtained the results on the posttest shown in Table 1.[1] Note that the difference between the two means is 5 raw-score points.

Table 1
Statistics Obtained in Experiment A (Treatment X)

Group	m	sd
Experimental group ($n = 50$)	12.00	4.00
Control group ($n = 50$)	7.00	4.00
Difference between two means	5.00	

Suppose that Experimenter B administered Treatment Y to an experimental group while treating the control group with the standard treatment. Furthermore, suppose Experimenter B used a 30-item scale with choices from "Strongly agree" to "Strongly disagree" with possible scores from 0 to 120 and obtained the results in Table 2, which shows a difference of 10 raw-score points in favor of the experimental group.

Table 2
Statistics Obtained in Experiment B (Treatment Y)

Group	m	sd
Experimental group ($n = 50$)	80.00	14.00
Control group ($n = 50$)	70.00	14.00
Difference between two means	10.00	

Which treatment is superior? Treatment X, which resulted in a 5-point raw-score difference between the two means, *or* Treatment Y, which resulted in a 10-point raw-score difference between the two means? Of course, the answer is not clear because the two experimenters used different measurement scales (0 to 20 versus 0 to 120).

To make the results of the two studies comparable, they need to be *standardized* so that both differences can be expressed on the same scale. The most straightforward way to do this is to express

both differences in terms of their *standard-deviation units* (instead of their raw-score units).[2] In Experiment A, *one standard-deviation unit* equals 4.00 raw score points. By dividing the difference between the means (5.00) by the size of the standard-deviation unit for Experiment A (4.00 points), an answer of 1.25 is obtained. This value is known as d and is obtained by the following formula in which m_e stands for the mean of the experimental group, and m_c stands for the mean of the control group:

$$d = \frac{m_e - m_c}{sd} = \frac{12.00 - 7.00}{4.00} = 1.25$$

The result indicates that the experimental group exceeded the control group by 1.25 (one and one-quarter) standard-deviation units. For all practical purposes, there are only three standard-deviation units on each side of the mean. Thus, d is expressed in standard-deviation units and has an effective range from 0.00 (no difference between the means) to 3.00 (the maximum difference between the means).[3] Thus, for Experiment A, the experimental group is one and one-quarter standard deviations above no difference (0.00) on a standardized scale that ranges from 0.00 to only 3.00. On such a limited scale, a value of d of 1.25 indicates that the difference is substantially above 0.00.

Using the formula for Experiment B, the difference between the means is divided by the standard deviation (10.00/14.00), yielding $d = 0.71$, which is almost three-quarters of the way above 0.00 on the three-point scale. The following is what is now known about the differences in the two experiments when both are expressed on a common (i.e., standardized) scale called d. Clearly, the difference in Experiment A (1.25) is greater than the difference in Experiment B (0.71).

0.00 0.50 0.75 1.00 1.50 1.75 2.00 2.50 2.75 3.00
         ↑   ↑
      Exp. B Exp. A

Table 3 summarizes the differences. Remember that the two raw-score differences are not directly comparable because different measurement scales

---

[1] Note that in the experiments in this topic, the researchers used instruments that yield *higher* scores when there is *less* depression.

were used (0 to 20 points versus 0 to 120 points). By examining the standardized values of d, which range from 0.00 to 3.00, a meaningful comparison of the results of the two experiments can be made.

Within each of the two examples in this topic, the two standard deviations are equal. When they are unequal, a special averaging procedure that results in the "pooled standard deviation" should be used. See Appendix E for more information.

Now for an important definition: *Effect size* refers to the *magnitude* (i.e., size) of a difference when it is expressed on a standardized scale. The statistic d is one of the most popular statistics for

describing the effect size of the difference between two means. In the next topic, the interpretation of d is discussed in more detail. In Topic 60, an alternative statistic for expressing effect size is described.

Table 3
Differences Expressed in Raw Scores and in Values of d

Group	Raw-score difference	Standardized differences (d)
Experimenter A	5 points	1.25
Experimenter B	10 points	0.71

EXERCISE ON TOPIC 58

1. In this topic, which experimenter had the smaller range of possible raw scores? Explain.

2. In this topic, the raw-score differences between the means (5 for Experimenter A and 10 for Experimenter B) were standardized by dividing each of them by what statistic?

3. When comparing the results of two experiments, is it possible for the experiment with the smaller raw-score difference to have a larger difference when the differences are expressed as d?

4. Suppose a researcher obtained a value of d of 2.95. Should this be characterized as representing a large difference? Explain.

5. Suppose you read that the mean for an experimental group is 20.00 and the mean for the control group is 22.00. Based on this information alone, can you calculate the value of d? Explain.

6. Suppose a researcher conducted an experiment on improving algebra achievement, and the experimental posttest raw-score mean equaled 500.00 ($sd = 100.00$), and the control group raw-score mean equaled 400.00 ($sd = 100.00$). What is the value of the effect size for the experiment?

7. What is the definition of *effect size*?

Question for Discussion

8. In your own words, briefly explain why it is desirable to compute d when comparing the results of two experiments that use different measurement scales.

For Students Who Are Planning Research

9. Do you plan to report value(s) of d in the results section of your research report? Explain.

TOPIC 59 INTERPRETATION OF EFFECT SIZE (d)

In the previous topic, effect size expressed as d was introduced. The two examples in that topic had values of d of 0.71 and 1.25. Obviously, the experiment with a value of 1.25 had a larger effect than the one with a value of 0.71.

While there are no universally accepted standards for describing values of d in words, many researchers use Cohen's (1992)[1] suggestions: (1) a value of d of about 0.20 (one-fifth of a standard deviation) is "small," (2) a value of 0.50 (one-half of a standard deviation) is "medium," and (3) a value of 0.80 (eight-tenths of a standard deviation) is "large." (Keep in mind that in terms of values of d, an experimental group can rarely exceed a control group by more than 3.00 because the effective range of standard-deviation units is only three on each side of the mean. Thus, for most practical purposes, 3.00 [or –3.00] is the maximum value of d.)[2]

Extrapolating from Cohen's suggestions, a value of 1.10 might be called "very large," and a value of 1.40 or more might be called "extremely large." Values this large are rarely found in social and behavioral research.

Table 1 summarizes the new material covered so far in this topic.

Table 1
Labels for Values of d

Value of d	Label
0.20	Small
0.50	Medium
0.80	Large
1.10	Very Large
1.40+	Extremely Large

Using the labels in Table 1, the value of d of 0.71 in the previous topic would be described as being closer to "large" than "medium," while the value of 1.25 would be described as being between "very large" and "extremely large."

Cohen (1992), who proposed the labels for the first three values in Table 1, noted that he originally established them subjectively but that they subsequently have been found to be useful by other researchers in various fields of study.

The labels being discussed should not be used arbitrarily without considering the full context in which the values of d were obtained and the possible implications of the results. This leads to two principles: (1) a small effect size might represent an important result and (2) a large effect size might represent an unimportant result.

Consider the *first principle*. Suppose that researchers have been frustrated by consistently finding values of d well below 0.20 when trying various treatments for solving an important problem (such as treatments for a new and deadly disease). If a subsequent researcher finds a treatment that results in a value of about 0.20, this might be considered a very important finding. At this low level (0.20), the effect of the treatment is small, but it might be of immense importance to ill individuals helped by the treatment—however small the effect size. In addition, the results might point the scientific community in a fruitful direction for additional research on treatments for the problem in question.

The *second principle* is that a large value of d—even one above 1.40—might be of limited importance. This is most likely when the results lack practical significance in terms of cost, public and political acceptability, and ethical and legal concerns. (See Topic 57 for considerations in determining the practical significance of research results.)

Here are three steps for interpreting the difference between two means. First, determine whether the difference is statistically significant at an acceptable probability level such as $p < .05$. If it is not, the difference should usually be regarded as unreliable and should be interpreted as such. Second, for a statistically significant difference, consider the value of d and consider the labels in Table 1 for describing the magnitude of the difference. Third, consider the implications of the difference for validating any relevant theories as well as the practical significance of the results.

Of course, before beginning to follow the three steps outlined in the previous paragraph, the adequacy of the research methodology employed by the researcher should be considered. Woefully inadequate sampling (such as a very biased sample), clearly invalid instrumentation (such as a test that measures a variable other than the one the re-

---

[1] Cohen, J. (1992). A power primer. *Psychological Bulletin, 112*, 155–159.

[2] A negative is obtained when the control group's mean is higher than the experimental group's mean. Note that less than one-half of one percent of a normal distribution lies above +3.00 and below –3.00, which means that it is technically possible—but highly unlikely—to obtain values larger than +3.00 and –3.00.

searcher wanted to study), and/or a very poor research design (such as a design that will not answer the research question) would lead to very serious questions regarding the validity of the results. In such cases, consideration of values of d might be meaningless.

EXERCISE ON TOPIC 59

1. Are there universally accepted standards for describing effect sizes?

2. What is the "effective range" of standard deviation units on both sides of the mean? Explain.

3. If the value of d for the difference between two means equals 1.00, the experimental group's mean is how many standard-deviation units higher than the control group's mean?

4. What value of d is associated with the label "extremely large"?

5. According to Cohen, what label should be attached to a value of d of 0.80?

6. Under what circumstance will a negative value of d be obtained?

7. Should a test of statistical significance be conducted "before" *or* "after" computing d and interpreting its value using labels?

Questions for Discussion

8. As noted in this topic, a small value of d might be associated with an important result. Name a specific problem that is currently confounding researchers and for which even a small value of d might indicate a result of great practical importance.

9. Is it possible for a large value of d to be associated with a difference that is unimportant? Explain.

For Students Who Are Planning Research

10. Will you be comparing the difference between two means in your analysis? If so, do you expect to find a statistically significant difference? Do you expect to find a large value of d? Explain.

TOPIC 60   EFFECT SIZE AND CORRELATION (r)

Cohen's d is so widely used as a measure of effect size that some researchers use the term "effect size" and "d" interchangeably—as though they are synonyms. However, "effect size" refers to any statistic that *describes the size of a difference on a standardized metric*. For instance, d describes the size of the difference between two means.[1] Furthermore, d is *standardized* because regardless of what variables are being studied and regardless of what raw-score scale is being used to express the difference, the value of d is always expressed on a standard-deviation scale that almost always ranges only from –3.00 to +3.00.[2] (See the previous topic to review d.)

In addition to d, a number of other measures of effect size have been proposed. One that is very widely reported is "effect-size r," which is simply the Pearson correlation coefficient (r), which is described in Topic 53. As indicated in that topic, r indicates the direction and strength of a relationship between two variables expressed on a scale that ranges from –1.00 to +1.00, where 0.00 indicates no relationship. Values of r are interpreted by first squaring them (r^2). For instance, when $r = 0.50$, $r^2 = .25$ (i.e., $0.50 \times 0.50 = 0.25$). Then, the value of r^2 should be multiplied by 100%. Thus, $0.25 \times 100\% = 25\%$. This indicates that the value of r of 0.50 is 25% greater than 0.00 on a scale that extends up to a maximum possible value of 1.00.

In simple, straightforward studies, the choice between reporting *means* and the associated values of d (which can range from –3.00 to 3.00) and reporting *correlation coefficients* and the associated values of r^2 (which can range from 0.00 to 1.00)[3] is usually quite straightforward. If a researcher wants to determine which of two groups is superior *on the average*, a comparison of means using d is usually the preferred method of analysis. On the other hand, if there is one group of participants with two scores per participant and if the goal is to determine the

degree of relationship between the two sets of scores, then r and r^2 should be used. For instance, if a group of students was administered a vocabulary knowledge test and a reading comprehension test, it would not be surprising to obtain a correlation coefficient as high as 0.70, which indicates a substantial degree of relationship between two variables (i.e., there is a strong tendency for students who score high on vocabulary knowledge to score high on reading comprehension). As indicated in Topic 53, for interpretative purposes, 0.70 squared equals 0.49, which is equivalent to 49%. Knowing this allows a researcher to say that the relationship between the two variables is 49% higher than a relationship of 0.00.

When reviewing a body of literature on a given topic, some studies present means and values of d while other studies on the same topic present values of r, depending on the specific research purposes and research designs. When interpreting such a set of studies, it can be useful to think in terms of the equivalence of d and r. Table 1 shows the equivalents for selected values.

Table 1
Equivalent Values of d, r, and r^2

d	r	r^2	% for r^2
0.20	0.100	0.010	1.0%
0.50	0.243	0.059	5.9%
0.80	0.371	0.138	13.8%
1.20	0.514	0.264	26.4%
1.50	0.600	0.360	36.0%
2.00	0.707	0.500	50.0%

Consider an example that illustrates the usefulness of Table 1. Suppose a researcher was examining the literature on anxiety and depression and found a study in which one group was administered scales that measured the two variables, and $r = 0.37$ was obtained. Suppose that in another study, an experimental group was administered a treatment designed to induce anxiety while the control group received a neutral treatment. Then, all participants were administered a depression scale (to see whether anxiety induces depression). Further, suppose that the experimenter reported that $d = 0.80$ for the difference between the posttest means for the two groups. Using Table 1, it can be seen that the effect sizes (i.e., magnitude of the differences) in the two studies are the same (i.e., for a value of d of

---

[1] If the means of two groups are identical, $d = 0.00$.

[2] Note that it is mathematically possible for d to exceed 3.00 because a very small percentage of the cases lies above three standard deviations above the mean. Such values are seldom seen in the social and behavioral sciences.

[3] Note that all values of r^2 are positive since squaring a negative correlation coefficient results in a positive product. Thus, the bottom of the range for values of r^2 is 0.00, not –1.00.

0.80 in the first column, the corresponding value of r in the second column is 0.371).

For values not shown in Table 1, it is often sufficient to locate the closest values and make mental approximations. To obtain more precise equivalent values of d and r, use the formulas provided near the end of Appendix E.

EXERCISE ON TOPIC 60

1. According to this topic, what are the two measures of effect size that are very widely reported?

2. Correlation coefficients are expressed on a standard scale that always ranges from –1.00 up to what value?

3. A value of r should be interpreted by doing what?

4. A value of r equal to 0.40 is what percentage of the distance above zero?

5. If there is one group of participants and a researcher wants to determine the strength of the relationship between two sets of test scores, which measure of effect size would typically be the more appropriate?

6. A value of d of 1.20 corresponds to what value of r^2?

7. A value of r of 0.600 corresponds to what value of d?

Question for Discussion

8. Briefly describe a hypothetical study in which it would be more appropriate to compute a value of d instead of a value of r as a measure of effect size.

For Students Who Are Planning Research

9. In this topic, there is an example of an experiment and an example of a correlational study. Will you be conducting either type of study? Explain.

Meta-analysis is a set of statistical methods for combining the results of previous studies.[1] To understand its basic premise, consider the following example. Suppose a researcher (named W) randomly assigned 50 students to an experimental group that received one-on-one remedial tutorial reading instruction. The remaining 50 children were the controls. At the end of the experiment, the experimental group had a mean of 22.00, and the control group had a mean of 19.00 on a standardized reading test. Subsequently, three other experimenters conducted strict replications of the first experiment using the same research methods, the same type of tutorial reading instruction, and the same number of second-grade students drawn at random from the same pool of students (e.g., second-graders in a particular school district). The posttest means of the four experiments are shown in Table 1.

Table 1
Results of a Meta-Analysis of Two Experiments

	Experimental Group	Control Group	Mean Difference
Researcher W	$m = 22.00$	$m = 19.00$	$m_{difference} = 3.00$
Researcher X	$m = 20.00$	$m = 18.00$	$m_{difference} = 2.00$
Researcher Y	$m = 23.00$	$m = 17.00$	$m_{difference} = 6.00$
Researcher Z	$m = 15.00$	$m = 16.00$	$m_{difference} = -1.00$

In Table 1, there are differences in the results from study to study. The differences could be caused by one or more of the following types of errors:

1. Random sampling errors created by assigning participants at random to the two groups, such as having more motivated students assigned (quite at random) to the experimental group in one or more of the experiments.
2. Random errors of measurement such as participants guessing on the multiple-choice test, and some students not feeling well on the day the test was administered.
3. Systematic errors known to one or more of the researchers, such as the unavailability of experienced tutors for one or more of the experiments.
4. Systematic errors of which one or more of the researchers are unaware, such as tutors not following the curriculum when the researcher or researchers were not present.

All four types of errors are possible in any experiment. Hence, the results of any one experiment should be interpreted with caution. However, in this particular example, there are four experiments, which should provide more confidence in any overall conclusions than any single study could provide. In a *traditional, subjective narrative review of these studies*, it would be reasonable to synthesize these four experiments with a statement such as, "Three of the four experiments on the tutorial instruction showed positive results, with one experiment showing a six-point difference in favor of the experimental group. However, the one negative case in which the control group exceeded the experimental group by one point reduces confidence in the effectiveness of this program."

In a *meta-analysis*, a reviewer might also make comments such as the one in the previous paragraph. However, the main thrust of the conclusions in a meta-analysis is based on a *mathematical synthesis* of the statistical results of the previous studies. The synthesis can be obtained by averaging the results by summing the four mean differences (3.00 + 2.00 + 6.00 – 1.00 = 10.00) and then dividing the sum by four because there were four studies (10.00/4.00 = 2.50). Thus, in a meta-analysis, the author would state that the best estimate of the effectiveness of the program is 2.50 points.[2]

At this point, it should be clear that a meta-analysis estimate of 2.50 points has two important characteristics. The first one is that the statistical result (e.g., 2.50) is based on a sample of 400 students. (Note that each of the four individual studies had 50 in each group for a total of 100 in each

---

[1] The prefix "meta" means occurring later and/or being later and more highly organized. Meta-analysis is conducted on previous results and mathematically synthesizes them.

[2] For reasons discussed in the next topic, those who conduct meta-analyses usually convert their results to one or more measures of effect size (such as *d* or *r*), which were discussed in the previous three topics.

study.) Statistics based on larger samples (such as 400 versus 100) yield more *reliable* results.

It is important to note that *reliable results* are not necessarily *valid results*. A systematic bias that skews the results (such as the experimental group having access to the answer key for the test) will yield invalid results no matter how large the sample is.

The second important characteristic of meta-analysis is that it typically synthesizes the results of studies conducted by *independent* researchers (i.e.,

researchers who are not working together). Thus, if one researcher makes a *systematic error* (such as using poorly trained tutors), the effects of his or her erroneous results will be moderated when they are averaged with the results obtained by other independent researchers who have not made the same error.

In short, the process of averaging when conducting a meta-analysis tends to decrease the effects of both the random and systematic errors listed earlier in this topic.

EXERCISE ON TOPIC 61

1. What is the meaning of the prefix "meta" as used in this topic?

2. Meta-analysis is a "set of statistical methods" for doing what?

3. Two types of random errors tend to be canceled out in the process of conducting a meta-analysis. What are the two types of random errors discussed in this topic?

4. In the report of a meta-analysis, the "main thrust of the conclusions" is based on what?

5. Very briefly state the "second important characteristic" of meta-analysis.

Question for Discussion

6. Based on what you have learned about meta-analysis in this topic, to what extent do you think that it is a good method for advancing knowledge on a topic? Explain.

For Students Who Are Planning Research

7. Some institutions (and journals) consider a meta-analysis to be a work of original research even though it is based on a reanalysis of the research results created by others. If you are planning to conduct research, would you be interested in conducting a meta-analysis as your research project (based on what you know about it at this point)? Explain. (Note: After reading the next two topics, reconsider your answer to this question.)

TOPIC 62 META-ANALYSIS AND EFFECT SIZE

For instructional purposes, the example in the previous topic illustrated a meta-analysis on four studies that were as similar as possible (i.e., a study by Researcher W plus three strict replications). In practice, it would be difficult to find even one perfectly strict replication of a study. One very important way that various studies on a given topic often differ is that various researchers frequently use different measures of the same variable. To see the importance of this issue when conducting and interpreting a meta-analysis, consider the values in Table 1, which are based on a study in which Experimenter A used a test with possible score values from 200 to 800 (like the *SAT*) while Experimenter B used a test with possible score values from 0 to 50.

Table 1
Results Used in Conducting a Meta-Analysis

	Experimental Group	Control Group	Mean Difference
Exp. A $n = 50$	$m = 500.00$ $sd = 200.00$	$m = 400.00$ $sd = 200.00$	$m_{difference}$ $= 100.00$
Exp. B $n = 50$	$m = 24.00$ $sd = 3.00$	$m = 22.00$ $sd = 3.00$	$m_{difference}$ $= 2.00$

If the average of the mean differences is computed ($100.00 + 2.00 = 102.00/2 = 51.00$), the average lacks meaning because the results are expressed on different scales. In other words, the answer of 51.00 does *not* refer specifically to the scale that goes from 200 to 800 *nor* does it refer specifically to the scale that goes from 0 to 50. When locating additional studies on the same topic, other tests with other score-point ranges are likely to be found, making a simple average of the mean differences entirely uninterpretable.

The solution to the problem being considered is to use a measure of *effect size*. One of the most popular is Cohen's *d*, which is expressed on a standardized scale that typically ranges from –3.00 to +3.00. (This statistic was discussed in Topics 58 through 60.) Calculating *d* for all studies to be included in a meta-analysis permits the averaging of the values of *d* to get a meaningful result.

As indicated in Topic 58, to obtain *d*, divide the difference between the means by the standard deviation. For Experiment A, $d = 100.00/200.00 = 0.50$. For Experiment B, $d = 2.00/3.00 = 0.67$. When the results of the two experiments are expressed on a common scale (*d*), it becomes clear that Experiment B (with a *d* of 0.67) had a larger effect than Experiment A (with a *d* of 0.50), which was not clear by a simple inspection of Table 1.

To proceed with the meta-analysis, the two values of *d* can be averaged to get a mathematical synthesis of the results [$(0.67 + 0.50)/2 = 0.58$]. Thus, **0.58** is the best estimate of the overall effect. Referring to Table 1 in Topic 59, a researcher can say that the overall result of the meta-analysis is somewhat above medium in strength.

In the example in this topic, the standard deviations for both groups in each experiment were the same. In reality, they will almost always differ. Those who plan to conduct a meta-analysis and want more information on several possible solutions to this problem should consult Appendix E.

Also in the example in this topic, the two experiments had the same number of participants ($n = 50$ in each). Suppose an additional published experiment (Experiment C) in which 300 participants were used is located. A researcher would, of course, calculate *d* for this experiment (assume that $d = 0.90$, which is "large" according to Table 1 in Topic 59). By summing the three values of *d* and dividing by 3 (the number of studies), each study is given an equal weight. In other words, the three values of *d* are being treated as though they were equally important even though the value of *d* for Experiment C is based on a much larger sample than that of the other two experiments. Using statistical methods that are beyond the scope of this book, researchers can "weight" the average value of *d* to take into account the varying numbers of participants, giving more weight to those studies with more participants in the final average. Thus, consumers of research should look to see whether a meta-analysis is based on "weighted averages," which is almost always desirable.

As indicated in Topic 60, *r* is also a measure of effect sizes. Like *d*, it is expressed on a standardized scale. However, the scale for *r* has values that can range from –1.00 to 1.00. Like *d*, values of *r* reported in various studies can be averaged while weighting the average to take into account varying sample sizes. (The mathematics of the weighting procedure for *r* are beyond the scope of this book.)

In this topic and the previous one, very simple examples were used to illustrate the purposes of meta-analysis and its interpretation. These simple examples may have failed to fully convey the importance of meta-analysis, so briefly consider two published meta-analytic studies. First, in one meta-analysis, researchers located 162 studies that reported on the gender differences in smiling. Combined, these studies contained a total of 109,654 participants. By averaging the effect sizes across the 162 studies, the researchers found that women smiled more than men, with an overall weighted mean value of d of 0.41, which is close to "medium" in strength according to Table 1 in Topic 59.[1] Note that this result is based on a large number of studies and a very large combined sample size.

In another meta-analysis, researchers reported a weighted average value of r of .48 for the relationship between posttraumatic stress disorder and anger based on 29 studies involving 7,486 participants. With such a large sample, the result of this meta-analysis is highly reliable.[2]

In conclusion, meta-analysis provides a statistical method that can synthesize multiple studies on a given topic. Thus, meta-analytic studies are an important adjunct to traditional, more subjective narrative reviews of literature, which are largely non-mathematical (i.e., reviews of literature in which some particular statistics may be mentioned but the results of the studies being reviewed are not mathematically synthesized).

EXERCISE ON TOPIC 62

1. According to this topic, is it easy to find perfectly strict replications of previous studies?

2. What is "one very important way" that various studies on a given topic differ?

3. Computing a mean difference across studies that used measurement scales with different possible numbers of score points is meaningless. What is suggested in this topic to overcome this problem?

4. What should usually be done when the studies to be used in a meta-analysis have different sample sizes?

5. Is d the only standardized measure of effect size used in meta-analytic studies? Explain.

Question for Discussion

6. In this topic, a meta-analytic study that reported a weighted average value of r of 0.48 for the relationship between posttraumatic stress disorder and anger is cited. Based on what you know about correlation, how would you interpret the direction and strength of this relationship?

For Students Who Are Planning Research

7. Reconsider your answer to Question 7 in the previous topic in light of what you learned in this topic. Has your answer changed? Explain.

[1] LaFrance, M., Hecht, M. A., & Paluck, E. L. (2003). The contingent smile: A meta-analysis of sex differences in smiling. *Psychological Bulletin, 129,* 305–334.

[2] Orth, U., & Wieland, E. (2006). Anger, hostility, and posttraumatic stress disorder in trauma-exposed adults: A meta-analysis. *Journal of Consulting and Clinical Psychology, 74,* 698–706.

Meta-analysis has both strengths and weaknesses. A major strength mentioned in the previous topic is that it produces results based on large combined samples—sometimes very large samples. The previous topic cited a meta-analysis of 162 studies that produced a mathematical synthesis involving 109,654 participants, which is very much larger than the typical number in research reports in academic journals. Such very large samples yield very reliable (although not necessarily valid) results. However, if the studies subjected to a meta-analysis have serious methodological flaws (resulting in a lack of validity), then the mathematical synthesis of their results will also lack validity.

As indicated in Topic 61, a strength of meta-analysis is that it can be used to synthesize the results of studies conducted by *independent* researchers (i.e., researchers who are not working together). Whether or not meta-analysis is used, independent confirmation of results is an important standard that is applied when assessing the validity of the results reported on a given research topic.

An additional strength of meta-analysis is the objectivity of its conclusions.[1] After making subjective judgments regarding how to define a topic, how to search for relevant studies, and what criteria should be used to select studies from the available pool of potential studies, the remaining steps in a meta-analysis are mathematical, leading to an objectively obtained result (such as an average value of d or r). Note that in a traditional qualitative literature review (i.e., a review that consists of a narrative discussion without averaging measures of effect size), the conclusions are expressed in words. The phrasing, emphasis, and other characteristics of written communication used to express the conclusions in a nonmathematical, traditional review are not "objective" from a mathematical point of view.

A potential weakness occurs if a researcher is not careful in the selection of studies to include in a meta-analysis. Poor selection might produce results that are difficult to interpret (at best) or meaningless (at worst). For instance, a meta-analysis involving all studies of tutoring in reading regardless of grade

level (from first grade through high school) would not be very helpful in reaching conclusions that have implications for program implementation at any given grade level. This is because different types of results might be obtained at different levels (e.g., tutoring might be more helpful at the primary level than at the high school level). When combined into one grand mean, the poor effectiveness at the high school level might cancel out much of the effectiveness at the primary level (by pulling the grand mean down).

One way to handle the problem of diversity across a set of studies is to establish criteria for the inclusion of a subset of studies on a topic in a meta-analysis. For instance, a researcher might include only those that meet criteria such as employment of teachers as tutors, use of tutoring sessions that last at least 30 minutes per session, and tutoring of only primary-grade students.

Another solution to the problem of diversity is to conduct multiple meta-analyses within a single meta-analytic project. For instance, a researcher might conduct three separate analyses: one for studies involving primary-grade students, one for those involving middle-school students, and a third for high school students. Comparing results of the three analyses would provide insights into the effectiveness of the programs at different grade levels.

In a report in which separate analyses are conducted for various subgroups, the variable on which the studies were divided into subgroups (e.g., the various grade levels) is called a *moderator variable* because it may moderate the results so that the results for subgroups are different from the grand combined result. The use of moderator variables is very common in published reports of meta-analyses.

A final potential weakness of meta-analysis stems from what is known as "publication bias." Typically, researchers are looking for significant differences (and relationships). When they fail to find them, they may be inclined *not* to write reports on such studies for submission for publication. It is also possible that some journal editors may have a bias such that they tend to reject for publication studies with insignificant results. Hence, the body of published research available on a topic for a meta-analysis might be biased toward studies that have statistically significant results. (A researcher conducting a meta-analysis, of course, wants to in-

---

[1] Quantitative researchers value and strive for objectivity, while qualitative researchers tend to question whether objectivity is obtainable. Thus, qualitative researchers challenge the feasibility and desirability of seeking complete objectivity in scientific research.

clude all relevant studies whether the differences are significant or not in order to get an *overall* estimate of effectiveness.) A partial solution to this problem is for those conducting meta-analyses to search for studies that might be reported in dissertations, convention papers, government reports, and other nonjournal sources, where there might not be as much bias against studies with statistically insignificant results.

Despite the potential weaknesses, meta-analysis is an important tool for gaining mathematical perspectives on the results of the studies on a research topic. It shows what can be obtained "objectively," which can be compared and contrasted with more subjective qualitative literature reviews on the same research topic.

EXERCISE ON TOPIC 63

1. What was the sample size for the meta-analysis of the 162 studies mentioned in this topic?

2. According to this topic, is a "meta-analysis" *or* a "review" consisting of a narrative discussion of the literature more objective?

3. Even if a meta-analysis yields highly reliable results based on objective mathematical procedures, are its results necessarily valid? Explain.

4. What is the name of the "final potential weakness of meta-analysis"?

5. What is a partial solution to the problem you named in your response to Question 4?

Question for Discussion

6. Is meta-analysis completely objective? Explain.

For Students Who Are Planning Research

7. Based on what you know about meta-analysis, would you be interested in conducting one in the near future? At some later point in your professional career? Explain.

PART H

QUALITATIVE RESEARCH

Topics 9 and 10 in the first part of this book describe some of the major distinctions between quantitative and qualitative research. In this part, techniques used by qualitative researchers are explored in more detail. Topics 64 and 65 describe sampling in qualitative research, Topics 66 and 67 describe methods used to collect data, and Topic 68 describes specific techniques qualitative researchers use to ensure the quality of their research. This part ends with Topics 69 and 70, which describe two frequently used general approaches to the analysis of qualitative data.

NOTES

In Part C of this book (i.e., Topics 20 through 26), the emphasis is on sampling from the point of view of quantitative researchers. However, Topic 23 briefly described **purposive sampling**, which is widely used by qualitative researchers. To select a purposive sample, a researcher must first identify a research topic of interest and then seek individuals who are likely to have relevant information. This is sometimes described as seeking individuals who will be "rich sources of information." In other words, qualitative researchers make subjective judgments regarding the individuals to select based on the likelihood that they will be able to provide the needed information. Example 1 illustrates purposive sampling in which department chairs are asked to nominate potential participants. In the example, notice that the department chairs were asked to use their "judgment" rather than some objective criteria such as GPAs.

EXAMPLE 1
Purposive sampling: To identify a sample of Asian American college students majoring in clinical psychology who have the potential to become highly successful clinicians, letters were sent to chairs of departments of psychology soliciting nominations. The letters asked the chairs to nominate Asian American students who, in the chairs' judgment, had the greatest potential for success as clinical psychologists, without regard to the students' grades or test scores.

Purposive sampling is the correct term to use when the researchers seek participants who fit into a broad category such as "Asian American students with the greatest potential to succeed as clinical psychologists." In contrast, when there are a number of criteria to be applied in the selection of a sample, the sampling technique is more properly called **purposive criterion sampling**. This is illustrated in Example 2.

EXAMPLE 2
Purposive criterion sampling: To identify a sample of distinguished elementary school teachers, a list of all elementary school teachers in a school district who had received merit raises in the past five years was obtained. From those on the list, teachers were selected who met these criteria: (1) at least three years of teaching experience at the elementary school level, (2) hold full credentials issued by the state in which they taught, (3) hold master's degrees in education, and (4) had supervised at least one student teacher in

the past three years. The last criterion was included because student teachers are typically assigned only to experienced teachers whom school administrators believe to be master teachers.

Sometimes, qualitative researchers seek diversity in their samples. Thus, for instance, in Example 2, the researchers might purposively select teachers who are diverse in their ages, ethnic/racial backgrounds, and in their majors as undergraduates in college. Using a diverse sample introduces additional variables that might need to be accounted for during the analysis of participants' responses (e.g., analyze separately the data from older versus younger teachers). Hence, some qualitative researchers seek fairly homogeneous samples in order to simplify their research.

Regardless of whether diversity is sought while sampling, qualitative researchers should collect **demographic information** that will help consumers of research "see" the participants. Example 3 lists the demographics collected for a qualitative study on the working lives of women living in a shelter due to domestic abuse. Note that these demographics were *not* a basis for selecting the women. The demographic data were collected at the onset of the study (after the participants were selected) so that the sample could be described in detail for consumers of the research.

EXAMPLE 3
Demographics of a sample: The demographic variables were: (1) age (e.g., average age was 35.4 years), (2) race/ethnicity, (3) marital status, (4) number of children, (5) highest educational level achieved, (6) type of employment, and (7) length of employment.[1]

Sometimes, qualitative researchers are silent on the issue of how their samples were selected and provide little demographic information in their research reports. For instance, they might simply say, "Fifteen male students enrolled in an introductory sociology class were interviewed." When this is encountered, it may be safe to assume that a sample of convenience (not a purposive sample) was used. This should be regarded as a flaw in sampling.

---

[1] Wettersten, K. B. et al. (2004). Freedom through self-sufficiency: A qualitative examination of the impact of domestic violence on the working lives of women in shelter. *Journal of Counseling Psychology, 51*, 447–462.

EXERCISE ON TOPIC 64

1. Is purposive sampling widely used by "qualitative researchers" *or* by "quantitative researchers"?

2. Qualitative researchers make subjective judgments regarding the individuals to select based on the likelihood of what?

3. What is the proper name for purposive sampling when there are a number of criteria to be applied in the selection of a sample?

4. Do all qualitative researchers seek diversity in their samples?

5. In a qualitative study, is the sole purpose for collecting demographic data to assist in the selection of participants?

Question for Discussion

6. Name a general topic on which a qualitative researcher might conduct research. Then, name at least four demographic variables for which it would be appropriate to collect data in light of the topic. At least two of them should be variables other than those mentioned in Example 3.

For Students Who Are Planning Research

7. If you are planning to conduct qualitative research, do you plan to use "purposive sampling" *or* "purposive criterion sampling"? Explain your choice. If you plan to use purposive criterion sampling, name some of the criteria you plan to apply.

Sometimes, qualitative researchers are interested in researching a problem that exists in a particular location or institution. For instance, they might want to understand why few women on the campus at which they teach are majoring in engineering. For such a study, sampling women only from that campus would be appropriate.

When qualitative researchers are interested in results that may have broader applications, they should seek participants from a variety of sources. For instance, college women might be solicited from several different colleges in order to study why so few major in engineering. The use of participants from *diverse sources* is a methodological strength of a qualitative study when the researcher has a broader interest than just a single source (such as a single college campus). Example 1 illustrates how one group of researchers sought participants from diverse sources for a qualitative study.

EXAMPLE 1

Obtaining participants from diverse sources: A questionnaire assessing self-handicapping and defensive pessimism (see Martin, 1998) was administered to 584 first-year education students enrolled in three universities in metropolitan Sydney (Australia). Included in the questionnaire was an invitation for students to record their names and phone numbers if they were willing to be interviewed at a later time. In total, 134 students volunteered this information.[1]

One method to obtain data from diverse sources (including a national sample) is to rent a list of names and addresses of potential participants.[2] For instance, most major professional associations, such as the American Sociological Association, will rent lists for a reasonable fee to individuals who are conducting legitimate research. Its lists are segmented so that, for instance, a list of only those who belong to a particular interest group within the organization can be rented. Example 2 illustrates the use of a rented list to reach out to diverse sources for participants.

EXAMPLE 2

Obtaining participants from diverse sources using a rented list: Participants were selected based on purposive criterion sampling from a list, purchased[3] by the research team, that consisted of professionals who had managerial positions in business, governmental, or nongovernmental organizations in a western Canadian city. The criteria for participation included....[4]

Qualitative researchers usually use fewer participants than quantitative researchers. A brief survey of sample sizes in a random sample of quantitative and qualitative research articles in five journals published by the American Psychological Association was conducted by this writer. The results of the survey are shown in Example 3.[5]

EXAMPLE 3

Sample sizes in five journals, each of which publishes both quantitative and qualitative research:

For qualitative research: Sample sizes ranged from 10 to 36, with a median (i.e., average) of 13.

For quantitative research: Sample sizes ranged from 25 to 766, with a median (i.e., average) of 82.

The major reason qualitative researchers use smaller samples than quantitative researchers is that qualitative data collection methods are often more expensive (including the expense of labor) and time-consuming than quantitative ones. For instance, a questionnaire for quantitative research can be distributed to hundreds of students in an auditorium relatively inexpensively. In contrast, individual interviews with students, each of which might last an hour or more, might make it possible to use only a dozen students, unless the researcher has major funding for the research.

---

[1] Martin, A. J., Marsh, H. W., Williamson, A., & Debus, R. L. (2003). Self-handicapping, defensive pessimism, and goal orientation: A qualitative study of university students. *Journal of Educational Psychology, 95,* 617–628.

[2] To locate specialized lists, use the term "list broker" (including the quotation marks) in a computer search using any major search engine. At the time of this writing, 80,800 Web sites for list brokers were identified by conducting such a search.

[3] While some lists can be "purchased" for unlimited use, typically they are "rented" for a specific purpose and for a specific number of times that they may be used.

[4] Iwasaki, Y., MacKay, K. J., & Ristock, J. (2004). Gender-based analyses of stress among professional managers: An exploratory qualitative study. *International Journal of Stress Management, 11,* 56–79.

[5] The journals are: *Journal of Counseling Psychology, Journal of Educational Psychology, Cultural Diversity and Ethnic Minority Psychology, American Journal of Orthopsychiatry*, and *Professional Psychology: Research and Practice*.

In addition, quantitative researchers often hope for statistically significant results using significance tests such as the *t* test. As indicated in Topic 54, the larger the sample, the more likely the results will be statistically significant. Qualitative researchers almost never test for statistical significance, and thus do not need to use large samples for this purpose.

A criterion many qualitative researchers use for determining their sample size is called **saturation**. Briefly, this is how it is applied: As the data are collected (such as while conducting interviews), the qualitative researcher conducts a preliminary, in-formal analysis, noting the major and minor themes that are emerging. At the point at which several additional participants fail to respond with new information that leads to the identification of additional themes, the researcher might conclude that the data collection process has become "saturated." At that point, no additional participants are studied because new types of information are unlikely to be obtained by increasing the sample size. Thus, the "point of saturation" may determine the final sample size.

EXERCISE ON TOPIC 65

1. Are qualitative researchers always interested in problems that extend beyond one location or institution?

2. The use of participants from *diverse sources* is a methodological strength of a qualitative study when the researcher has what?

3. How might a qualitative researcher obtain names and addresses for a national sample?

4. Based on the brief survey reported in this topic, what was the average sample size for qualitative studies?

5. Do "qualitative researchers" *or* "quantitative researchers" tend to use more expensive data collection methods?

6. At what point might a qualitative researcher conclude that the data collection process has become "saturated"?

Question for Discussion

7. Are you surprised by the results reported in Example 3 on the previous page? Explain.

For Students Who Are Planning Research

8. If you are planning to conduct qualitative research, do you plan to sample from diverse sources? Will you collect data until you reach "saturation"? Explain.

Semi-structured interviews are by far the most widely used type of instrument for collecting data for qualitative research. Typically, these are face-to-face interviews, which are often tape recorded. The obvious advantages of tape recording the interviews are that they can be examined carefully at a later date and can be examined by other researchers who are collaborating on the research project.

There should be an **interview protocol** consisting of written directions for conducting the interview as well as a standard set of predetermined questions to be asked of all participants. Ideally, the questions should be pilot-tested with at least a few individuals who will not be participants in the study. Based on the pilot test, the questions should be revised, if necessary. Also, when possible, the predetermined questions should be reviewed by experts in the area being investigated and revised as needed.

The initial questions should be designed to *establish rapport*. Example 1 shows three of the nine questions researchers asked in order to establish rapport with first-year university students at the beginning of an interview. Notice that the questions are quite general and do not deal with the direct topic of the research (i.e., self-handicapping, defensive pessimism, and goal orientation). These might also be thought of as "warm-up" questions.

EXAMPLE 1
Sample interview questions to establish rapport with first-year university students:

So now that you're at the university, what do you think?

Is the university what you expected?

Are you enjoying the university?[1]

Example 2 shows how a research team described their use of predetermined questions. Notice that they commenced with "broad, open-ended questions," followed by increasingly specific questions as the data collection progressed.

EXAMPLE 2
Use of predetermined questions in a semi-structured interview: A set of predetermined questions guided

but did not limit the conversation. Interviews were about half an hour in length and commenced with broad, open-ended questions inviting participants to describe in their own words what assisted or impeded recovery during the 6 months immediately following discharge from treatment. As data collection progressed and emerging categories became apparent, participants were asked increasingly specific questions. In addition, summary statements and reflections were frequently made to validate responses and verify accurate understanding.[2]

"Semi-structured" refers to the fact that the interviewer does not need to ask only the predetermined questions. First, if a participant does not seem to understand a question, it can be reworded by the interviewer. Second, if a response is too terse, the interviewer can ask additional questions such as "Can you tell me more about it?" Third, the interviewer can probe with additional questions (in addition to the predetermined questions) in order to explore unexpected, unusual, or especially relevant material revealed by a participant.

It is especially important that qualitative interviewers be skilled in interviewing because they are not simply following a predetermined script. This skill is acquired through practice. A novice who is planning qualitative research should conduct some practice interviews with individuals who will not be participants in the study. If possible, these practice interviews should be observed by an experienced qualitative researcher, who provides feedback to the novice.

It is also important that an interviewer be unbiased. An interviewer can achieve an unbiased attitude through the process of **self-disclosure**. This refers to considering the research problem in relation to the interviewer's background and attitudes before conducting the interviews. For instance, if a team of qualitative researchers is planning to study child-rearing practices of recent emigrants from Asia, the researchers should consciously think about how they themselves were raised, their own experiences raising children, and any attitudes they have toward Asian Americans that might predispose them to skew the interview. The purpose of self-disclosure is to "clear the air" as well as to "clear

---

[1] Martin, A. J., Marsh, H. W., Williamson, A., & Debus, R. L. (2003). Self-handicapping, defensive pessimism, and goal orientation: A qualitative study of university students. *Journal of Educational Psychology, 95*, 617–628.

[2] Cockell, S. J., Zaitsoff, S. L., & Geller, J. (2004). Maintaining change following eating disorder treatment. *Professional Psychology: Research and Practice, 35*, 527–534.

the mind" before conducting the interviews. In some published reports of qualitative research, brief summaries of the researchers' self-disclosures are described.

Note that some of the predetermined questions should ask for **demographic information** (i.e., background information such as age, highest level of education), which will allow the researchers to describe the participants in a research report.

The next topic explores additional issues in measurement in qualitative research.

EXERCISE ON TOPIC 66

1. Are semi-structured interviews widely used for collecting data in qualitative research?

2. An "interview protocol" consists of what?

3. With whom should a pilot test of the interview questions be conducted?

4. The initial questions should be designed to do what?

5. In a semi-structured interview, is it ever acceptable for an interviewer to ask questions not included in the list of predetermined questions?

6. What is the name of the process through which an interviewer can "clear the air" and "clear the mind"?

Question for Discussion

7. In your opinion, does the flexibility afforded by semi-structured interviewing open the possibility that the interviewer might bias the interview so that the interviewer obtains results along the lines that he or she already expected to find? Do you think that fully structured interviews (with only predetermined questions) might provide more valid data?

For Students Who Are Planning Research

8. If you are planning to conduct qualitative research, do you consider yourself to be a "novice"? If yes, how do you plan to gain experience before conducting your research? Explain.

Basic characteristics of semi-structured interviews are described in the previous topic. This topic explores some additional issues regarding them and then describes other measurement methods used in qualitative research.

The use of interview data to explore complex issues raises the issue of "reality." For instance, when participants describe how they were treated in some situation, the interview primarily exposes how participants "perceive" these matters. To many quantitative empiricists, *perception* is important but may not be as important as "reality." To most qualitative researchers, however, "objective factual reality"[1] is not as interesting or informative as participants' perceptions. Examining perceptions is known as a **phenomenological approach** to acquiring knowledge. Almost all qualitative researchers are in some sense "phenomenologists."[2,3]

In addition to one-on-one semi-structured interviews, qualitative researchers sometimes use **focus groups**. A focus group usually consists of six to twelve participants who are gathered to discuss a topic. The group is led by a **facilitator**,[4] as opposed to an "interviewer." The facilitator describes the topic to be discussed and tries to create a nonthreatening environment in which all group members feel free to express their opinions, attitudes, and experiences even if they differ from those of other participants. The facilitator should have a predetermined set of questions (also known as a "questioning route") to ensure that all relevant aspects of the topic are discussed. In addition, the facilitator should probe for additional information when needed.

Typically, a focus group lasts for about an hour. Also, it is typical to use two or more focus groups in a given research project.

A clear advantage of using focus groups is that it reveals *the evolution of perceptions in a social context*. It is interesting to note that the focus group method began as a business marketing research tool when marketing researchers realized that the perceptions of an individual in isolation may be different from their perceptions as they develop in a social context. For instance, a new product that initially seems satisfactory to an individual may be seen as less desirable after discussing it with other individuals who may have different perspectives on it.

Example 1 shows a brief description of how data were collected using the focus group method in a study on stress.

EXAMPLE 1
Description of data collection using focus groups:
The moderator followed a focus group questioning route…developed by the research team and guided by the research objectives. The questioning route outlined opening comments about the topic of stress, introductory questions to engage the participants in the topic, transition questions related to evaluations of stress, key questions on the causes of stress and coping strategies, and ending questions to summarize the discussions and confirm main points…. At each stage of questioning, the moderator gave sufficient time for all the participants to share their views….[5]

Appendix F at the end of this book shows the "question route" used by the authors of Example 1. Notice that the questions in the appendix move logically from broad to more specific questions, with the exception of the "ending questions," which are broad.

Although it is widely discussed in research methodology textbooks, the use of direct, physical observation is seldom used in published qualitative research reports in the social and behavioral sciences. Nevertheless, direct observation can provide valuable data. In qualitative observational studies, an important distinction is made between **nonparticipant observation** and **participant observation**. In *nonparticipant observation*, the qualitative researcher observes individuals as an outsider such as

---

[1] Both qualitative and quantitative researchers realize that "objective factual reality" is elusive. The distinction here is in whether the researchers strive to obtain it.

[2] Both qualitative and quantitative researchers are interested in "perceptions." The distinction here is in the degree to which the two types of researchers rely on perceptions for understanding a research topic.

[3] A full discussion of these issues is beyond the scope of this book. However, it is helpful to consider a trial in a court of law, in which a jury attempts to determine the reality of a situation, often relying heavily on witnesses' perceptions and recollections as well as any physical evidence.

[4] Facilitators are also sometimes called **moderators**.

[5] Iwasaki, Y., MacKay, K. J., & Ristock, J. (2004). Gender-based analyses of stress among professional managers: An exploratory qualitative study. *International Journal of Stress Management, 11*, 56–79.

by sitting at the back of a classroom to observe student/teacher interactions. A particular concern with this type of observation is that the participants' behavior may change from its normal course because the participants know they are being observed.

In *participant observation*, the researcher becomes (or already is) a member of the group being researched, and thus makes his or her observations as an insider. For instance, a teacher who is also a researcher who wants to study a high school that is widely known for academic achievement might arrange to teach at the school, providing an opportunity to observe while participating. Note that making participant observations without revealing to those who are being observed that research is being conducted may raise serious ethical problems.

Researchers who use observational methods often refer to their research as **field research**, which has historical roots in the field of anthropology. When the focus is on cultural issues, the research may be referred to as **ethnography**.

EXERCISE ON TOPIC 67

1. Examining perceptions is known as what type of "approach" to acquiring knowledge?

2. A focus group usually consists of about how many participants?

3. What are the two names for the individual who leads a focus group?

4. According to this topic, what is a "clear advantage" of using focus groups?

5. What is the name of the type of observation in which the researcher observes as an outsider?

6. When the emphasis in field research is on cultural issues, the research may be referred to as what?

Question for Discussion

7. Do you think that it would be easier to analyze and interpret data from "individual interviews" *or* from "focus group discussions"? Explain.

For Students Who Are Planning Research

8. If you are planning to conduct qualitative research, do you anticipate using focus groups? Explain.

This topic describes some of the specific techniques that qualitative researchers use to establish the dependability and trustworthiness of their data.[1]

One technique is to use multiple sources for obtaining data on the research topic. The technical name for this is **data triangulation**. For instance, for a qualitative study of discrimination in an employment setting, a researcher might interview employees, their supervisors, and the responsible personnel officers. To the extent that the various sources provide similar information, the data can be said to be corroborated through data triangulation.

The methods used to collect data can also be triangulated. For instance, a researcher might conduct individual interviews with parents regarding their child-rearing practices and then have the same participants provide data via focus groups. This would be an example of **methods triangulation**.

Note that in *data triangulation*, typically two or more types of participants (such as employees and supervisors) are used to collect data on a research topic. In contrast, in *methods triangulation*, only one type of participant (such as parents) is used to provide data, but two or more methods are used to collect the data.

An important technique to assure the quality of qualitative research is to form a *research team*, with each member of the team participating in the collection and analysis of data. This can be thought of as **researcher triangulation**, which reduces the possibility that the results of qualitative research represent only the idiosyncratic views of one individual researcher.

Sometimes, it is helpful to form a **team of researchers with diverse backgrounds**. For instance, for a study on the success of minority students in medical school, a team of researchers that consists of both medical school instructors and medical school students might strengthen the study by providing more than one perspective when collecting and analyzing the data.

The issue of having diversity in a research team is addressed in Example 1, which is from a qualitative research report on gender issues. The researchers point out that gender diversity in their research team helps to provide a "comprehensive view."

EXAMPLE 1
Diversity in a research team: Gender and sexuality issues were analyzed by all three researchers. That our research team included one man and two women probably helped us have a comprehensive view of the different meanings of gender issues.[2]

Oral interviews and focus groups are typically audiotaped and then transcribed. Sometimes, transcription is difficult because some participants might not speak distinctly. In addition, transcribers sometimes make errors. Therefore, checking the accuracy of a transcription helps to ensure the quality of the data. In Example 2, a sample of segments was checked.

EXAMPLE 2
Checking the accuracy of transcriptions: Each audiotaped session was transcribed verbatim. Segments of the transcriptions were checked randomly against the audiotapes for accuracy.[3]

In the analysis of data, which is covered in the next two topics in more detail, each member of a research team should initially work independently (without consulting each other) and then compare the results of their analyses. To the extent that they agree, the results are dependable. This technique examines what is called **interobserver agreement**.[4] When there are disagreements, often they can be resolved by having the researchers discuss their differences until they reach a consensus. This process is described in more detail in Topic 70.

The use of an outside expert can also help to ensure the quality of the research. A researcher's peer (such as another experienced qualitative researcher) can examine the process used to collect data, the resulting data and the conclusions, and then provide feedback to the researcher. This process is called **peer review**. Under certain circumstances, the peer

---

[1] The terms "dependability" and "trustworthiness" in qualitative research loosely correspond to the terms "reliability" and "validity" in quantitative research.

[2] Rasera, E. F., Vieira, E. M., & Japur, M. (2004). Influence of gender and sexuality on the construction of being HIV positive as experienced in a support group in Brazil. *Families, Systems, & Health, 22*, 340–351.

[3] Lukens, E. P., Thorning, H., & Lohrer, S. (2004). Sibling perspectives on severe mental illness: Reflections on self and family. *American Journal of Orthopsychiatry, 74*, 489–501.

[4] In qualitative research, this is sometimes called *intercoder agreement*. In quantitative research, this concept is called *interobserver reliability*.

who provides the review is called an **auditor**, which is discussed in Topic 70.

The dependability of the results can also be enhanced by a process called **member checking**. This term is based on the idea that the participants are "members" of the research team. By having the participants/members review the results of the analysis, researchers can determine whether their results "ring true" to the participants. If not, adjustments can be made in the description of the results.

EXERCISE ON TOPIC 68

1. Suppose a researcher interviewed participants and then observed the behavior of the same participants. Is this an example of "data triangulation" *or* an example of "methods triangulation"?

2. In data triangulation, how many types of participants are used?

3. What is the name of the type of triangulation that reduces the possibility that the results of qualitative research represent only the idiosyncratic views of one individual researcher?

4. Is it ever desirable for a team of researchers to consist of individuals with diverse backgrounds?

5. In "peer review," what is a peer?

6. Who are the "members" in "member checking"?

Question for Discussion

7. Name a research topic for qualitative research for which it might be helpful to have a team of researchers with diverse backgrounds. Explain why it might be helpful for the research topic you name.

For Students Who Are Planning Research

8. If you are planning to conduct qualitative research, which of the techniques described in this topic, if any, do you plan to use? Explain your choice(s).

To guide their data analysis, qualitative researchers usually select a general, overarching approach. Perhaps the most frequently used approach is **grounded theory**. At first, the term "theory" in "grounded theory" can be a bit misleading because it does not refer to an existing theory of human behavior. Instead, it refers to an *inductive method* of analysis that can lead to theories of behavior. In the inductive approach, which is characteristic of all qualitative research, the results (including resulting "theories") emerge through consideration and analysis of the data. In other words, qualitative researchers start with the data and develop theories based on the data (i.e., grounded in the data). In contrast, many quantitative researchers start with an existing theory or deduce a new one from existing information and collect data to test the theory; they typically do not look to the data they have collected to develop new theories. Thus, quantitative researchers use a *deductive method*.

To put it more simply, quantitative researchers deduce theories from what is known and test the theories with research. In contrast, qualitative researchers collect data and analyze it in order to derive theories that explain the patterns noted in the responses of participants. In their seminal work on how to use the grounded theory approach, Strauss and Corbin said:

> It is through careful scrutiny of data, line by line, that researchers are able to uncover new concepts and novel relationships and to systematically develop categories in terms of their properties and dimensions.[1]

The grounded theory approach starts with **open coding**. In this stage, segments of the transcripts of the interviews are examined for distinct, separate segments (such as ideas or experiences of the participants) and are "coded" by identifying them and giving each type a name. For instance, in a study of adolescent delinquents, each statement referring to overt aggression by the participant might be coded with a certain color highlighter. Subcategories should also be developed, when possible. For instance, "overt aggression" might have two subcategories: "overt aggression toward peers" and "overt

aggression toward adults, including parents and teachers."[2] Preliminary notes on any overarching themes noticed in the data should also be made at this point.

The second step in the grounded theory approach to data analysis is called **axial coding**. At this stage, the transcripts of the interviews and any other data sources, such as memos written during data collection, are reexamined with the purpose of identifying relationships between the categories and themes identified during open coding. Some important types of relationships that might be noted are (1) temporal (X usually precedes Y in time), (2) causal (X caused participants to do Y),[3] (3) associational (X and Y usually or always occur at about the same time but are not believed to be causally connected), (4) valence (participants have stronger emotional reactions to X than to Y), and (5) spatial (X and Y occur in the same place *or* X and Y occur in different places).

In the final stages of the grounded theory approach to analysis, qualitative researchers develop a **core category**, which is the main overarching category under which the other categories and subcategories belong. They also attempt to describe the *process* that leads to the relationships identified in the previous stage of the analysis. A process description should describe how the categories work together (or in opposition to each other) in order to arrive at the conditions or behaviors contained in the core category.

A key element throughout the analysis of data using the grounded theory approach is **constant comparison**, which is a technical term that refers to constantly comparing each new element of the data with all previous elements that have been coded in order to establish and refine categories. While this is being done, the analysis focuses on similarities

---

[1] Strauss, A. L., and Corbin, J. (1998). *Basics of Qualitative Research: Techniques and Procedures for Developing Grounded Theory* (2nd ed.). Thousand Oaks, CA: Sage.

[2] In keeping with the inductive approach, categories and subcategories should be suggested by the data during data analysis, not developed prior to analyzing the data. Categories and subcategories developed at this stage should be regarded as preliminary and subject to change during the remainder of the analysis using the grounded theory approach.

[3] Participants' claims that "X caused me to do Y" should be viewed with caution because participants sometimes are not sufficiently insightful into the causes of their behavior.

and differences in the data that might be accounted
for by a core idea.

EXERCISE ON TOPIC 69

1. In the term "grounded theory," does the term "theory" refer to a theory that existed prior to conducting the research?

2. Does the grounded theory approach use the "inductive approach" *or* does it use the "deductive approach"?

3. The grounded theory approach starts with what type of coding?

4. What is the name of the second step in the grounded theory approach?

5. In which type of coding is there an emphasis on identifying relationships?

6. What is the technical term that refers to constantly comparing each new element of the data with all previous elements that have been coded in order to establish and refine categories?

Question for Discussion

7. Do you think that the inductive approach (such as grounded theory) *or* the deductive approach (such as quantitative research) is more likely to yield important information? Are they equally likely to do so? Explain.

For Students Who Are Planning Research

8. If you are planning to conduct qualitative research, do you anticipate using the grounded theory approach? Explain. How prepared do you feel to use it? If poorly prepared, how do you plan to learn more about it?

Topic 70 Consensual Qualitative Research: Analysis

As indicated in the previous topic, qualitative researchers usually select a general, overarching approach to the analysis of their data. In the previous topic, the grounded theory approach was described. In this topic, **consensual qualitative research (CQR)** is described.[1] Like all qualitative research, both approaches are *inductive* (see the previous topic for a discussion of the differences between the inductive and deductive approaches).

As its name implies, CQR strives to have a team of researchers arrive at a consensus on the meaning of the data collected (such as interview transcripts).

The first step in the CQR method is to **code into domains**. This refers to segmenting the data (such as interview transcripts) into groups according to the topics they cover. After each member of the research team has done this, they meet and discuss and refine the domains until they reach unanimous agreement on them.

The next step is to **develop core ideas within domains**. This is done by writing short summaries (i.e., abstracts) that reduce the original ideas of participants into fewer words. Notice that initially, the researchers work independently in developing core ideas.

The third step in CQR is called **cross-analysis**. In this step, the core ideas are grouped into categories based on similarities. This results in a higher level of generalization (i.e., the results are becoming less specific and more general).

Example 1 shows how one team of researchers described the above three steps.

Example 1
Description of the use of CQR by a research team:
...the consensual qualitative research (CQR) method was developed by Hill et al. (1997) with the understanding that complex issues discussed during interviews often involve "multiple perspectives and levels of awareness" (p. 523). Consequently, CQR requires that researchers on a team openly discuss any ambiguities in meanings that may exist in the data obtained during the interviews. This open discussion allows for clarification and often promotes more accurate conceptualizations of the data. CQR directs researchers to group data into domains (clusters of similar topics), constructs core ideas (summaries of

domain content), and conducts cross-analyses (identification of the themes in the core ideas across the cases) to determine the categories in which the core ideas fit.[2]

In CQR, there may be an external **stability check**, which can be done by examining data in addition to the interview transcripts (perhaps eyewitness accounts or physical evidence), if available.

Internal stability is examined in CQR by determining the extent to which each category was general, typical, or variant. Typically, domains that apply to all the participants are called **general**; those that apply to half or more of the participants are called **typical**; and those that apply to less than half but more than two participants are called **variant**. When writing up the results, researchers who use CQR usually use these labels throughout their results sections. Emphasis on enumerating the number of participants to which each domain applies is a distinctive feature of CQR. Example 2 shows a portion of the results section of a CQR study in which there is enumeration.

Example 2
Enumeration in the results of a CQR study (bold added for emphasis):
Results for European American therapists yielded one **typical** and two **variant categories** (neither of the variant categories emerged for the African American sample). As a **typical category**, these participants stated that, like their African American counterparts, they would address race when they deemed it relevant to the therapy process or relationship.... In the first **variant category**, these participants reported that if a client raised the topic of race, the therapist would respond....[3]

The CQR method requires the use of an **auditor**, who is an outside expert. The auditor usually reviews the work of the research team after each major step in a study, not just at its conclusion. In a

---

[1] For more information on CQR, see Hill, C. E., Thompson, B. J., & Williams, E. N. (1997). A guide to conducting consensual qualitative research. *The Counseling Psychologist, 25,* 517–572.

[2] DiGiorgio, K. E., Arnkoff, D. B., Glass, C. R., Lyhus, K. E., & Walter, R. C. (2004). EMDR and theoretical orientation: A qualitative study of how therapists integrate eye movement desensitization and reprocessing into their approach to psychotherapy. *Journal of Psychotherapy Integration, 14,* 227–252.

[3] Knox, S., Burkard, A. W., Johnson, A. J., Suzuki, L. A., & Ponterotto, J. G. (2003). African American and European American therapists' experiences of addressing race in cross-racial psychotherapy dyads. *Journal of Counseling Psychology, 50,* 466–481.

report on a CQR study, the following should be briefly described: the credentials of the auditor, the steps at which the auditor supplied feedback, and whether changes were made on the basis of the auditor's feedback. If changes were made, the types of changes made should be mentioned.

EXERCISE ON TOPIC 70

1. "Unlike the grounded theory approach in Topic 69, CQR is *deductive*." Is this statement true *or* false?

2. What is the first step in analyzing data using the CQR approach?

3. Which step includes writing short summaries of participants' ideas?

4. What is done in the cross-analysis?

5. In CQR, what term is used for domains that apply to all the participants?

6. Does the auditor review the work of the research team only at the conclusion of the study?

Question for Discussion

7. Do you think that CQR (as you understand it from this topic) is likely to produce studies that yield important and valuable information? Explain.

For Students Who Are Planning Research

8. If you are planning to conduct qualitative research, do you anticipate using CQR? Explain. How prepared do you feel to use it? If poorly prepared, how do you plan to learn more about it?

PART I

PREPARING RESEARCH REPORTS

This part of the book provides an overview of how to structure a research report as well as a discussion of the differences in reporting the results of quantitative and qualitative research. Note that variations will be found in published research reports. This part summarizes the common elements found in most such reports.

NOTES

TOPIC 71   THE STRUCTURE OF A RESEARCH REPORT

This topic describes the structure of a typical research report.

The first element is the **title**. A typical title is concise, consisting of about 10 to 15 words, and should name the major variable(s). Populations of special interest may also be mentioned in a title. In Example 1, the variables are "political activism" and "socioeconomic status," and the population consists of Asian American voters.

EXAMPLE 1
Title of a research report: The Relationship Between Political Activism and Socioeconomic Status Among Asian American Voters

The title is usually followed by an **abstract**, which is a brief summary, typically containing 100 to 150 words. A straightforward abstract starts with a statement of the research purpose, followed by (1) a very brief description of methods (e.g., a national survey of Asian American voters), (2) any highly distinctive characteristics of the study (e.g., the first survey on the topic to distinguish among various Asian nationalities), and (3) a summary of the general nature of the results. Sometimes an abstract concludes with a statement of the practical implications of the results. Appendix G shows three effective abstracts. Note that they differ somewhat from the recommendations made here, which is permissible. Also note that the authors of the third abstract used subheadings (in bold and italics) within their abstract, which is also permissible.

The abstract is followed by a **literature review**, which also serves as an introduction to the research. (See Part B of this book on reviewing literature).[1] The literature review should end with an explicit statement of the research purposes, questions, or hypotheses. Note that these should flow logically from the literature reviewed. In other words, the literature review should establish the context and serve as a "setup" for the purposes, questions, or hypotheses.

Following the combined introduction/literature review is the Method section, which usually has its own major heading of **Method** (bold and centered). Immediately under this heading is the subheading *Participants* (in italics and flush left). Under this subheading, researchers state (1) the number of participants, (2) the criteria for their inclusion (e.g., only Asian Americans who had voted in the last election), and (3) how they were selected and recruited (e.g., a random sample of registered voters contacted via mail). Any difficulties in recruitment/selection (e.g., only 42% returned the mailed surveys) should also be mentioned.

The next subsection under Method is *Instrumentation* (with its own flush-left subheading). If published instruments were used, they should be named and what is known of their validity and reliability (see Part D of this book) should be briefly summarized. If new instruments were devised for the research, the methods used in their development should be indicated. Regardless of whether published or newly devised instruments were used, it is usually desirable to provide sample items or questions (e.g., responding Strongly Agree to Strongly Disagree to 15 statements such as "I regard it as my duty as a citizen to vote.").

An optional subsection under the main heading of Method is *Procedure*. This subsection should follow *Instrumentation* and be used to describe any crucial steps taken by the researcher to conduct the research. For instance, if treatments were given in an experiment, the treatments could be described in detail in this subsection.

An additional optional subsection under the main heading of Method is *Data Analysis*, in which the method used to analyze the data is described. As indicated in the next topic, this subsection is most likely to be included by researchers reporting on qualitative research.

The next major heading is **Results** (bold and centered). Considerations in presenting the results of research are described in the next topic.

The final major heading is **Discussion** (bold and centered).[2] In long, complex research reports, the discussion might begin with a summary of the purposes and findings of the research. In addition to a possible summary, most discussions cover one or more of the following: (1) the interpretation of any unexpected findings (i.e., speculation on the reasons for them), (2) an acknowledgment of any limitations of the methods used in the research process

---

[1] In a traditional thesis or dissertation, Chapter 1 is an introduction to the research problem (with a limited number of citations to literature), while Chapter 2 is a literature review.

[2] In journal articles, some researchers use headings such as "**Discussion and Conclusions**" and "**Summary, Discussion, and Implications**."

(e.g., weaknesses in sampling) that should be taken into account in interpreting the results, (3) implications (i.e., what actions should be considered in light of the results), and (4) suggestions for future research.

A reference list concludes the report. (See Topic 19 for information on citing references.)

In outline form, here are the major components of a research report, as described above:

```
                Title
              Abstract
    Introduction/Literature Review
               Method
   Participants
   Instrumentation
   Procedure (optional)
   Data Analysis (optional)
               Results
             Discussion
             References
```

EXERCISE ON TOPIC 71

1. The title is usually followed by what?

2. An abstract typically contains how many words?

3. The literature review should end with an explicit statement of what?

4. Is "Participants" a "major heading" or a "subheading"?

5. Regardless of whether published or newly devised instruments were used, it is desirable to provide what?

6. Which subsection(s) under the main heading of Method is(are) optional?

7. An acknowledgment of weakness in research methodology should be provided in which section of a research report?

Question for Discussion

8. Examine the three abstracts in Appendix G. Note that the third one has subheadings within the abstract. In your opinion, are the subheadings helpful? Would the abstract be as effective without the subheadings? Explain.

For Students Who Are Planning Research

9. Examine a research article related to the topic for your research. Does it follow the *exact* structure described in this topic? Explain. (Note: This topic describes common practices frequently followed by researchers; variations in structure are often permitted by journal editors.)

TOPIC 72 REPORTING RESEARCH RESULTS

As indicated in the previous topic, the Results section should have a main heading of **Results** (bold and centered).

For research that has more than one research hypothesis, purpose, or question, it is usually best to report the results for each one separately and in the order in which they were first presented in the research report. For instance, if there were two hypotheses, restate the first one and present the data for it. Then, restate the second hypothesis and present the data for the second one.

In reports on *quantitative research*, researchers typically do not indicate how the statistical results were computed (e.g., they do not name the statistical computer program used) and they do not provide a reference for standard statistical formulas. For instance, a researcher would simply report the means and standard deviations relating to a hypothesis without discussing computational details. In these reports, descriptive statistics (e.g., mean, standard deviation, and percentage) should be reported first, followed by the results of tests of statistical significance (e.g., chi-square, t test, and ANOVA). This is illustrated in Example 1. Note that when there are hypotheses, the research should explicitly state whether the hypothesis was supported by the data.

EXAMPLE 1
Beginning of the Results section in a quantitative research report:

The first hypothesis was that participants who attended the extended training sessions would report more satisfaction with the program than those who attended the abbreviated session. The mean satisfaction score for the extended group was higher ($m = 24.00$, $sd = 1.50$) than the mean for the abbreviated group ($m = 22.00$, $sd = 1.40$). The difference between the two means is statistically significant at the .05 level ($t = 3.30$, $df = 21$). Thus, the first hypothesis was supported.

The second hypothesis was that participants....

When there are a number of related statistics to be reported, it is usually best to present them in a table (instead of reporting them in sentences). Example 2 shows a table with a number of descriptive statistics. Highlights of the contents of statistical tables should be described in the Results section with statements such as "The means in Table 2 show that the supervised practice group outperformed the unsupervised practice and control groups."

EXAMPLE 2
Table 2
Posttest Statistics for Three Groups

Group	n	m	sd
Supervised practice	21	55.78	8.27
Unsupervised practice	20	49.02	7.66
Control group	22	46.35	9.36

The Results sections for *qualitative research* differ from those for quantitative research in a number of respects. First, in reports on qualitative research, there is usually a discussion of the steps taken to analyze the data (such as the results of semi-structured interviews), usually under the subheading *Data Analysis* (see the outline at the end of the previous topic).[1] Here, the method of analysis (such as grounded theory or consensual qualitative research) should be named and the steps taken to implement the method (e.g., how many coders were used and how a consensus was reached) should be described. This should include a description of what steps were taken to ensure the dependability and trustworthiness of the results of the analysis (see Topic 68 on quality control in qualitative research).

In the Results section of reports on qualitative research, there are usually few, if any, statistics reported. Instead, qualitative researchers discuss the primary themes that emerged from the data as well as any theories developed during the analysis. Example 3 shows the beginning of the Results section of a qualitative research report. Note that each of the themes mentioned in the example was used as a subheading within the Results section. Under each subheading, the researchers described the theme and illustrated it with verbatim quotations from participants to illustrate the meaning of the theme.

EXAMPLE 3
Beginning of the Results section for a qualitative research report:[2]

In this study we investigated the questions: What is collaborative health care? What occurs? and How

---

[1] This subsection seldom appears in reports on quantitative research when standard statistical methods are employed.
[2] Todahl, J. L., Linville, D., Smith, T. E., Barnes, M. F., & Miller, J. K. (2006). A qualitative study of collaborative health care in a primary care setting. *Families, Systems, & Health*, 24, 45–64.

167

is it experienced? Qualitative data analysis produced six cultural themes: (a) characteristics of the environment, (b) characteristics of therapists, (c) the referral process, (d) characteristics of collaboration, (e) the psychotherapy process, and (f) social considerations. Taken together, they describe, at least in part, how collaborative health care is practiced at this site. The content and meaning of each cultural theme will be described via a summarized version of patient, therapist, physician, and staff statements.

Because statistics can be used to very concisely summarize quantitative data, the Results sections of reports on quantitative research tend to be much shorter than the Results sections of qualitative research reports.

EXERCISE ON TOPIC 72

1. For research that has more than one research hypothesis, purpose, or question, is it usually best to report the results for each one separately and, if so, in what order?

2. In reports on *quantitative research*, do researchers typically indicate how the statistical results were computed (e.g., do they name the statistical computer program used)?

3. Should "descriptive statistics" *or* "results of tests of statistical significance" be reported first?

4. When statistical tables are included in a Results section, which of the following is true?
   A. The tables should be presented without commentary.
   B. Highlights of the contents of statistical tables should be mentioned.

5. Is a subsection titled Data Analysis more likely to appear in reports on "quantitative research" *or* "qualitative research"?

6. Are verbatim quotations more likely to appear in reports on "quantitative research" *or* "qualitative research"?

7. Do reports on "quantitative research" *or* "qualitative research" tend to have shorter results sections?

Questions for Discussion

8. If you have access to a published report on quantitative research, examine it to answer these questions: Are statistics reported in tables? If yes, does the researcher describe the highlights of the results in the tables? Does the researcher discuss how he/she computed the statistics (e.g., give formulas and citations for them)?

9. If you have access to a published report on qualitative research, examine it to answer these questions: Is the Results section organized around themes? Does the Results section contain verbatim quotations from participants? If yes, are there many quotations?

For Students Who Are Planning Research

10. Examine a research article related to the topic for your research. Is the organization of the Results section in the article similar to the organization you plan to use? Explain.

APPENDIX A
ELECTRONIC DATABASES FOR LOCATING LITERATURE

Access Note

Access to all the following electronic databases can usually be obtained free of charge through your college or university library, which probably maintains license agreements with the database publishers. Consult with your reference librarian for information on their availability at your library. Note that the *ERIC* database and *MEDLINE* database are available free of charge to all individuals via the Internet.

Databases Discussed in Topic 15

The *ERIC* database contains more than one million abstracts of unpublished documents and published journal articles on educational research and practice. The *AskERIC* version of the database can be accessed on the Internet free of charge by any individual. A unique, free feature of this database is the "Ask an ERIC Expert" feature, which allows users to pose free-form questions and receive information based on bibliographic sources in response. Visit www.eric.ed.gov for more information.

PsycINFO indexes and abstracts journal articles from more than 1,800 journals, which constitute more than 77% of the database. Books, dissertations, and university and government reports are also included. An online thesaurus is available. Members of the public can access this database via the Internet for a daily service charge (charged to a credit card) at www.apa.org. Consult with the reference librarian at your college or university for information on accessing this database free of charge through your library's license agreement.

PsycARTICLES (a database that is related to *PsycINFO*) contains more than 3,100 full-text articles (not just abstracts) from more than 50 journals and selected chapters from books published by the American Psychological Association. Members of the public can access this database via the Internet for a daily service charge (charged to a credit card) at www.apa.org. Consult with the reference librarian at your college or university for information on accessing this database free of charge through your library's license agreement.

Sociological Abstracts indexes and abstracts (i.e., summarizes) articles in 1,800 international journals, and indexes and abstracts books and chapters in books. *Sociological Abstracts* indexes dissertations, book reviews, film reviews, and game reviews. An online thesaurus is available. Consult with the reference librarian at your college or university for information on accessing this database free of charge through your library's license agreement.

Other Electronic Databases

The *ABI/Inform* (*ProQuest*) database is a business and management database with abstracts and many full-text articles from over 1,000 U.S. and international publications. Topics include advertising, marketing, economics, human resources, finance, taxation, and computers.

The *Chicano Database* identifies all types of material about Chicanos. It incorporates the *Spanish Speaking Mental Health Database*, which covers psychological, sociological, and educational literature. Also included (1992 to the present) are the broader Latino experiences of Puerto Ricans, Cuban Americans, and Central American immigrants.

Child Development Abstracts and Bibliography includes abstracts from professional periodicals and book reviews related to the growth and development of children from 1927 to the present. It is divided into seven sections: biology, health, and medicine; cognition, learning, and perception; education; psychiatry and clinical psychology; social psychology and personality; theory, methodology, and book reviews; and book notices.

Contemporary Women's Issues provides full-text access to journals, hard-to-find newsletters, reports, pamphlets, fact sheets, and guides on a broad array of gender-related issues published since 1992.

Criminal Justice Periodical Index contains full-text articles from criminology and criminal justice journal articles on law enforcement, corrections administration, social work, drug rehabilitation, criminal and family law, industrial security, and other related fields. There is also indexing and abstracts for 150 U.S. and international journals.

Dissertation Abstracts Online is a definitive subject, title, and author guide to virtually every American dissertation accepted at an accredited institution since 1861. Selected master's theses have been included since 1962. The electronic version indexes doctoral records from July 1980 (*Dissertation Abstracts International*, Volume 41, Number 1) to the present. Abstracts are included for master's theses from Spring 1988 (*Master's Abstracts*, Volume 26, Number 1) to the present. This database has very wide subject matter coverage including, but not limited to, business and economics, education, fine arts and music, geography, health sciences, political science, language and literature, library and information science, psychology, and sociology.

Family Studies contains citations and abstracts for journal articles, books, popular literature, conference papers, and government reports in the fields of family science, human ecology, and human development since 1970.

International Index to Black Periodicals Full Text (*IIBP Full Text*) draws its current content from more than 150 international scholarly and popular periodicals. It covers a wide array of humanities-related disciplines including art, cultural criticism, economics, education, health, history, language and literature, law, philosophy, politics, religion, and sociology, among others. All records in the current file (1998 forward) contain abstracts.

MEDLINE is the National Library of Medicine's (NLM) premier bibliographic database covering the fields of medicine, nursing, dentistry, veterinary medicine, the health care system, and the preclinical sciences. *MEDLINE*, the primary subset of *PubMed*, is available on the Internet through the NLM home page at http://www.nlm.nih.gov and can be searched free of charge. No registration is required. Additional *MEDLINE* services are also provided by organizations that lease the database from NLM. Access to various *MEDLINE* services is often available from medical libraries and many public libraries.

Social Sciences Citation Index (*SSCI*®) and *Social SciSearch*® provide access to current and retrospective bibliographic information, author abstracts, and cited references found in over 1,700 of the world's leading scholarly social science journals covering more than 50 disciplines. They also cover individually selected, relevant items from approximately 3,300 of the world's leading science and technology journals. Note that the *Citation Index* lists cited authors and their works together with all authors who have discussed the cited works in their publications. This can be very helpful in conducting a literature search if a researcher starts with a classic older article that is highly relevant to the topic. By searching for all publications in which it was subsequently cited, the researcher can quickly build a collection of references that are likely to be very specific to the topic. Examining these sequentially permits the researcher to trace the history of thought on a topic or theory.

APPENDIX B

ELECTRONIC SOURCES OF STATISTICAL INFORMATION[1]

When writing literature reviews, writers need up-to-date information. Because of the ease of electronic publishing, the Web usually has more up-to-date information than conventionally printed materials. (Note that it is not uncommon for a journal article or book to be published a year after it was written.)

It is often a good idea to begin literature reviews with current statistics on how many individuals (and/or the percentage of individuals) have a certain characteristic or a particular problem. Suppose, for instance, that the general topic for a literature review is cigarette smoking by pregnant women. Examine Box A, which shows two possible first sentences for a review. The second one, which cites current statistics found on the Web, is stronger and more compelling than the first one.[2]

BOX A
The beginning of two possible first paragraphs for a literature review. The second one cites recent statistics found on the Web.

> 1. Many pregnant women continue to smoke despite warnings from the medical community. This makes it important to review literature to identify effective programs that....
>
> 2. Approximately 17 percent of pregnant women smoked cigarettes within the last month, according to a recent national survey (NHSDA, 1999).[3] This makes it important to review literature to identify...effective programs that....

Even if you do not begin your literature review with statistics, including specific statistics (e.g., "5,421 students" and "55.6% of the students") at some point in your literature review will make it more convincing than a review in which only vague references to statistics are made (e.g., "many individuals" and "a majority").

Note that many sources on the Web post the latest available information, which may not be completely up-to-date. For instance, the information in Box A was the most current available (for 1999) when retrieved for use in this book. Nevertheless, a journal article or book published in 1999 would probably contain even older statistics given the publication lag in conventional, hard-copy publishing.

Note that Web addresses (i.e., URLs) frequently change, Web sites are often discontinued, and access that might be free at the time of this writing might not be free by the time you try to access them. If you have difficulties locating Web sites given in this book, use a general search engine such as www.Google.com to locate newer sites, additional free sites, and so on.

✎ Guideline 1 FedStats is a very important source of statistical information.

At www.FedStats.gov, you will be able to access statistics from more than 100 Federal agencies.[4] Prior to establishment of this Web site, writers needed to search for statistics agency by agency. While the FedStats site still allows you to do this, you can also search by *topic* and the FedStats search engine will automatically search all agencies for relevant links to federal statistics. This is important for two reasons: (1) you do not have to search each agency separately and (2) an agency that you are not aware of may have statistics relevant to your topic.

For example, conducting a search by first clicking on Topic links – A to Z produced a screen with the letters of the alphabet underlined. (As you may know, Web links to other sites are usually underlined and/or are sometimes identifiable by other means such as the use of a different color, such as blue, for a link.) By click-

---

[1] This appendix was adapted from Chapter 4 of *Preparing Literature Reviews*: *Qualitative and Quantitative Approaches* (2nd ed.) by M. Ling Pan (pp. 33–38). Copyright © 2004 by Pyrczak Publishing. All rights reserved.
[2] Using simple, compelling statistics is appropriate in both qualitative and quantitative reviews.
[3] Retrieved at http://www.samhsa.gov/oas/2k2/PregAlcTob/PregAlcTob.htm on September 19, 2002.
[4] Be sure to go to www.FedStats.*gov* and *not* www.FedStats.*com*. The latter is *not* a government site.

ing on the letter <u>C</u>, the extensive set of links shown in Box B was obtained. By clicking on the <u>Breast</u> link (the second link from the top), the links in Box C were obtained.

Box B
FedStats links for the letter C.

Cancer:
-- *Atlas of Cancer Mortality in the United States*
-- Breast
-- Cervical
-- Lung
-- Mortality maps
-- Prostate
Charitable trusts
Children:
-- Administration for Children programs and services
-- Adoption
-- *America's Children* (ChildStats)
-- Behavior and social environment indicators
-- Child care
-- Child support enforcement
-- Cigarette smoking
-- Delinquency and victimization
   -- Delinquency case records (data and analysis software
     package)
   -- Juvenile arrests
   -- Juveniles as offenders
   -- Juveniles as victims
   -- Juveniles in court
   -- Juveniles in detention and corrections
-- Drug use
-- Economic security indicators
-- Education indicators
-- Foster care
-- HeadStart
-- Temporary Assistance for Needy Families
Health:
-- Child and infant
-- Indicators
-- Insurance
-- Population and family characteristics
-- Nutrition
-- WIC
Civil justice statistics
Coal
Commodity flow
Common cold
Communications:
-- Broadcast radio and television
-- Cable television providers by community served (size 9M)
-- Telephone industry and telephone usage
-- Wireless communications services
Computer and Internet use
Construction
Industry tax statistics:
-- Corporations
-- Exempt organizations' unrelated business
-- Partnerships
-- Sole proprietorship

Consumer Credit
Consumer product safety
Consumer Price Indexes
Consumption, energy
Corporations
Country profiles
Crime (See also *Law enforcement*):
-- Characteristics of crime
-- Children
-- Crime in schools
-- Crimes reported to the police
-- Criminal offenders
-- Drugs
-- Firearms
-- Hate
-- Homicide
-- Prison inmates
-- Terrorism
-- Victims
-- Violent
Criminal justice:
-- Corrections
   -- Capital punishment
   -- Inmates
   -- Jails
   -- Prisons
   -- Probation and parole statistics
-- Courts and sentencing
   -- Court organization
   -- Criminal case processing
   -- Pretrial release and detention
   -- Sentencing
-- Criminal record systems
-- Employment and expenditure
-- Federal justice statistics
-- Indigent defense statistics
-- Law enforcement
   -- Campus law enforcement
   -- Federal law enforcement
   -- State and local law enforcement
-- Prosecution
Crops:
-- Crop progress and weather, weekly
-- Data by county
-- Data by state, historic
-- Field
-- Fruits and nuts
-- Vegetables

BOX C
A large sample of the links obtained by clicking on Breast, which is the second link in Box 4B (under the main heading "Cancer").

Treatment
Information about treatment, including surgery, chemotherapy, radiation therapy, immunotherapy, and vaccine therapy
       • Breast Cancer Treatment
[patients] [health professionals]
       • Male Breast Cancer Treatment
[patients] [health professionals]
 • Breast Cancer and Pregnancy
[patients] [health professionals]
• More Information

Prevention, Genetics, Causes
Information related to prevention, genetics, risk factors
 • Breast Cancer Prevention
[patients] [health professionals]
• Genetics of Breast and Ovarian Cancer
       • Digest Page: Menopausal Hormone Use
• More Information

Screening and Testing
Information about methods of cancer detection including new imaging technologies, tumor markers, and biopsy procedures
 • Breast Cancer Screening
[patients] [health professionals]
• NCI Statement on Mammography Screening
• HHS Affirms Value of Mammography
• Get a Mammogram
• More Information

Clinical Trials
Information on clinical trials and current news on trials and trial-related data
       • Breast Cancer Trial Results
 • Search for Clinical Trials

Cancer Literature
Resources available from the PubMed database
    • Cancer Topic Searches: Breast Cancer
    • Cancer Topic Searches: Cancer Genetics
    • Cancer Literature in PubMed

Related Information
Other information, including reports about NCI priorities for cancer research and initiatives
    • Breast Cancer Progress Review Group
    • Early Reproductive Events and Breast Cancer

Statistics
Information related to cancer incidence, mortality, and survival
    • Probability of Breast Cancer in American Women
    • Breast: U.S. Racial/Ethnic Cancer Patterns
  • Finding Cancer Statistics

✍ Guideline 2   State and local governments and their agencies often post very current statistics on the Web.

While information at the local level can be obtained at FedStats.gov, researchers can sometimes obtain more current statistical information from nonfederal governmental sources. Example 4.2.1 shows the latest statistics on property crimes in Buffalo, New York, posted on FedStats at the time of this writing as well as the latest ones obtained by going directly to the City of Buffalo Web site.[5] Note that the federal statistics are current as of 1999, while the City's statistics are two years more current than the federal ones.

EXAMPLE 2.1
Property-crime statistics for Buffalo, New York, from federal and local sources:

Year	FedStats Web Site	City of Buffalo Web Site
2001	not available	16,185
2000	not available	16,591
1999	17,436	17,436

---

[5] Retrieved September 19, 2002, from www.city-buffalo.com/Files/1_2_1/Police/Crime%20Statistics.htm

✍ Guideline 3   Use the raw statistics from governmental agencies, not statistics filtered by individuals or groups with special interests.

Government statistics are usually collected by civil service employees (not political appointees). While there may be errors in their work, there is no more reason to suspect them of deliberately biasing their data collection procedures than to suspect any other type of researcher of doing so. However, some individuals (such as politicians and others with special interests) may understandably be selective (and perhaps misleading) in choosing which statistics to report. Hence, it is usually best to obtain the original government reports either in print or via the Web. However, as shown in Guideline 4, those with vested interests in statistical information sometimes provide useful links or primary-source information (via the Web), which can be helpful when writing a literature review.

Note that in some cases, it is appropriate to present original government statistics in a literature review *and* to discuss how they are interpreted by individuals and organizations with varying special interests.

✍ Guideline 4   Consider consulting the Library of Congress's Virtual Reference Shelf on the Web.

The Library of Congress maintains a Web site titled the Virtual Reference Shelf. It is an excellent site for general references such as dictionaries, general history, abbreviations, genealogy, and so on. It can be found at www.loc.gov/rr/askalib/virtualref.html.[6] Box D shows the main links at that site. At the bottom of the home page (not shown in the box but clearly visible on the Web site) is a link for "Ask a Librarian," which can be a very useful service if you are struggling to find specialized information to use in your literature review.

Box D
Links on the home page of the Library of Congress's Virtual Reference Shelf.

Virtual Reference Shelf
Selected Web resources compiled by the Library of Congress

• Abbreviations	• Education
• Almanacs and Fast Facts	• Encyclopedias
• Arts and Music	• Genealogy, Biography, and Archaeology
• Associations	• Grant Resource
• Awards/Prizes	• Health/Medical
• Books, Periodicals, and Publishing	• History (General)
• Business	• Language and Literature
• Calculators	• Law
• Calendars	• Libraries
• Clocks/Times	• Maps/Driving Directions
• Consumer Information	• Political Science and Government
• Current Events on the Web	• Quotations
• Dictionaries/Thesauri	• Science, Technology, and Engineering
• Directories	• Statistics

Library of Congress Research Tools

Internet Public Library Reference Center * Other Reference Sites * In the News

---

[6] Rather than typing (and risk mistyping) long URLs, it is sometimes faster to do a quick search on a major search engine such as www.Google.com using a term such as "Virtual Reference Shelf." Use the quotation marks around the terms (e.g., "Virtual Reference Shelf") to conduct an exact phrase match and exclude other Web sites that might have only one of the words, such as "virtual."

↳ Guideline 5   Consider accessing information posted on the Web by associations and businesses.

A wide variety of associations post information (and statistics) on the Web. Following the link called "Associations" in the Virtual Reference Shelf (see the fourth link in Box D), you can identify hundreds of associations, many of which are quite specialized. For instance, there are employee associations such as the Southern California Association of Fingerprint Officers at www.scafo.org, which publishes an on-line journal titled *The Print* in which there are original articles as well as reprints of articles from other sources. In addition, there are Web sites maintained by political lobbying and advocacy associations such as the American Civil Liberties Union at www.aclu.org, which publishes a newsletter and sells inexpensive special reports such as *Unequal, Unfair, and Irreversible: The Death Penalty in Virginia*.

You should also consider accessing information posted on the Web by businesses. Suppose you are writing a literature review on allergies for a health education class. Going to the home page for the drug Flonase® will provide you with a reference to an article in an academic journal.

You should be cautious when citing information found on Web sites maintained by associations and businesses. On the other hand, because of their special interest in certain topics, they may have more information (and newer information) than other sources.

Keep in mind that complete objectivity in research cannot be achieved. All associations and businesses that sponsor research have points of view that might influence what is researched, how questions are worded, how the sample is drawn, how the information is presented, and so on. Your job is to try to understand their points of view and identify which information on the Web is reliable and useful for the purposes of your literature review.

NOTES

APPENDIX C
EXCERPTS FROM LITERATURE REVIEWS

The following excerpts show the beginning paragraph(s) of literature reviews. They should be referred to while answering Question 7 in the Exercise for Topic 16 (Organizing a Literature Review).

Betrayal in Romantic Relationships

Betrayal is one of the most devastating experiences in a romantic relationship. A betrayal is defined as an act committed by a relational partner that goes against the other partner's expectations of the relationship and, as a result, causes pain to that individual (Jones & Burdette, 1994). As Jones and Burdette point out, betrayal has the potential for psychological damage because it "implies that something of realized value has been lost" (p. 246). That something may be the relationship itself, the benefits generated by the relationship, the time and effort that were invested to build the relationship, and the feelings of companionship and closeness with the partner. But perhaps the most consequential casualties of betrayal are trust and commitment (Couch, Jones, & Moore, 1999).

The discovery of a partner's transgression may create a range of negative emotions including anger, sadness, disappointment, and a loss of self-esteem (Jones & Burdette, 1994). Acts of betrayal are especially hurtful because they are unexpected and are performed by people whom we trust. In addition, betrayal signifies the painful truth that the perpetrator does not value the relationship...as much as we do (Leary, 2001). In a sense, betrayal may be considered a total rejection of the relationship and the person.

Source

Haden, S. C., & Hojjat, M. (2006). Aggressive responses to betrayal: Type of relationship, victim's sex, and nature of aggression. *Journal of Social and Personal Relationships*, *23*, 101–116. (Excerpt from page 102.) Copyright © 2006 by Sage Publications.

Notes:

_____

_____

_____

_____

_____

Family-Based Interventions for Pediatric Obesity

The U.S. Centers for Disease Control estimate that approximately 16% of youth ages 6–19 years are overweight (Hedley et al., 2004). Associated health problems, such as increased cholesterol, hypertension, Type II diabetes, and sleep apnea, and psychosocial problems, such as depression, disturbed body image, social isolation, and low self-concept, underscore the need to reverse the current trends (Dietz, 1998; Eisenberg, Neumark-Sztainer, & Story, 2003; Freedman, Dietz, Srinivasan, & Berenson, 1999; Latner & Stunkard, 2003; Srinivasan, Myers, & Berenson, 2002; Strauss & Pollack, 2003).

Weight-gain prevention and weight-loss programs for children are often more successful than similar programs targeting adults (Epstein, Valoski, Kalarchian, & McCurley, 1995; Wilson, 1994). In the current review, we focus on a subset of interventions that are known as family-based. Family-based interventions for pediatric obesity are programs that focus on changing the behavior of multiple family members, not only that of the overweight child (Epstein, Myers, Raynor, & Saelens, 1998). These programs recognize that children's weight problems develop and are maintained in a family context (Golan & Weizman, 2001), that parents play a role in shaping children's health behaviors (Davison & Birch, 2001), and that parent functioning can influence the course of treatment (Epstein, Wisniewski, & Weng, 1994; Favaro & Santonastaso, 1995).

Source

Kitzmann, K. M., & Beech, B. M. (2006). Family-based interventions for pediatric obesity: Methodological and conceptual challenges from family psychology. *Journal of Family Psychology*, *20*, 175–189. (Excerpt from page 175.) Copyright © 2006 by the American Psychological Association.

Notes:

_____

_____

_____

_____

_____

Adolescent Girls' Problem Behavior

Adolescent problem behaviors, such as externalizing symptoms and substance abuse, can result in marked functional impairment (e.g., school failure), adverse health outcomes, and societal costs (Chassin, Ritter, Trim, & King, 2003; Hinshaw, 1992). Conduct problems and substance abuse have become an increasing problem among adolescent girls. Between 1993 and 2002, arrests of females younger than 18 years old increased more or decreased less than males for most offenses (e.g., simple assault, curfew, and loitering; Office of Juvenile Justice and Delinquency Prevention, 2004). In the same period, drug-abuse violations grew at twice the rate for adolescent girls (120%) than boys (51%).

Considerable research has attempted to elucidate the risk factors that predict emergence of these problem behaviors in an effort to illuminate etiologic processes and inform the design of more effective prevention programs targeting these disturbances. However, theory on the development of problem behavior in adolescents has evolved primarily from studies relying on samples of boys (Calhoun, Jurgens, & Chen, 1993; Silverthorn & Frick, 1999). Surprisingly little research has specifically examined the development of problem behavior with adolescent girls. The increasing prevalence of externalizing problems and substance abuse among adolescent girls illustrates a need to test theoretical models with females.

Source

Huh, D., Tristan, J., Wade, E., & Stice, E. (2006). Does problem behavior elicit poor parenting? A prospective study of adolescent girls. *Journal of Adolescent Research*, *21*, 185–204. (Excerpt from pages 185–186.) Copyright © 2006 by Sage Publications.

Notes:

_____

_____

_____

_____

Family Relationships and Substance Abuse

Understanding the role of family relationships in the causes and course of substance abuse problems in adolescence is critical for two main reasons. First, adolescent substance use is a growing problem, with recent population-based surveys identifying high rates of drug use and national trends toward increased rates of use (PRIDE, 1995; SAMHSA, 1998; USDHHS, 1995). Moreover, reports suggest that adolescents are initiating use at earlier ages (Johnston, Bachman, & O'Malley, 1997) and overall rates of illicit drug use appear to be increasing (Johnston, Bachman, & O'Malley, 1995). Second, family relationships have been found to play a major role in adolescent drug abuse. Among the list of parent-centered and family functioning variables implicated in the etiology and symptom picture of adolescent drug use, researchers have identified family relationship characteristics such as parental support and closeness (Hays, Stacy, Widaman, DiMatteo, & Downey, 1986), parental hostility (Johnson & Pandina, 1991), parenting style (Baumrind, 1991; Fletcher, Darling, & Steinberg, 1995), aspects of the parent–adolescent attachment relationship (Brook, Brook, Gordon, Whiteman, & Cohen, 1990; Brook, Whiteman, Gordon, & Cohen, 1986), and levels of family cohesion (Piercy, Volk, Trepper, Sprenkle, & Lewis, 1991).

Given the array of evidence that indicates family factors are influential in this serious, growing social problem, family relations are a critical developmental context for understanding adolescent substance abuse.

Source

Samuolis, J., Hogue, A., Dauber, S., & Liddle, H. A. (2005). Autonomy and relatedness in inner-city families of substance abusing adolescents. *Journal of Child & Adolescent Substance Abuse*, *15*, 53–86. (Excerpt from page 54.) Copyright © 2005 by The Haworth Press.

Notes:

_____

_____

_____

_____

Health Care for Women with Disabilities

The decades prior to the 1990s were notable for the paucity of research conducted on women's health and health care (Public Health Service Task Force on Women's Health Issues, 1985). Concerns about these critical deficits eventually led the National Institutes of Health to create the Women's Health Initiative (Pinn & LaRosa, 1992). Despite these advances, attention to women's health has generally excluded consideration of women with disabilities (Krotoski, Nosek, & Turk, 1996).

The dearth of extant research that has examined the health care needs of women with disabilities indicates the critical need for more research targeting this significant, but often overlooked, percentage of the population. In 1995 females with disabilities (defined as having functional limitations in daily living activities) were estimated at nearly 29 million, or 21 percent of the female population (Jans & Stoddard, 1999).

Source

Parish, S. L., & Huh, J. (2006). Health care for women with disabilities: Population-based evidence of disparities. *Health & Social Work*, *31*, 7–15. (Excerpt from page 7.) Copyright © 2006 by the National Association of Social Workers.

Notes:

_____

_____

_____

_____

Marital Conflict and Child Maladjustment

Marital conflict is among the most universal problems children face (Katz & Gottman, 1997). Almost all children experience some degree of conflict between their parents, and most identify marital conflict as a source of distress (Lewis, Siegel, & Lewis, 1984). Research consistently shows that the consequences of marital conflict on children's psychological and emotional development are complex, with unresolved marital conflict potentially negatively affecting many areas of children's functioning (e.g., Cummings & Davies, 1994). Moreover, the deleterious effects of marital conflict appear to last well beyond the childhood years (Glenn & Kramer, 1985). Therefore, it is imperative that the processes that account for the association between marital conflict and child maladjustment be identified and understood.

Source

Kaczynski, K. J., Lindahl, K. M., Malik, N. M., & Laurenceau, J.-P. (2006). Marital conflict, maternal and parental parenting, and child adjustment: A test of mediation and moderation. *Journal of Family Psychology*, *20*, 199–208. (Excerpt from page 199.) Copyright © 2006 by the American Psychological Association.

Notes:

_____

_____

_____

_____

NOTES

APPENDIX D
A CLOSER LOOK AT THE STANDARD DEVIATION

In this appendix, some rules for interpreting the standard deviation in relation to the normal curve are described. In addition, the computation of the standard deviation is considered.

As indicated in Topic 51, going out one standard-deviation unit on both sides of the mean captures 68% of the cases in a normal distribution. It turns out that by going out two units on both sides of the mean captures approximately 95% of the cases.[1] For the distribution considered in Topic 51 with $M = 70$ and $S = 10$, it was noted that 68% lies between scores of 60 and 80. Going out $2 \times 10 = 20$ points (which is two standard-deviation units), scores of 50 and 90 (i.e., the mean of 70 *minus* 20 = 50, and the mean of 70 *plus* 20 = 90) are reached. This is illustrated in Figure 1.

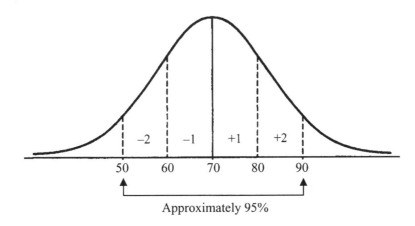

Figure 1. Normal curve illustrating approximate 95% rule.

Going out three standard-deviation units captures 99.7% of the cases, which is essentially all of the cases. Thus, there are about three standard-deviation units on each side of the mean in a normal distribution.

Considering how the standard deviation is calculated may help in understanding the standard deviation. As the formula below indicates, it is the *square root of the mean squared deviation from the mean*. Thus, the larger the deviations from the mean are, the larger the standard deviation is. Conversely, the smaller the deviations from the mean are, the smaller the standard deviation is.

The formula that defines the standard deviation is:

$$S = \sqrt{\frac{\sum x^2}{N}}$$

The lowercase x stands for the deviation of a score from the mean of its distribution. To obtain it, first calculate the mean (in this case, 78/6 = 13.00) and subtract the mean from each score, as shown in Example 1 on the next page. Then, square the deviations and sum the squares, as indicated by the symbol Σ. Then, enter this value in the formula along with the number of cases (N) and perform the calculations as indicated in Example 1 on the next page.

---

[1] To capture precisely 95%, go out 1.96 (a little less than 2.00) standard deviations. Going out 2.58 standard deviations captures 99% of the cases.

EXAMPLE 1

Scores (X)	Deviations ($X - M$)	Deviations Squared (x^2)
10	$10 - 13.00 = -3$	9.00
11	$11 - 13.00 = -2$	4.00
11	$11 - 13.00 = -2$	4.00
13	$13 - 13.00 = 0$	0.00
14	$14 - 13.00 = 1$	1.00
19	$19 - 13.00 = 6$	36.00
		$\Sigma x^2 = 54.00$

Thus, for these data:

$$S = \sqrt{\frac{54}{6}} = \sqrt{9.00} = 3.00$$

APPENDIX E
A CLOSER LOOK AT EFFECT SIZE

Reporting effect sizes in research reports has become common only in recent years, and they still are not universally reported. Hence, consumers of research (who typically do not need to compute statistics) may find it beneficial to be able to calculate some simple statistics that will allow them to interpret more accurately results in which effect sizes have been omitted in research reports.

In Topic 59, the calculation of Cohen's *d* was illustrated in the examples in which the two standard deviations were equal. When they are not equal, most researchers divide the difference between means by the "pooled standard deviation," which is a special type of average standard deviation that can be obtained using the following formula. Its use is illustrated for an experiment in which the experimental group's standard deviation is 10.00 (with 15 participants, $n = 15$), and the control group's standard deviation is 14.00 (with 12 participants, $n = 12$). Note that for an experiment, the subscript "1" designates the experimental group, and the subscript "2" designates the control group.

$$sd_{pooled} = \sqrt{\frac{(n_1 - 1)sd_1^2 + (n_2 - 1)sd_2^2}{n_1 + n_2 - 2}} = \sqrt{\frac{(15-1)10.00^2 + (12-1)14.00^2}{15+12-2}} = 11.93$$

(Note that the pooled standard deviation of 11.93 is very close to the simple average of the standard deviations [10.00 + 14.00 = 24.00/2 = 12.00]. The larger the difference between the numbers of participants in the two groups and the larger the difference between the two standard deviations, the greater the difference between the pooled standard deviation and the simple average of the standard deviations.)

The usual formula for Cohen's *d* is the difference between the means divided by the pooled standard deviation, which is shown here in symbols:[1]

$$d = \frac{m_1 - m_2}{sd_{pooled}}$$

As a practical solution for consumers of research who do not want to engage in extensive calculations, a good *estimate* of *d* will usually be obtained by dividing the difference between the means by the *simple average* of the standard deviations. As indicated in the example above, the simple average of the standard deviations is 10.00 + 14.00 = 24.00/2 = 12.00. Divide the difference between the two means by 12.00 for an estimate. Another practical solution when conducting meta-analyses on experiments is to use only the standard deviation of the control group (and hence avoid averaging standard deviations altogether), as discussed in the next paragraph.

When analyzing the difference between an experimental group and a control group, some researchers prefer to divide the difference between the means by the standard deviation of the control group only (as opposed to the pooled standard deviation for both groups). The resulting statistic is widely known as Glass's delta (Δ), although it is sometimes also referred to as *d* in research literature. This is understandable because the value of *d* and the value of Δ are very similar when the two standard deviations are very similar. For instance, in a perfect case in which the two standard deviations are identical, the standard deviation of the control group will equal the pooled standard deviation of the two groups, so *d* and Δ will have exactly the same value.

In Topic 59, the examples were *experiments* (with experimental and control groups). Cohen's *d* is also appropriate for describing the difference between two means in *nonexperimental studies*. For instance, a

---

[1] Students who have taken statistics should note that the population value of the standard deviation (computed without the minus one [−1] in the denominator of the computational formula) should be used to obtain Cohen's *d*. If the sample standard deviation is used, the result is Hedge's *g*, which, for small samples, can differ noticeably from Cohen's *d*. Values of *g* can be converted to values of *d* using the following formula:

$$d = g\sqrt{N/df}$$

researcher could survey a random sample of girls and a random sample of boys (without any physical treatments), compute a mean and standard deviation for each group, and compare the two groups using d. In such a study, it is usually best to subtract the smaller mean from the larger mean (so that the difference is a positive number) and then divide by either the pooled standard deviation (for an exact value of d) or by the simple average of the two standard deviations (for an estimate of the value of d).

As indicated in Topic 60, when examining a body of literature, it is sometimes helpful to be able to directly compare the effect sizes represented by values of d with effect sizes represented by values of r. The following formula yields a good approximation of the value of d corresponding to a value of r.

$$d = \frac{2r}{\sqrt{1-r^2}}$$

The following formula is recommended for calculating the "effect size r" from a value of d. The subscript "es" for "effect size" is used in the formula to distinguish the result from a value of r that is computed directly from raw scores (as opposed to being computed from a value of d).

$$r_{es} = \frac{d}{\sqrt{d^2 + 4}}$$

APPENDIX F
OUTLINE OF QUESTION ROUTE FOR A FOCUS GROUP STUDY[1]

Opening comments:

Welcome and statements regarding the purpose of the study, focus group procedures, and ethical issues.

Opening comment:

"Please tell us a little bit about yourself."

Introductory question:

"Stress is prevalent in our everyday lives because many people feel stressed. In thinking about your daily life, what does stress mean to you?"

Transition questions:

"Is stress a negative factor in your life? If so, explain how it is negative."
"Is stress a positive factor in your life? If so, in what ways is it positive?"
   Subprobe: "What is it about stress that makes it good or bad?"

Key questions:

"What are the things that contribute to stress in your life?"
   Subprobe: (a) "How does this work? Does one thing contribute to stress more than others, or does the combination of many things contribute to stress?" (b) "Do you have any particular health concerns that contribute to your feelings of stress? Can you tell us more about this?" (c) "Besides possible health concerns, is there anything else that adds to your feelings of stress?" (d) "Does being a manager contribute to your feelings of stress? If so, describe how."

Ending questions:

"All things considered, what would you say is the major cause of stress in your life?"
"Is there anything about stress that we haven't talked about that you would like to raise before we leave tonight?"

---

[1] Reprinted from page 62 of Iwasaki, Y., MacKay, K. J., & Ristock, J. (2004). Gender-based analyses of stress among professional managers: An exploratory qualitative study. *International Journal of Stress Management*, *11*, 56–79.

NOTES

APPENDIX G

SAMPLE ABSTRACTS OF RESEARCH REPORTS

This appendix contains three sample abstracts, which appeared at the beginning of published research reports. Note that all indicate the nature of the findings, which is highly desirable. These abstracts should be referred to when answering Question 8 for Topic 71.

Abstract 1: Abstract of a Survey

This study examines ethical dilemmas and problems that are encountered by psychologists across rural and urban communities. A survey instrument was created on the basis of previous surveys of ethical practices. A national sample of 1,000 psychologists stratified into urban and nonurban practitioners was surveyed; 447 usable surveys were returned. Data analysis revealed significant differences between small town/rural and urban/suburban groups for several ethical categories. Notably, small town/rural psychologists are more likely to encounter several types of multiple relationships than their urban counterparts. Small town/rural practitioners are also more likely to be highly visible, or well-known, in their communities. Qualitatively, respondents described their struggles with dual relationships, and several offered suggestions to cope with boundary issues. These findings suggest the need to study the practice of psychology in rural communities in more depth, to study the impact of rural characteristics on clients and practitioners, and to create a conceptual model of best practices for rural practitioners.

Source

Helbok, C. M., Marinelli, R. P., & Walls, R. T. (2006). National survey of ethical practices across rural and urban communities. *Professional Psychology: Research and Practice, 37,* 36–44. Copyright © 2006 by the American Psychological Association.

Notes:

_____
_____
_____
_____

Abstract 2: Abstract of an Experiment

This research examines the multiple effects of racial diversity on group decision making. Participants deliberated on the trial of a black defendant as members of racially homogeneous or heterogeneous mock juries. Half of the groups were exposed to pretrial jury selection questions about racism and half were not. Deliberation analyses supported the prediction that diverse groups would exchange a wider range of information than all-white groups. This finding was not wholly attributable to the performance of black participants, as whites cited more case facts, made fewer errors, and were more amenable to discussion of racism when in diverse versus all-white groups. Even before discussion, whites in diverse groups were more lenient toward the black defendant, demonstrating that the effects of diversity do not occur solely through information exchange. The influence of jury selection questions extended previous findings that blatant racial issues at trial increase leniency toward a black defendant.

Source

Sommers, S. R. (2006). On racial diversity and group decision making: Identifying multiple effects of racial composition on jury deliberations. *Journal of Personality and Social Psychology, 90,* 597–612. Copyright © 2006 by the American Psychological Association.

Notes:

_____
_____
_____
_____

Abstract 3: Abstract of a Program Evaluation

Objective: To evaluate the impact of a consumer-driven rehabilitation program on perceptions of loss and gain of interpersonal relationships, energy, material objects, work benefits and opportunities, well-being, and experiences of mastery in persons with chronic fatigue syndrome. *Study Design*: Participants were randomly assigned to a program group (*n* = 23) or a control group (*n* = 24). Outcomes were assessed (a) at baseline, (b) after program participants completed an illness management group, and (c) after they completed one-on-one peer counseling. *Setting*: A community-based advocacy organization for individuals with disabilities. *Interventions*: Four months of illness management groups followed by 7 months of one-on-one peer counseling emphasizing goal setting and goal attainment. *Main Outcome Measure*: The Conservation of Resources Evaluation scale. *Results*: Significant gains were observed for program participants across all categories of resource gain—interpersonal, energy, material, work, well-being, and mastery resources. Effect sizes were moderate to large. *Conclusions*: Programs in which participatory action research methods are used may have a positive impact on resource acquisition for individuals with chronic fatigue syndrome.

Source

Taylor, R. R., Jason, L. A., Shiraishi, Y., Schoeny, M. E., & Keller, J. (2006). Conservation of resources theory, perceived stress, and chronic fatigue syndrome: Outcomes of a consumer-driven rehabilitation program. *Rehabilitation Psychology, 51,* 157–165. Copyright © 2006 by the American Psychological Association.

Notes:

_____

_____

_____

_____

_____

Table 1
Table of Random Numbers

Row #						
1	2 1 0	4 9 8	0 8 8	8 0 6	9 2 4	8 2 6
2	0 7 3	0 2 9	4 8 2	7 8 9	8 9 2	9 7 1
3	4 4 9	0 0 2	8 6 2	6 7 7	7 3 1	2 5 1
4	7 3 2	1 1 2	0 7 7	6 0 3	8 3 4	7 8 1
5	3 3 2	5 8 3	1 7 0	1 4 0	7 8 9	3 7 7
6	6 1 2	0 5 7	2 4 4	0 0 6	3 0 2	8 0 7
7	7 0 9	3 3 3	7 4 0	4 8 8	9 3 5	8 0 5
8	7 5 1	9 0 9	1 5 2	6 5 0	9 0 3	5 8 8
9	3 5 6	9 6 5	0 1 9	4 6 6	7 5 6	8 3 1
10	8 5 0	3 9 4	3 4 0	6 5 1	7 4 4	6 2 7
11	0 5 9	6 8 7	4 8 1	5 5 0	5 1 7	1 5 8
12	7 6 2	2 6 9	6 1 9	7 1 1	4 7 1	6 2 0
13	3 8 4	7 8 9	8 2 2	1 6 3	8 7 0	4 6 1
14	1 9 1	8 4 5	6 1 8	1 2 4	4 4 2	7 3 4
15	1 5 3	6 7 6	1 8 4	3 1 8	8 7 7	6 0 4
16	0 5 5	3 6 0	7 1 3	8 1 4	6 7 0	4 3 5
17	2 2 3	8 6 0	9 1 9	0 4 4	7 6 8	1 5 1
18	2 3 3	2 5 5	7 6 9	4 9 7	1 3 7	9 3 8
19	8 5 5	0 5 3	7 8 5	4 5 1	6 0 4	8 9 1
20	0 6 1	1 3 4	8 6 4	3 2 9	4 3 8	7 4 1
21	9 1 1	8 2 9	0 6 9	6 9 4	2 9 9	0 6 0
22	3 7 8	0 6 3	7 1 2	6 5 2	7 6 5	6 5 1
23	5 3 0	5 1 2	1 0 9	1 3 7	5 6 1	2 5 0
24	7 2 4	8 6 7	9 3 8	7 6 0	9 1 6	5 7 8
25	0 9 1	6 7 0	3 8 0	9 1 5	4 2 3	2 4 5
26	3 8 1	4 3 7	9 2 4	5 1 2	8 7 7	4 1 3

NOTES

Table 2

Table of Recommended Sample Sizes (n) for Populations (N) with Finite Sizes[1]

N	n	N	n	N	n
10	10	220	140	1,200	291
15	14	230	144	1,300	297
20	19	240	148	1,400	302
25	24	250	152	1,500	306
30	28	260	155	1,600	310
35	32	270	159	1,700	313
40	36	280	162	1,800	317
45	40	290	165	1,900	320
50	44	300	169	2,000	322
55	48	320	175	2,200	327
60	52	340	181	2,400	331
65	56	360	186	2,600	335
70	59	380	191	2,800	338
75	63	400	196	3,000	341
80	66	420	201	3,500	346
85	70	440	205	4,000	351
90	73	460	210	4,500	354
95	76	480	214	5,000	357
100	80	500	217	6,000	361
110	86	550	226	7,000	364
120	92	600	234	8,000	367
130	97	650	242	9,000	368
140	103	700	248	10,000	370
150	108	750	254	15,000	375
160	113	800	260	20,000	377
170	118	850	265	30,000	379
180	123	900	269	40,000	380
190	127	950	274	50,000	381
200	132	1,000	278	75,000	382
210	136	1,100	285	100,000	384

[1] Adapted from: Krejcie, R. V., & Morgan, D. W. (1970). Determining sample size for research activities. *Educational and Psychological Measurement, 30*, 607–610.

NOTES

INDEX

NOTES

NOTES

NOTES

NOTES

NOTES

NOTES